Globalization, the Nation-State and the Citizen

Routledge Research in Education

Globalization, the Nation-State and the Citizen

Dilemmas and Directions for Civics and Citizenship Education

Edited by Alan Reid, Judith Gill, and Alan Sears

Routledge
Taylor & Francis Group
New York   London

First published 2010
by Routledge
270 Madison Avenue, New York, NY 10016

Simultaneously published in the UK
by Routledge
2 Park Square, Milton Park, Abingdon, Oxon OX14 4RN

Routledge is an imprint of the Taylor & Francis Group, an informa business

© 2010 Taylor & Francis

Typeset in Sabon by IBT Global.
Printed and bound in the United States of America on acid-free paper by IBT Global.

Library of Congress Cataloging in Publication Data
    Globalization, the nation-state and the citizen : dilemmas and directions for civics and citizenship education / edited by Alan Reid, Judith Gill and Alan Sears.
        p. cm.—(Routledge research in education ; 34)
    Includes bibliographical references and index.
    1. Citizenship—Cross-cultural studies.   2. Citizenship—Study and teaching.   I. Reid, Alan (Alan D.)   II. Gill, Judith.   III. Sears, Alan M.
    LC1091.G45 2010
    370.11'5—dc22
    2009039540

ISBN10: 0-415-87223-5 (hbk)
ISBN10: 0-203-85511-6 (ebk)

ISBN13: 978-0-415-87223-2 (hbk)
ISBN13: 978-0-203-85511-9 (ebk)

Contents

Acknowledgments

The editors would like to acknowledge:

- the support given to them by the Hawke Research Institute (HRI), University of South Australia, in the development of this book;
- the CitizEd group whose conferences have been a regular source of inspiration for our work and whose membership includes many of the contributors;
- the sterling work of Anne Morrison in organising the manuscript for submission to the publisher; and
- all the contributors whose readiness to participate in the book and meet all the deadlines was greatly appreciated.

Part A
Introduction

1 The Forming of Citizens in a Globalising World

Alan Reid, Judith Gill and Alan Sears

CIVICS EDUCATION AS A PROJECT OF SCHOOLING

If citizenship is understood to be 'the system of values, efforts and institutionalized practices required for creating and maintaining conditions for living together in a complex society' (Dimitrov & Boyadjieva 2009, p. 156), then clearly individuals need a significant set of capabilities if they are to function as active and responsible citizens. Of course, the type and nature of these capabilities will vary according to the society and the context—but in most societies the burden of developing these capabilities falls to the institutions of formal education, particularly schools.

This connection between schooling and the state has been a major preoccupation of educational literature over the past three decades, particularly that of the sociology of the curriculum where the relationship between the state, education policy and curriculum practice is an ongoing problematic (e.g. Bernstein 1971; Apple 1996; Pinar 2006). One of the recurring themes in this literature is the role of schools in nurturing civic values and nationalist sentiment for the purposes of social order and control. Grundy, for example, refers to school lessons in the Australian context as the official story lines of a society where 'portrayed modes of being are given wide social approval' (1994, p. 17); and De Cillia and colleagues use a Bourdieuian perspective within a European case study to argue that:

> it is to a large extent through its schools and education system that the state shapes those forms of perception, categorization, interpretation and memory that serve to determine the orchestration of the habitus which are in turn the constitutive basis for a kind of national common-sense. (De Cillia, Reisigl & Wodak 1999, p. 156)

If a civics and citizenship education (hereafter referred to as CCE) function is embedded in the 'grammars' (Tyack & Tobin 1994) or the 'scripts' of the project of schooling (Barton & Levstik 2004), then schools can tell us a lot about the form of democracy and understanding of citizenship extant in a society at a particular point in time. Of course this is not a one-way relationship: in any society, the ways in which citizenship is constructed will shape the forms of education in a society, just as education will contribute to the nature of citizenship. Whilst the dominant understanding of citizenship is usually consistent with that of the power elites in the society, it is rarely uncontested and is often the outcome of political battles involving different groups (Bernstein 1971; Apple 1996). It follows then that every country will differ in understanding citizenship and the ways in which the CCE function of schools is constructed and practised, since these will be specific to the history, context, forms and structures of government in each society.

Notwithstanding the specificities of context, there do appear to be some elements of the relationship between citizenship, schooling and the state that have been common across nation-states. First, schools are used by the state for purposes of legitimation and stability, especially during times of perceived crisis. They both serve and help to shape the prevailing educational settlement. This settlement is expressed in and through the aims and purposes of education and the policy and practice which flows from these purposes. Formal educational institutions like schools have always served a number of purposes. Some purposes seek to advance the interests of society as a whole; others promote the interests of individuals. Following Labaree (1997), there are three broad purposes of schooling:

1. *Democratic equality*, which is about a society preparing all of its young people to be active and competent citizens. When this purpose is dominant, the citizen is understood as an active participator in the polity.
2. *Social efficiency*, which is about preparing young people to be competent and productive workers. When this purpose is dominant, the citizen is understood as human capital.
3. *Social mobility*, which is about providing individuals with a credential which will advantage them in the competition for desirable social positions. This goal constructs education as a commodity which can be traded in, say, the labour market. When this purpose is dominant it constructs the citizen as a consumer.

In any society, state-funded educational institutions will always serve a range of purposes: it is a matter of balance. Different historical times invariably result in shifts in emphasis, and the new settlement will shape the discourses and practices of schools and education systems. The question of whether the right balance has been achieved at any point in time is an important, although neglected, one in debates about public policy generally and CCE specifically.

The second factor common across nation-states seems to be that the CCE function of schools is delivered through at least three modalities of the schooling project. These include the *structure of schooling*, such as the ways in which formal schooling is organised and funded in a society, which contain hidden messages about how the society is/should be structured, ordered and maintained; the *formal representations of civics and citizenship in the curriculum*, such as the subjects which purport to teach the knowledge, skills and dispositions needed for participation in the polity and civil society; and the *culture and processes of education systems and schools*, such as ceremonies, class organisation and pedagogy, discipline structures, traditions and relationships which inculcate certain values and dispositions associated with citizenship. In our view, attention to each of these modalities is necessary for a complete analysis of the civics and citizenship function of schools.

The third common element across nation-states is that no matter how tightly the state seeks to prescribe educational practice to conform with the educational settlement, there is always 'wriggle room' for educators, creating possibilities for contestation and resistance. That is, there is never a one-to-one correspondence between the state's agenda and its realisation in the classroom.

In summary, we argue that the CCE function of schooling both reflects and produces the dominant version of citizenship in any society, and that this version is inscribed in the grammars of schools as well as taught formally through subjects in the official curriculum—but it is never fixed. This means that an analysis of CCE which starts and ends with the subject of 'civics' is a partial analysis only. In our view, a study of CCE in schools must include a study of the (changing) relationship between the state, education, citizenship and democracy at the macro-level, as well as the content of the curriculum at the micro-level, if it is to realise its potential as a window into the health of the structures and processes of civil society and the polity in any nation-state.

The fact that the challenges of globalisation have injected a new dynamic into these relationships presents a unique opportunity to explore them further and to test the efficacy of the framework we have described. Thus, the purpose of this book is to use CCE, as practised in twelve different nation-states, as a lens into understanding the dynamic relationship between globalisation, the nation-state and the citizen. Before exploring this further, we need to briefly locate the studies in the context of globalisation.

GLOBALISATION AND THE NATION-STATE.

In the past twenty years, globalisation has produced a new set of challenges for nation-states. For example:

1. Flows of capital, goods and people have produced challenges of diversity and questions of cohesion for nation-states.
2. The growth of transnational organisations and bodies (e.g. the European Union, United Nations, OECD, World Bank, NGOs,

multinational firms) have constrained the power of nation-states and posed a number of democratic dilemmas, such as how citizens might have a say in decisions that are taken beyond the nation-state.

3. The rapid expansion of technology has tended to fragment the spaces for public discussion, making it difficult to speak of a single public when there are many publics, some intersecting and overlapping.

Hobsbawm (2007) suggests that democracies are ill-equipped to handle such challenges:

> In short, we shall be facing the problems of the 21st century with a collection of political mechanisms dramatically ill-suited to dealing with them. They are effectively confined within the borders of nation-states, whose numbers are growing, and confront a global world which lies beyond their range of operation . . . They face and compete with a world economy effectively operating through quite different units (transnational firms) to which consideration of political legitimacy and common interest do not apply, and which bypass politics. Above all, they face the fundamental problems of the future of the world in an age when the impact of human action on nature and the globe has become a force of geological proportions. (p. 113)

Such challenges are of concern to the governments of nation-states whose legitimation role, as we have argued, requires a stable democratic system and who are therefore casting about for solutions. They understand that as the democratic system adjusts to these new challenges, change is also needed for the concept of what it means to be a citizen in a nation-state in the twenty-first century. Since schooling is seen as a major vehicle through which citizenship can be shaped and developed, it is not surprising that in many countries there has been a renewed focus on civics and citizenship in schools.

So, how have nation-states responded and are the responses adequate to meeting the sorts of challenges of globalisation spelt out by Hobsbawm? In this book we use the lens of schooling and CCE to explore this question from the perspective of twelve nation-states in very different parts of the world, and with very different contexts and histories. The twelve case studies in this collection represent the situation for CCE in relation to very different forms and styles of government and population movements against a range of pressures, such as political instability, terrorism, global financial crisis, changes in governance and so on. No doubt variants of these conditions apply to many other countries; our collection is not intended to be representative but rather to suggest the range of possible outcomes and to provide some deeper understandings about democracy, citizenship and the common good in globalising times. In addition, the collection provides a basis for generating some new ways in which CCE might be understood and practised. In this chapter we want to take the opportunity to canvass some of the general issues raised by the case-study chapters, and in so doing suggest a framework for your reading.

NATION-STATE RESPONSES TO GLOBALISATION: EVIDENCE FROM THE CASE STUDIES

The chapters in this collection set out a substantial range of responses by nation-states to globalisation, particularly in the areas of citizenship and citizenship education. That range is well illustrated by comparing the chapters on the United States (Chapter 11, this volume) and South Africa (Chapter 4, this volume). Both nations are diverse and multiethnic and, like other nations around the world, struggle with building policies and approaches to citizenship and citizenship education that are inclusive. Particular contextual factors, however, are shaping those struggles in very different ways.

Scott and Cogan (Chapter 11, this volume) argue that the election of Barack Obama as president of the United States represents not only a change of political regime in Washington but also 'a paradigm shift' in terms of how citizens understand their place in the nation. These authors hold that the juggernaut of popular engagement that swept Obama to power will also break down the last vestiges of resistance to more active and progressive approaches to CCE. American citizens will demand an education that prepares them all for active civic life.

Kogila Moodley (Chapter 4, this volume), on the other hand, contends that progressive and inclusive approaches to CCE in South Africa are 'undermined by a public discourse on corruption, crime and mortality that contradicts the values taught in schools'. She reminds us that democracy remains a government of the privileged; of those whose days are not overwhelmed by the search for food, shelter, security and basic health care. The full participation of citizens requires more than high-minded constitutions and progressive rhetoric in curriculum documents, it also requires that citizens have the basic means of life available in order to allow them the time and energy required to engage in shaping civic life. Yet while conditions on the ground challenge the efficacy of civic education, Moodley concludes by arguing that civic education is also 'the main hope of overcoming the current malaise'.

Like the United States and South Africa, the other chapters in the book demonstrate clearly that, while globalisation has common features and manifestations, context does matter in terms of how these impact nation-states and how those states respond. Nations emerging from periods of totalitarian rule, Mexico, Brazil, Singapore and Russia, for example, have different issues than longer established Western democracies. One of those issues is resistance to the domination of Western conceptions of citizenship and particularly the emphasis on individualism. As Levinson

(Chapter 12, this volume) points out, conceptions of democracy in Mexico 'include a strong emphasis on group work, solidarity and the collective good'. This is true for a number of the nation-states described here. In his response to the chapters, Walter Parker (Chapter 14, this volume) uses the tool of semiotic squares to explore two of the binaries that cause tension for citizenship across the countries described here: nationalism/multiculturalism and nationalism/cosmopolitanism. He could have added another: individualism/collectivism.

Context matters not only in terms of differences between Western and non-Western democracies, but also between and among nations in those categories. Ireland's response to its relatively new experience with immigrant diversity, for example, stands in contrast to that of Australia and Canada, which have been immigrant nations from the start. While Hong Kong and Singapore are both, in a sense, city-states and important international centres of commerce, their particular political and social contexts mean they face many different issues in terms of CCE. Hong Kong's independence is restrained by its status as a territory of the People's Republic of China and Singapore has a much greater range of ethnic diversity among its citizenry. These factors are critical in shaping approaches to CCE.

While the chapters clearly demonstrate contextual differences in policy and practice related to citizenship and citizenship education they also reveal several common themes. Space does not permit detailed exploration of them all so we will focus on two: the continuing centrality of the nation-state as the primary site for citizenship and the degree to which fear or sense of crisis often drives policy in the area.

Sears (Chapter 13, this volume) argues that diversity has been a central focus for citizenship and citizenship education in Canada from before the formation of the nation-state. In recent years there has been a move away from seeing internal diversity as a problem to be managed to seeing it as a strength that should be explored and understood. Even with that, however, the overweening focus has been on finding ways to make diversity serve the interests of the nation-state either by assimilating it or by making it the central feature of national identity. Pakistan, Dean contends in Chapter 5 of this volume, has taken a very different approach to diversity than Canada by essentially ignoring or pathologising it. Most of the nations described in these chapters fall somewhere between these positions, but in virtually every one diversity is seen as a problem or issue to be managed in the service of the nation-state. Nowhere is the potential for cosmopolitan or global citizenship explored in any depth. Ironically, prior to World War II and long before contemporary concerns about globalisation, both Australia and Canada had a sort of global approach to citizenship rooted in what both countries saw as the potential of the British Empire for world leadership (Sears, Davies & Reid 2008), but this is long forgotten. As Kennedy points out in his response in Chapter 16 of this volume, far from fading away, the nation-state seems to be in a period of resurgence.

The degree to which policy and practice in CCE is driven by crisis is striking (see also Sears & Hyslop-Margison 2007). As these case studies make clear, perceived threats to social cohesion are ubiquitous across nations and often drive reform initiatives. In Chapter 9 of this volume, Nelli Piattoeva, for example, details increasingly draconian attempts by the Russian state to 'create and defend a national narrative' that will serve to subvert growing restiveness among minorities across the country. According to Davies (Chapter 8, this volume), recent reforms to the English national curriculum which increase the focus on identity and diversity are much more positive, but Osler (Chapter 15, this volume) calls for them to be subject to critical analysis as they do flow from a concern about terrorism and a more general worry about diversity as a problem. Related to concerns about the breakdown of social cohesion generally are specific worries about vanishing traditional values that have generated curricular and extra-curricular responses in a number of the nations reviewed here.

WHAT DO THE CASE-STUDY CHAPTERS TELL US ABOUT THE PROJECT OF CCE?

These chapters make it abundantly clear that CCE is not only education about politics; it is itself a political enterprise. McCowan and Puggian (Chapter 3, this volume) address this explicitly by pointing out that education is a contested field where political and social groups engage 'in disputes to defend their particular interests'. In Brazil, this has been manifest both in neo-liberal reforms that appear antithetical to democracy and in educators finding space 'to engage in counter-ideological work' even in the face of those reforms. Similarly, Reid and Gill (Chapter 2, this volume) argue that the Howard government in Australia 'used schooling, and specifically civics education, as an important plank in the government's attempt to consolidate a particular approach to democratic processes and to understandings of citizenship'. The case studies presented in this book also illustrate that the contest for democratic approaches to citizenship education go on across the three modalities of schooling: the structure of schooling; the culture and processes of schools; and formal representations of CCE in the curriculum.

In terms of the structure of schooling, both the chapters on Hong Kong (Chapter 7, this volume) and Brazil (Chapter 3, this volume) make the case that a decentralised approach to schooling opens up democratic possibilities in the face of state repression. In the case of Hong Kong, Kwan-choi Tse contends that the provision of education by civil society organisations during the colonial period provided possibilities for developing democratic citizens outside of strict state structures that worked against that project. In Brazil, according to McCowan and Puggian, a range of NGOs, trade unions and social movements provide both formal and non-formal education programmes designed to foster more radical approaches to citizenship. Sears (Chapter 13, this volume) also contends that the decentralised nature of Canadian schooling has allowed for resistance to neo-liberal reforms that threatened CCE at a number of levels.

Highly centralised systems raise both problems and possibilities for CCE. Dean (Chapter 5, this volume) details a system in Pakistan that has systematically moved away from fostering inclusive approaches to democracy toward a more xenophobic, nationalist agenda. This has taken the shape not only of curricular reform but of undercutting the professional autonomy of teachers who 'are not viewed as professionals able to make decisions about what to teach and how to teach, rather they are seen as implementers of other peoples ideas'. On the other hand, the centralised nature of English education played a critical role in bringing to bear the political will and resources necessary for the development and implementation of a national curriculum in citizenship.

In terms of the culture and processes of schools, most chapters report attempts, albeit often tentative ones, to move away from citizenship as indoctrination to citizenship education. The former seeks to inculcate a fixed set of values, ideas and processes while the latter engages students in the exploration and construction of ideas and process with the view to fostering civic agency: one narrows possibilities the other opens them up (see also Sears & Hughes 2006). The most radical examples of the move to more democratic approaches to schooling are the alternative schools described by McGowan and Puggian (Chapter 3, this volume) in Brazil. These range from those established by local governments to those founded by trade unions and other social groups. All include substantive attention to democracy in establishing school policies, determining curricula and carrying out instruction. As interesting as these are, they remain isolated examples. Davies (Chapter 8, this volume), on the other hand, describes recent initiatives by the Department for Education and Skills in England designed to foster system-wide attention to democratic schools and classrooms. While he questions the degree of success attributed to these efforts, it is significant that attention to these matters is receiving such sustained and widespread official interest as well as the resources designed to move the cause forward. That is not the case in many of the jurisdictions described.

CCE remains a contested area in terms of its curricular manifestations. In some jurisdictions it is a separate subject; in others it is embedded in other subjects such as history or social studies; and in still others it exists as a cross-curricular theme. In virtually all there is significant difficulty figuring out exactly what it is. One of the key areas of dispute with regard to the latter is the relationship among moral or values education (sometimes broadly referred to as character education), health education and political education. Levinson (Chapter 12, this volume), for example, details attempts in Mexico to use civic education as a vehicle for promoting lawfulness and keeping students from getting involved in criminal activity, particularly that around drug use. Similarly, Baildon and Sim (Chapter 6, this volume) argue that values education, particularly the promotion of 'Asian' values vis-à-vis 'Western' values, has been central to citizenship education in Singapore. Davies (Chapter 8, this volume) contends that the tension between attention to private and personal character concerns and civic education is a key challenge facing curriculum planners in England. It would seem from these chapters that England is not alone in facing that challenge. Across the world there is considerable ambiguity about just what constitutes CCE.

THE POSSIBILITIES FOR A NEW AGENDA IN CCE

The case studies of citizenship education presented here were deliberately sought as symptomatic of nation-states undergoing significant change processes at socio-political, cultural and constitutional levels. The question immediately posed by the collection is one of commonalities and differences—to what degree do the similarities in the debates around citizenship and civics education lend themselves to generalisable themes? And yet any attempt at categorisation seems fraught with problems. For example, in some cases the countries selected are more or less established Western democracies which, as a consequence of globalising movements, have had occasion to renegotiate their social contracts to accommodate an increasing and increasingly different population. It would seem that Australia, the United States, England and Canada fit loosely within this category with the added dimension of political change further impacting on the social and political settlement.

In other cases, newly emerging nation-states—possibly Mexico, Brazil and Singapore—seek to establish and maintain an identity in their own right as national players on the global stage. Still others—perhaps Russia, South Africa, Pakistan and Ireland—have undergone significant social and political change and are confronting the need to reassess their capacity to maintain themselves as separate states within a rapidly globalising world. Even this loose grouping leaves Hong Kong as the outlier with its particular set of conditions, such as the need to acknowledge its recent colonial past and to celebrate its reunion with Mainland China while maintaining its impressive trade location and entrepreneurial capacities. Each of the nation-states presented here comprises a particular set of conditions that throw questions of the link between global movements and state-oriented citizenship into stark relief, for example the outcomes of the global financial crisis in terms of Ireland (Bryan, Chapter 10, this volume). In fact, we would caution against any ready categorisation and insist that each must be taken on its own terms in order to develop a multilayered understanding of the factors brought to bear on the development of CCE in each place. However, in acknowledging the specificities of location and culture, there are some general points to be made.

Firstly, the reader is urged to see the processes of globalisation as comprising force fields that provoke changes in population, constitution and culture and lead to a necessary reassessment of what it means to be a citizen in current times. These processes are ongoing, multidirectional and unlikely to be reversed in any foreseeable future. What we have attempted in this collection is to capture the effects of the ongoing developments toward CCE at particular historical moments in order to gain a broader picture of the whole process across different sites. Importantly, another consequence of global movements and globalised communication systems has meant that there is considerable diversity within the majority of the countries listed, with differences of race and class compounded by culture and language making each a microcosm of the set as a whole.

Secondly, the complexity of the topic is compounded by the fact that the conception of *citizen* is likely to be different according to place and historico-political culture. The very notion of *citizen* was once popularly understood as co-terminous with some typification of person and culture, such as the British gentleman, the American businesswoman, the Russian grandmother and so on. Nowadays the population movements that have provoked renewed interest in the topic of schooling and citizenship education have disrupted those earlier stereotypes and taken-for-granted assumptions. And even within one nation-state, as Scott and Cogan point out (Chapter 11, this volume), there are different conceptions of citizen. In the academic literature citizenship is seen as a multilayered complex of identities and belonging, a felt response as well as a system of rights and responsibilities, a formally legal mechanism and a shorthand descriptor, a narrative of identity and culture that connotes both sameness and difference. It falls to CCE to translate this revisioning of citizen into the perceptions and life-worlds of teachers and students.

In the face of this definitional complexity we believe that this collection does lend itself to providing some valuable insights into the ways in which CCE has been constructed across cultures and nations and through this to some better understanding of its processes.

Taken collectively the cases reiterate the close connection between dominant political forces and the modalities through which citizenship education is produced—the education system and structure, the culture and practices of schools and the curriculum arrangements. The case studies also demonstrate that these modalities have changed markedly in recent decades and that there remains a good deal of potential for further change and development. These accounts show that there is room for action but they also carry a warning. New approaches to citizenship education, like any 'new' educational approach, may fail if out of step with other developments in youth culture, educational theory and current teacher professionalism. For example, the more progressive approach to education for critical democracy in some sections in Brazil (see Chapter 3, this volume) appeared to work well in the supportive context of the Plural School and the Landless

Movement, where the initiative was supported by pedagogies informed by constructivist learning theory and an ideology of social inclusion. In a similar vein, Chapter 11 of this volume from Cogan and Scott demonstrates the radical new approach in the recent U.S. election in which technological literacy proved to be a dominant force in getting the message across in ways previously unexperienced and constituted a lively avenue for youth engagement. While these examples may be less successful in other contexts, they do share, along with other accounts here, a commitment to agency and constructivism. By this we mean the idea of building on the local scene and the particular historical moment to develop young people's capacity for seeing themselves as participants in their local contexts. While these two factors, agency and constructivism, appear as recurrent themes in this collection of accounts of CCE arrangements, it seems they emerge more often as an idealised best practice than the actuality of the conditions that govern educational possibilities. Much of this material deals with repressive regimes which constrain education, but there is also a sense in which a new vision involving students and teachers co-constructing their learning and its articulation into community action is presented as ideal.

Furthermore, there appears to be some consensus about the need for CCE to involve more than text-book learning. All contributors were drawn to comment first on features of the political landscape which they saw as impacting on the sort of educational experience students received. In this the implication is that no education takes place in a vacuum and in particular CCE has to include and involve the local context. Thus Moodley (Chapter 4, this volume) writes of the desperate situation of overweening inequality in South Africa against which the pious vision of education for social justice and citizenship can seem like empty rhetoric however well intentioned. Elsewhere, contributors look to CCE as leading to knowledge plus action, a desire to get involved and a capacity to take part and to see oneself in terms of societal membership. The learning environment for CCE ideally is one in which new knowledge has to be talked through, alternatives debated, reflected on and discussed, along with traditional exercises of writing and taking action.

Because the dominant voices in the writing on CCE to date have largely come from Western first world countries (see Sears, Chapter 13, this volume) there is a danger in a collection such as this to have the voices from these countries reinforce a white Western form of CCE and a Western-style democracy as best practice. This collection can be seen to remediate this possibility insofar as the voices from the less developed nation-states appear at times to offer a keener vision of what CCE might ideally entail, even if they have not realised this vision yet. For instance, while the situations in Canada (Chapter 13, this volume) and Australia (Chapter 2, this volume) are described in terms of the specific sets of problems currently encountered in developing CCE, the burden of their own high level of development provides a good deal of background noise, such as colonial past, multiculturalism and its meanings, indigenous rights *inter alia*, that can sometimes obscure the clear vision of what CCE might be in, say, Brazil or Mexico. While most writers see the ideal in the form of a grass roots movement, many also affirm the need for support from senior levels of government if the initiative is to succeed. The challenge will be to achieve that necessary support but to also retain sufficient autonomy to develop a form of educational practices and schooling systems that is openly committed to democratic participation and is informed by and appropriate to the local setting.

Another clear message from the combination of accounts presented here is the need for CCE to involve more than a dedicated subject area incorporated into the curriculum. In order to be effective, CCE must involve the whole school and there must be a clear and reiterated rationale for the idea of shared governance and distributed responsibility if participatory democracy is to prosper in the classroom and in the institution. Moreover these ideas must be incorporated into the state-wide school system to consciously counter the elitist and separatist tendencies that are endemic in some school systems, especially those in the developed world.

The three modalities that have been identified as central to education— the school system, the culture of schooling and the curriculum—have in recent times been oriented around individual achievement and competitive entrepreneurialism. From the standpoint of CCE we argue on the basis of the material presented in these case studies that the purposes of schooling in general and citizenship education in particular need to be revisioned in terms of the common good. Of course this does not mean that students will comprise an undifferentiated mass but rather that educational equity be promoted as a conscious goal of schooling for an inclusive society characterised by reciprocity and mutuality. Schooling structures that divide students are to be avoided. Thus, school choice can only operate if different schools are equally available to all students. In the interest of promoting a global citizenry the curriculum should embrace global as well as local and national perspectives so that students develop an understanding of their membership in multiple levels of societal arrangement. Present-day young people happily claim multiple layers of identities comprising the various cultural and racial mixes in their familial worlds, indicating that identity is fluid and changing rather than unitary and fixed in space and time (Gill & Howard 2009). In comparison with the parent generation they are much more accustomed to a rich cultural mix. CCE must celebrate these new ways of being together and belonging without the imposition of sameness. The curriculum should promote the processes of teaching and learning in a deliberative and constructive manner. In this context learning becomes not so much driven to find the 'right' answer but rather to operate in a space in which thinking and critical dialogue are encouraged in mutually respectful ways. Differences are to be explored and discussed and the idea of a common humanity encompassing needs, goods and feelings is celebrated. Such a learning environment would welcome the concept of multiculturalism as offering a chance to investigate the different pathways taken by others to arrive at a similar place or goal and from which to journey again.

All too often in discussions of CCE and the terms of its engagement the voices of politicians, administrators, school leaders and teachers are prominent and the voices of children are rarely heard if at all. Even in this collection we hear the policy makers and the government officials, educational leaders and political philosophers much more often than young people. As argued by Gill and Howard (2009), any serious curriculum development in CCE must begin with what the current generation of young people understand about the ways in which the world is organised. Ideally, learning would progress from the level of the local and immediate environment through the state to the idea of a global community.

The project that gave rise to this collection provokes educators to envisage a number of ways through which CCE could be progressed from a global perspective. This progression in the CCE curriculum would ideally be accompanied by a much greater degree of teacher collaboration and sharing of perspectives using an approach which rejects policy transfer or borrowing and which recognises differences in context, history, cultures, structures and values across countries. Using electronic communications, teachers could share resources, ideas and experiences across national borders. Research projects designed across national boundaries would promote greater exploration of local identities and specificities as well as more dialogue about education for global citizenship. Students in classrooms would be encouraged to use their technological skills to work on common problems with students from other nation-states. Such approaches would involve exciting educational possibilities for developing global awareness involving local and global patterns of action—thinking beyond the nation-state while working within it.

One real achievement of this work lies in its suggestion that the case of CCE stands as a particular instance of the issues that confront education more generally. Of course, CCE is evidently more clearly linked to political climate than some of the other subjects. However, by the twenty-first century the perception of education as a political process is hardly radical (Chapter 3, this volume). What has been shown here is that CCE is far from a simple linear transmission of particular ideology, but rather ideally comprises a space in which the best opportunities for critical dialogue can operate and model best practice for all educational endeavours. The collection is remarkable insofar as it displays the case for CCE as an ongoing struggle in which there are few right answers and no golden rules. Rather, in CCE the teachers and learners are involved in a mutual quest for finding better, more compelling ways to answer Bruner's fundamental question to educators working towards a well-educated citizenry: 'What shall we teach and to what end?' (1977, p. 1). For CCE it seems the goal of creating a participatory democracy has been a little clearer than the means. We hope that this book will contribute to a better understanding of how it is to be achieved.

REFERENCES

Apple, Michael (1996) *Cultural Politics and Education*. Buckingham, Open University Press.

Barton, Keith & Linda Levstik (2004) *Teaching History for the Common Good*. Mahwah, NJ, Lawrence Erlbaum Associates.

Bernstein, Basil (1971) On the classification and framing of knowledge, in Michael F.D. Young (ed.) *Knowledge and Control*. Basingstoke, Collier-Macmillan, pp. 47–69.

Bruner, Jerome (1977) *The Process of Education*. London, Harvard University Press.

De Cillia, Rudolf, Martin Reisigl & Ruth Wodak (1999) The discursive construction of national identities, *Discourse and Society*, 10(2), pp. 149–173.

Dimitrov, Georgi & Pepka Boyadieva (2009) Citizenship education as an instrument for strengthening the state's supremacy: An apparent paradox? *Citizenship Studies*, 13(2), pp. 153–169.

Gill, Judith & Sue Howard (2009) *Knowing Our Place: Children Talking about Power, Identity and Citizenship*. Camberwell, ACER Press.

Grundy, Shirley (1994) Being and becoming Australian: Classroom discourse and the construction of identity, *Discourse*, 15(1), pp. 14–23.

Hobsbawm, Eric (2007) *Globalisation, Democracy and Terrorism*. London, Little, Brown.

Labaree, David (1997) *How to Succeed in School without Really Learning: The Credentials Race in American Education*. New Haven, Yale University Press.

Pinar, William (2006) *The Synoptic Text Today and Other Essays: Curriculum Development after the Reconceptualization*. New York, Peter Lang.

Sears, Alan, Ian Davies & Alan Reid (2008) From Britishness to nothingness and back again. Paper presented at Britishness, The View from Abroad, University of Huddersfield, Huddersfield, UK, 5–6 June.

Sears, Alan & Andrew S Hughes (2006) Citizenship: Education or indoctrination, *Citizenship Teaching and Learning*, 2(1), pp. 3–17.

Sears, Alan & Emery Hyslop-Margison (2007) Crisis as a vehicle for educational reform: The case of citizenship education, *Journal of Educational Thought*, 41(1), pp. 43–62.

Tyack, David & William Tobin (1994) The grammar of schooling: Why has it been so hard to change? *American Educational Research Journal*, 31(3), pp. 453–480.

Part B
Case Studies

2 In Whose Interest?

Australian Schooling and the Changing Contexts of Citizenship

Alan Reid and Judith Gill

CIVICS EDUCATION AS A PROJECT OF SCHOOLING: THE HISTORICAL CONTEXT

In this chapter we want to assess the educational responses to globalisation in Australia in terms of their consistency with the kind of democracy and citizenship that we will argue is needed to meet the challenges of a globalising world. In particular we will critically explore how Australian governments over the past decade have understood the challenges to Australian democracy and the ways in which these understandings have been reflected in policy related to civics and citizenship education in schools. In order to place the task in context, we begin with a brief historical overview of the role that civics and citizenship education has played in Australian education.

As was argued in the introduction to this book, issues of civics and citizenship have been central across the curriculum and in the forms and structures of schools ever since the start of formal schooling in Australia (Grundy 1994). That is, constructing a national identity is embedded in the 'grammars' of schooling (Tyack & Tobin 1994). Thus, the introduction of state-provided education (public schools) by the Australian colonies in the 1870s was motivated by the need for social order (especially among the working classes), and for social cohesion (Grundy 1970; Miller 1986). For the next fifty years, state schools were elementary (primary) schools, at the end of which stage most working-class students left. The children of the middle classes and elites, on the other hand, largely attended private (church) schools which offered post-primary education and formed the pathway to university and white-collar employment (McCalman 1993). Even as state-provided, post-primary opportunities expanded in the first half of the twentieth century to meet the needs of an industrialising economy, so school structures were stratified with technical schools (trade and domestic) for working-class boys and girls, and high schools for the more socially mobile (Hyams & Bessant 1972; Miller 1986). In this way the structure of schooling reflected, normalised and reproduced the unequal power and social relationships that existed, first in the colonies and, following Federation in 1901, in the states. This situation constituted a powerful and continuing form of pedagogy for citizenship, brought to life through the very structure and organisation of schooling. It taught students, from an early age, about their proper place in society.

At the same time, throughout the period until the 1950s, the culture and processes of schools, and the official curriculum, melded two apparently contradictory roles in relation to civics and citizenship education. They taught and reinforced loyalty to the mother country (Great Britain) and to the British Empire. In addition, and with increasing intensity after Federation, they inculcated a sense of nationalism, fanned by writers and artists around the turn of the century, which developed pride in a new country that was free from some of the ingrained customs and divisions of the old: 'a new land is for new ideas!' (Goldstein 1918).

In the first half of the twentieth century at weekly assemblies, school-children sang the national anthem ('God Save the King/Queen'); recited the Oath of Allegiance ('I will serve the King/Queen, honour the flag and cheerfully obey my parents, teachers and the laws'; Education Department of South Australia 1953); raised the flag and marched in to class to the steady beat of a fife and drum band. When in class, students were instructed in a small number of tightly prescribed subjects, including arithmetic, English literature and British history. It was through these subjects, and particularly the stand-alone subject of civics, that young people were taught to become loyal subjects of the King and Empire, to vote and pay taxes and, if the need arose, to enlist and fight for country and Empire (Education Department of South Australia 1953). In these and other ways, schools were sites for nation-building and national identity formation—mediating a particular view of what it meant to be an Australian citizen, based on strong ties to Great Britain and an awareness of a new 'Australianness' (Musgrave 1979).

Over time the emphasis on the strong ties to Great Britain and the Empire weakened. The profound social changes that began in the post–World War II period were accompanied by an influx of non-British peoples from southern and eastern Europe who brought with them cultures and customs distinctly different from the dominant British culture. This influence, and the social and cultural revolutions of the 1960s, resulted in Australia slowly becoming, from the early 1970s, a more tolerant and cosmopolitan society—at least on the surface. There was a growing awareness of Australia's place in Asia, a focus on multiculturalism rather than assimilation or integration and a growing appreciation of the need for reconciliation with Aboriginal Australians (Manne 2001).

These developments inevitably challenged accepted practices in education. By the mid to late 1970s, most young people were experiencing at least two or three years of secondary schooling, increasing numbers of girls were completing secondary school, the stratified technical and high schools divisions were abandoned in favour of comprehensive high schools and the traditional competitive academic curriculum came under challenge (Connell et al. 1982). In addition, by the late 1980s the Australian university system had become a mass system, which encouraged a greater proportion of the population to think of themselves as university material, entitled to attend and take out degrees. Thus, education structures systematically began to mirror the social changes that were occurring in the wider society.

With the relative prosperity brought about by the population increase and the ready availability of work, more Australian families began to look to extended educational experiences as an important means of upward mobility for their children. Developments in the discipline of psychology lent weight to the idea that learning should be understood as an individual endeavour and that educational achievement was produced in terms of a good relationship between teacher and individual student. Teachers also embraced the idea of needing to gear their classroom treatments to each student rather than the group and 'treat them as individuals' became the new credo in teacher education (Grundy & Hatton 1996).

In this environment the older style of teaching for civics and citizenship education—both across the curriculum and as a stand-alone subject—appeared increasingly irrelevant. Schools became less regulated in terms of ritual ceremonies; Monday assemblies gradually abandoned the Oath of Allegiance and children no longer marched into class. The rigid seating patterns that had dominated classrooms in the pre-war years were replaced by more casual arrangements. The organisational culture of the school was no longer characterised by a military discipline but rather an atmosphere that included alternative elements, open space classrooms and group work.

Formal areas of study were also changing. By the 1970s, teachers were gaining a larger share of popular respect as professionals and were increasingly empowered to develop their own curricula in keeping with the perceived needs of the students and the teachers' particular skills (Jones 1971). Student demands for curricula to be relevant added to the push for education to become more flexible, with much attention to process as well as to the repeatedly stated commitment to maximise individual student potential. By the 1980s then, the civics and citizenship education function of the school, as represented in the hidden curriculum of school structures and process, was now a very different function from the one that had been performed in the first half of the twentieth century.

One outcome of these changes was to cause the study of civics to fall into serious decline as a formal area of study in schools. It had tended to be rejected by students as dry and boring and was an early victim of the progressive movement in education, which championed the call for relevance of curriculum content to student experience. The subject of civics was now subsumed by the broader, interdisciplinary subject of social studies where it dealt more with current issues than the structure and functions of government. As the Civics Expert Group was to note later:

There is no clear point at which Civics was submerged in Australian schooling, but by the late 1960s, social studies was disowning its civic function and declaring itself to be more concerned with 'current realities' than with the formal institutions and methods by which they were shaped. (Civics Expert Group 1994, p. 31)

This brief sweep across Australian educational history has served two purposes. First, it demonstrates that there is a close connection between the state, forms of democracy and school curricula. This is not a one-way relationship involving state-imposed policy and compliant teachers. Curriculum policy is always and rightly a site of struggle. But the dominant elites do have an edge in this struggle, and in the last instance the state will serve their interests (Bernstein 1971; Apple 1996). We have shown how schooling is organised, structured and practised by the state to serve particular versions of what it means to be a citizen in Australian democracy at specific historical moments. Second, our historical overview confirms the proposition put in the introduction to this volume: that the civics and citizenship function of schools is delivered through at least three modalities of the schooling project:

1. *The structure of schooling*: The ways in which formal schooling is organised in a society—the balance of public and private schools, funding arrangements, types of schools, processes of policy making and so on—which contain powerful messages about how the society is/should be structured, ordered and maintained.
2. *The culture and processes of schools*: The inculcation of the values and dispositions associated with citizenship seen in the organisational culture of the schools through such processes and events as its ceremonies, class organisation and pedagogy, discipline structures, traditions and relationships.
3. *Formal representations of civics and citizenship in the curriculum*: The formalised knowledge represented in the curriculum as 'civics and citizenship', usually concerned with the structures of power and governance, citizens' rights and responsibilities, and the skills and dispositions for participation in the polity and civil society. This area may have constituted a separate subject as in the first half of the twentieth century, but since the 1960s it has usually been taught across the curriculum, particularly within social studies or through a strand of what is now known as Studies of Society and the Environment (SOSE), as well as through the more traditional subjects such as history, geography, literature, science and the arts.

In the next section we use these three modalities as the theoretical framework for an analysis of contemporary approaches to civics and citizenship education. But since these modalities occur in and indeed are shaped by the wider context in which the state functions, we will start by describing some of the features of political life during the eleven years of the Howard government (1996–2007). We will then explore the extent to which these features influenced education, and specifically curriculum, policy.

THE CONTEMPORARY PERIOD: CHANGING GOVERNMENT IDEOLOGY, CHANGING SCHOOLING?

The Context

In 1996 the Liberal/National Party Coalition won government under the leadership of John Howard and the direction of Australian politics changed dramatically. Bearing an amalgam of neo-liberal and neo-conservative ideology, successive Howard governments reconfigured the multicultural settlement of the 1980s and challenged the ways in which concepts like *citizen* and *citizenship* are understood and used in the public sphere. Not surprisingly, attempts were made to co-opt schools into the service of this agenda, particularly their role in forming the citizen subject.

Before Howard's election, the Hawke and Keating Labour governments (1983–1996) had been attempting to complete Prime Minister Gough Whitlam's project from twenty years earlier—described by Manne as 'the transformation of Australia from a postcolonial British settler society to fully independent nationhood' (2001, p. 2). This included an embrace of multiculturalism, recognition of the need for Australia to have deeper links with countries in the Asian region, a proposal for Australia to free itself from its colonial past by becoming a republic and an assertion of the need for reconciliation with Indigenous Australians. From the outset, the new Howard government set about dismantling these policy directions.

Within a decade of winning government, Howard was able to boast in his 2006 Australia Day speech that Australia had now successfully rebalanced national identity and cultural and ethnic diversity:

> We've drawn back from being too obsessed with diversity to a point where Australians are now better able to appreciate the enduring values of the national character that we proudly celebrate and preserve. (Howard 2006)

Behind this triumphalist tone lay a trail of policy initiatives and political rhetoric based on a mixture of fervent Australian nationalism, fear of external threats, attacks on 'political correctness' and so-called 'black armband'[1] views of Australian history. There is not the space here to tell the full story. Rather, for current purposes, we will draw attention to the ways in which democratic processes and the concept of 'citizenship' were narrowed and diluted.

Howard's legitimation of an antipolitical correctness line changed the tenor and tone of public conversation: indeed, some described the new form of public discourse as being a 'war on democracy' (Lucy & Mickler 2006). For example, radio shock jocks and conservative media commentators attacked the so-called 'social elites' and 'chattering classes' for holding progressive views claimed to be at odds with the interests and views of the 'Aussie battlers' upon whose behalf they purported to speak; and left-leaning public intellectuals were named and derided under Parliamentary privilege (Hamilton & Maddison 2007).

At the same time there were ongoing efforts to narrow the definition of Australian citizenship. Thus refugees fleeing repressive regimes—the so-called 'boat people'—were constructed as the 'other' through exclusionary discourses and strategies; placed under detention orders in far-flung detention centres for indeterminate periods of time; and accused by the government of being a threat to 'border security'. From positions of safety, radio shock jocks and the conservative commentariat described the asylum seekers as 'queue jumpers' and 'terrorist sympathisers' (Crock, Saul & Dastyari 2006).

Of course, all of this was played out against the backdrop of 9/11, the 'war on terror' and the Iraq war—events which underlined the message of fear that was the bedrock of government policy. In 2001, Prime Minister Howard garnered substantial public support when he refused to allow the *Tampa*, a Norwegian vessel which had saved a sinking boatload of refugees on their way to Australia, to land on Australian soil. Not long after, he falsely accused another boatload of refugees in a sinking vessel of throwing their children overboard to advance their chances of arriving in Australia. Howard's famous claims during the 2001 election that 'we will decide who comes to this country and the manner in which they come' fed the picture of a government protecting rightful Australians from an alien threat and made a major contribution to the re-election of the Liberal/National party government (see Marr & Wilkinson 2003).

In such a climate it was inevitable that understandings about citizenship would change significantly. Calls from senior government ministers for a focus on 'Australian values' confirmed a sense of 'us' and 'them'. The treasurer, Peter Costello, for example, observed that those immigrants who don't like 'our' values should go home (Lateline 2005). With citizens being defined through a much narrower lens, the stage was set for a new version of Australian citizenship, one that placed greater emphasis on sameness than on difference.

For some time there had been a consistent attack on the concept of multiculturalism which, according to the government, placed too great a focus on diversity at the expense of national cohesion. Bipartisan support from the major parties resulted in an act which established a compulsory test for citizenship based on the view that Australian values are not optional—migrants who refuse to accept them, or learn them, should be refused citizenship. A multiple-choice test—which expected new citizens to learn and regurgitate under test conditions disparate knowledge about Australian iconic events, people, values and customs—was introduced in the Australian Citizenship Act of 2007.

Such changes were emblematic of the attempts to redefine what it meant to be a citizen in Howard's Australia. They eschewed difference, assuming a homogenous Australian culture with an agreed set of values; and disciplined the most vulnerable citizens in the community. In this way Australian citizenship was constituted through a discourse of exclusion which distinguished between 'us' and 'them' and which characterised the 'other' as people not to be trusted. As a number of researchers have pointed out, such an approach is consistent with the project of nation-building, including the formulation of nation, national identity and citizenship (e.g. Hall 1997; Urry 1998; Christie & Sidhu 2006). To use Hannah Arendt's powerful image, such an outcome represents the 'conquest of the state by the nation' (Arendt 1951, p. 275, quoted in Isin & Turner 2007, p. 12).

Although schools have a certain relative autonomy, they are state apparatuses, and are therefore caught in a tension between their role in establishing the conditions for capital accumulation and for democratic practice (Althusser 1971). This legitimation role whereby schools reflect and refract the guiding principles of dominant social groups is usually shaped by the prevailing political settlement (Apple 1996). Nonetheless, it has long been recognised that when the state is reshaping the social and cultural practices of a society, as the Howard government did in Australia for over a decade, it is inevitable that the organisational and curricula structures and processes of schools will be expected to bear the burden of some of this change (Bernstein 1971; Pinar 2006). How was civics and citizenship education constructed in this environment?

THE THREE MODALITIES OF CIVICS AND CITIZENSHIP EDUCATION

During the Howard decade, each of the three federal ministers of education—Kemp, Nelson and Bishop—used schooling, and specifically civics education, as an important plank in the government's attempt to consolidate a particular approach to democratic processes and to understandings of citizenship. We will argue that this created a form of civics and citizenship education that is redolent of the early years of the last century—one that is manifestly out of step with the challenges of citizenship and political participation in a globalising world. We will employ the heuristic of the three modalities to demonstrate how this occurred, spending the most time on the third.

The Structure of Schooling

The messages contained in the federal government's schooling policy constituted a form of civics education in the broadest sense. The central platform was the concept of individual choice, where parents and students are understood as consumers and education as a commodity. On the basis of this logic, the Howard federal government increased funding to private schools, thus speeding up the drift of students from public to private schools and leading to the current position in which just over 66 percent of students nationally attend government schools, a decline from 70.4 percent in 1997 (Australian Bureau of Statistics 2008).

Much empirical research from around the world demonstrates the social effects of constructing education around individual choice. Such research shows that marketised schooling systems result in a loss of the diversity of student populations and a significant growth in the disparity of resources between schools. And these differentiations are invariably organised on the basis of socio-economic status, ethnicity, religion and race. Already, the focus on individual choice within education markets is creating a number of tendencies in Australia. Such choices create an educational environment which promotes competition between schools and the imperative to market schools; the re-creation of curriculum hierarchies as schools seek to establish market niche; and the residualisation of public education (Caro & Bonner 2007).

An approach like this foregrounds the private benefits of education at the expense of seeing education as a public good (Reid 2002). Such an environment projects a narrow, competitive and individualistic view of the world. In an educational culture where many schools are organised around single world-views, or where competition is valorised, it is difficult to promote educational outcomes that foster a sense of the common good, reciprocity and respect for difference. Accompanying the neo-liberal policy regime at the federal level has been a corporate managerialist approach to the administration of education at the state levels. The professional autonomy that teachers experienced in the 1970s and 1980s has been replaced by top-down processes of surveillance and accountability, where teachers are seen as technicians implementing the ideas of 'expert' policy makers who construct policy many steps removed from actual teaching practice (Hargreaves 2003).

In such a policy environment, the socialising messages of choice and technical rationality become a surrogate but powerful form of civics and citizenship education because they highlight what is valued (and not valued) in citizens and the processes of democracy. Far from participatory and engaged citizenship, these messages suggest that the ideal form of governance in society involves a quiet and compliant citizenry which limits its political involvement to voting every three or four years.

The Cultures and Processes of Schools

Although the Australian Constitution does not give the federal government responsibility for school education, in the past decade successive federal ministers of education have mounted sustained attacks on the supposed low quality of school education in the various states and territories, particularly of schools and teachers in the public system. The attacks have been accompanied by a similar campaign conducted by the national newspaper, the *Australian*. Using the language of crisis as a vehicle for reform (Sears & Hyslop-Margison 2007), both the government and some sections of the media constructed an educational environment in which any initiative which goes beyond a restricted set of discipline-based subjects, transmission pedagogy or external examinations was deemed to constitute a 'dumbing down' of the curriculum. State ministers were sensitive to the political effects of these claims, and, in the name of 'rigour' and 'standards', dismantled a number of progressive strategies designed to cater to diverse groups of students. All of these interventions have begun to shape the organisational structures and processes of schools in ways that resemble versions of schooling from the 1950s and before.

In 2004, the prime minister stepped up the 'culture wars' by claiming provocatively that public schools don't teach values because they are too 'politically correct and too values-neutral' (*Australian*, 20 January 2004), and it was not long before Minister Nelson was proposing a focus on values education. In the next few months his department developed a National Framework for Values which named nine 'values for Australian schooling'—freedom, honesty, respect, care and compassion, fair go, doing your best, integrity, understanding and tolerance, and inclusion. These were the centre-piece of a $29 million campaign involving school-based values projects and conferences. A values poster containing the silhouetted image of Simpson and his donkey (a once celebrated and partly mythical hero from World War I) as the background to the selected values was sent to every school in Australia.

To ensure that such developments were not ignored by the states, in 2005 the federal government moved to a form of coercive federalism where federal funding for schools was made conditional on the implementation of a number of federal initiatives, including the requirement that all schools must hang the values poster in the school foyer. Other expectations were that all schools have and use a fully functioning flagpole, (re)introduce a traditional 'A–E' grading system and publish the results of 'benchmark' tests to parents. Under the threat of losing funds, the states fell into line with these demands.

In all of these policies, the federal government was seeking to reach into schools and to influence pedagogical style. The templates it used for this intervention were the practices of earlier times in Australian education, characterised by order, certainty and classification. Inexorably, by returning to the past, the federal government was seeking to (re)create a version of Australian education that was designed, through the cultures and processes of schools, to produce the individual citizen subject: loyal, competitive and compliant.

Formal Representations of Civics and Citizenship in the Curriculum

In the late 1980s, two Senate Enquiries (Senate Select Committee on Employment, Education and Training 1989, 1991) produced evidence to show there was a low level of knowledge among eighteen-year-old Australians about the Australian political system. This caused a great deal of consternation in political circles and the then Labour government subsequently established a 'Civics Expert Group' to explore the problem and recommend some possible solutions. The subsequent report—*Whereas the People: Civics and Citizenship Education in Australia* (Civics Expert Group 1994)—provided the rationale for a significant federal intervention into civics education. It was clear that there was a determination that civics and citizenship education should return to being a more visible part of the school curriculum.

Dr. Kemp, who was appointed as Howard's first education minister in 1996, made it clear that he intended to pursue the civics agenda set in train by the previous Keating government. However, under Kemp, the civics project, now labelled 'Discovering Democracy', was reduced to the development of a set of materials which were sent to all schools in late 1998. The process of development and the nature of the materials made it clear that 'Discovering Democracy' represented a shift of ideological gears, consistent with the government's broader agenda outlined earlier. The package had a strong curriculum content focus for each year level of schooling, to be integrated across the curriculum, or as a stand-alone subject, and with a strong historical flavour. Although many of the materials were useful resources for teachers, their most notable feature was what they did *not* contain. Thus, the materials lacked almost any attention to diversity and what it means to be a citizen in a multicultural society; and almost totally neglected a consideration of the changing concept of citizenship in a globalising world. They also marginalised the development of political skills for active citizenship, particularly in the areas of environmental sustainability and social justice.

The 'Discovering Democracy' project was maintained as the federal flagship for civics and citizenship education until 2004, throughout which time its content emphasis continued. Associated with the project were a number of video kits that were developed and distributed to all Australian schools. The seemingly objective, factual nature of the material disguised its gendered construction. For example, one video featured the ANZAC story,[2] stressing the heroism of the soldiers who fought for king and country, their mateship and loyalty to their cause and to each other. Women, on the other hand, were included in reference to the baking of the Anzac cookie, a national symbol of this piece of military history. Another video took up the issue of Australia as a military power and ranged through the several wars in which Australian troops were involved. Once again the representations centred around men as the soldiers or leaders in war. Prefiguring some of these developments, Pettman wrote in 1996:

This routine invisibility of women . . . is also encouraged by the current recasting of Australian identity in militaristic associations of manhood, independence, bloodying and agency on the international scene . . . this history routinely masculinises nationalism and militarises citizenship. (p. 16)

Although the 'Discovering Democracy' project ceased being funded in 2004, the Howard government maintained, even increased, its determination to implement its version of civics and citizenship education in schools. In his Australia Day speech in 2006, Prime Minister Howard boasted that on his watch there had been a successful rebalancing of Australia's national identity and cultural and ethnic diversity. However, he claimed that there was much more to do and that education was central to this work. In particular, he called for a 'coalition of the willing' to promote a 'root and branch' renewal of teaching history which had 'succumbed to a postmodern culture of relativism where any object of achievement is questioned or repudiated'. Instead, said the prime minister, Australian schools must replace the fragmented stew of issues and themes that currently exist as historical education with a single structured historical narrative (Howard 2006). It was made clear that alternative narratives to the one that would be officially endorsed would not be acceptable.

Education Minister Bishop took the cue and in a speech opening the National History Teachers Conference in 2006, she attacked state curricula, announcing that she would convene a national history summit comprising the 'sensible centre of educators' (Bishop 2006). This summit was held in August 2006 and predictably recommended compulsory Australian history at years nine and ten in all Australian schools, organised around a chronologically structured narrative approach. History was now being co-opted in the service of a conservative model of citizenship focusing on the nation.

Just as in the first half of the twentieth century, the curriculum area of civics and citizenship was now being based on an inward-looking nationalism and an exclusionary concept of citizenship. It must be stressed here that we are not suggesting that the ideological slant of the federal government was simply implemented in the various states. Far from it. Although this chapter has been based on the official discourses about civics and citizenship education—mainly as represented in policy texts—at the level of the federal government, we appreciate that many of the curriculum developers in the states and territories, and teachers in schools, were putting in place far more expansive versions of civics. Indeed, at the political level, the Ministerial Council for Education, Employment and Youth Affairs (MCEETYA)—the regular meeting of the state education ministers—tried to wrest back a more progressive curriculum agenda through a proposal for nationally consistent statements of learning. The civics version of these statements, for example, included a quite clear focus on knowledge and skills for active citizenship. But this was a rearguard action and, by 2007, the increasing use of its financial muscle suggested that the federal government was going to get its way.

But in late 2007, the Howard government was defeated. The new Rudd Labour government is as yet untested in terms of its implications for schooling but this work will need to involve the recognition that Australian democracy has changed. In its first few months the new government has pledged an 'education revolution', setting in train proposals for a national curriculum, proposing new forms of 'transparent' accountability and committing significant expenditure to capital works and other infrastructure for every school in the country. Disappointingly, much of this work has a strong technocratic orientation; improved education outcomes are justified in terms of the economy; and the curriculum vision appears to be a return to a small number of stand-alone 'academic' subjects. However, the new government has stated a firm commitment to equity and a determination to work collaboratively with the states on national approaches. These approaches offer some space for more critical approaches to civics and citizenship education of the kind spelt out in the next section. Only time will tell.

CONCLUSION: CIVICS EDUCATION BEYOND THE NATION-STATE

In this chapter we have explored the relationship between the state and schooling in developing an officially sanctioned version of civics and citizenship education in Australia. We have argued, using examples from the history of Australian education, that the state has employed three key modalities to shape civics and citizenship education; and we have critically analysed how these modalities were employed during the years of the Howard government in the service of forming citizen subjects. The concerns raised about those directions were twofold.

First, we believe that it was based upon a constrained view of democracy which posited democracy as a thing, something to be discovered and accessed when needed, rather than as a process of ongoing engagement in critical and thoughtful deliberation in public arenas. The idea of deliberative democracy (Parker 2006; Young 2002) has never been more important than now. A multicultural society organised around enclaved communities of difference with civic engagement limited to voting every three or four years is doomed to fail. Unless citizens have the skills and the opportunities to engage in democratic dialogue across groups, and unless this dialogue is characterised by a sense of reciprocity, then ethnic tensions can only multiply. In order to meet the demands of a world of increasing diversity and interdependence, civics and citizenships education in Australia must be based upon more sophisticated notions of democratic theory. And importantly, education policy must recognise the powerful messages that the structure of schooling systems and the organisation and processes of schools give out about what and who is valued in society.

Second, we believe that the focus of civics and citizenship education as a preparation for civic life in a nation-state like Australia is a necessary but not a sufficient condition for citizenship in the twenty-first century. Since notions of citizenship are still defined by the rights and responsibilities that derive from living in sovereign nation-states, national and local identities cannot be ignored. But as many scholars have noted, the expanded global flows of goods, services and people, the increasing economic and environmental interdependence of all nation-states and the new and additional forms of influence and decision making at regional and global levels are making redundant old versions of citizenship and therefore citizenship education (e.g. Hobsbawm 2007). As Held (2001, quoted in Osler & Starkey 2003, p. 246) points out, we live in 'overlapping communities of fate'—local, regional, national, international and increasingly virtual.

In our view the concepts of cosmopolitan citizenship proposed by Osler and Starkey (2003), and of inclusive citizenship based on institutional multiculturalism (Kiwan 2008), hold potential for reimagining what it means to be a citizen of a nation-state in a globalising world. They offer a genuine alternative to the myopic policy direction that has been pursued in Australia over the past decade. Instead of a narrowly nation-state-focused civics education which ignores diversity and power differentials in society, we believe that there is an urgent need to begin the conversation about ways in which the three modalities of Australian schooling might be reconstituted to reflect a more cosmopolitan and identity-based conception of citizens and deeper forms of democratic engagement. This would include reorientating:

- *The structure of schooling*, to be based upon a rejuvenated notion of the public good and social reciprocity in place of market-based competitive individualism, with the professional expertise of teachers recognised, respected and employed in policy making.
- *The cultures and processes* of schools to reflect models of deliberative democracy where power differentials are recognised and the culture of the school is one that eschews certainty and dogmatism in favour of open, respectful and critical dialogue and analysis, and 'operationalises multiculturalism' (Kiwan 2008, p. 108).
- *Formal representations of civics and citizenship* in the curriculum to ensure that the curriculum engages with the actual experiences of learners who in a globalising world are likely to have multiple identities and a sense of belonging that is not necessarily expressed primarily in terms of the nation; and embraces global as well as local and national perspectives.

We have argued that the absence of these features from education policy at the federal level in the past decade has exacerbated the problems facing Australian democracy. Far from being a 'new civics' for contemporary times as described by Print (1996), Australian education has witnessed a rerun of earlier versions of civics and citizenship education—fiercely nationalistic, based on a limited understanding of democracy, an individualised and passive notion of *citizen* and a failure to take account of the diversity of the Australian population or the effect of globalisation in its various guises on Australian democracy. In our view, in the twenty-first century this curriculum trajectory can only lead to disaster, ignoring as it does the rich diversity of Australian society and the fact that Australia exists in a globalising world. But it doesn't have to be this way. Education (and specifically civics and citizenship education) can play a role in reshaping democracy, rather than simply reprising versions that were designed for different times and different circumstances.

ACKNOWLEDGMENTS

An earlier version of this chapter appeared as 'An arm of the state? Linking citizenship education and schooling practice', in the *International Journal of Citizenship Teaching and Learning* (2009), 5(1), pp. 3–17. Permission to use this material has been granted by the editor, Professor Ian Davies.

NOTES

1. The 'black armband' view of history is a pejorative term used by conservative commentators and intellectuals to describe interpretations of Australian history that are perceived to be too negative, such as histories that focus on the colonial dispossession of Indigenous Australians.
2. The ANZAC story concerns a WWI engagement at Gallipoli wherein the Australian and New Zealand forces were defeated. It was routinely retold in schools before the 1960s but had slipped from focus until its very recent revival with Prime Minister Howard leading pilgrimages of young people to ANZAC cove in Turkey.

REFERENCES

Althusser, Louis (1971) Ideology and ideological state apparatuses, in *'Lenin and Philosophy' and Other Essays*. London, New Left Books, pp. 123–173.
Apple, Michael (1996) *Cultural Politics and Education*. Buckingham, Open University Press.
Arendt, Hannah (1951) *The Origins of Totalitarianism*. New York, Harcourt Brace.
Australian Bureau of Statistics (2008) http://www.abs.gov.au/Ausstats/ABS@. nsf/Latestproducts/4221.0Main%20Features22008?opendocument&tabname=Summary&prodno=4221.0&issue=2008&num=&view (accessed 18 April 2008).
Bernstein, Basil (1971) On the classification and framing of knowledge, in Michael F.D. Young (ed.) *Knowledge and Control*. Basingstoke, Collier-Macmillan, pp. 47–69.

Bishop, Julie (2006) Address to the History Teachers' Association Conference, Fremantle, Western Australia, 6 October, http://www.dest.gov/au./Ministers/Media/Bishop/2006/10/B001061006.asp (accessed 18 April 2008).

Caro, Jane & Chris Bonner (2007) *The Stupid Country: How Australia is Dismantling Public Education.* Sydney, University of New South Wales Press.

Christie, Pam & Ravinder Sidhu (2006) Governmentality and 'fearless speech': Framing the education of asylum seeker and refugee children in Australia, *Oxford Review of Education,* 32(4), pp. 449–465.

Civics Expert Group (1994) *Whereas the People: Civics and Citizenship Education.* Canberra, Australian Government Publishing Service.

Connell, Robert W, Dean Ashenden, Gary Dowsett & Sandra Kessler (1982) *Making the Difference: Schools, Families and Social Division.* Sydney, Allen & Unwin.

Crock, Mary, Ben Saul & Azadeh Dastyari (2006) *Future Seekers II. Refugees and Irregular Migration in Australia.* Sydney, Federation Press.

Education Department of South Australia (1953) *Course of Instruction for Primary Schools.* South Australia, Government Printer.

Goldstein, Vida (1918) *Historical Manuscripts Commission: National Register of Archives, Historical Manuscripts Commission, 2002,* http://www.hmc.gov.uk/searches/pidocs.asp?P=P11498 (accessed 5 February 2005).

Grundy, Denis (1970) *Secular, Compulsory and Free: The Education Act of 1872.* Carlton, Melbourne University Press.

Grundy, Shirley (1994) Being and becoming Australian: Classroom discourse and the construction of identity, *Discourse,* 15(1), pp. 14–23.

Grundy, Shirley & Elizabeth Hatton (1996) Teacher educators, student teachers and biography, www.aare.edu.au/96pap/gruns96227.txt (accessed 12 June 2008).

Hall, Stuart (1997) Old and new identities, old and new ethnicities, in Anthony D. King (ed.) *Culture, Globalization and the World System.* Minneapolis, University of Minnesota Press, pp. 41–68.

Hamilton, Clive & Sara Maddison (2007) *Silencing Dissent.* Sydney, Allen & Unwin.

Hargreaves, Andy (2003) *Teaching in the Knowledge Society: Education in the Age of Insecurity.* New York, Teachers College Press.

Hobsbawm, Eric (2007) *Globalisation, Democracy and Terrorism.* London, Little, Brown.

Howard, John (2006) Australia Day Speech, http://www.australianpolitics.com/news/2006/01/06–01–25_howard.shtml (accessed 22 April 2007).

Hyams, Bernard & Bob Bessant (1972) *Schools for the People? An Introduction to the History of Sate Education in Australia.* Melbourne, Victoria, Longman.

Isin, Engin & Brian Turner (2007) Investigating citizenship: An agenda for citizenship studies, *Citizenship Studies,* 11(1), pp. 5–17.

Jones, Alby (1971) Freedom and Authority Memorandum, http://www.unisa.edu.au/hawkecentre/events/2007events/ATIR (accessed on 26/3/2008).

Kiwan, Dina (2008) *Education for Inclusive Citizenship.* Milton Park, Oxon, Routledge.

Lateline (2005) Transcript of Lateline interview with Peter Costello, 28 May, http://www.abc.net.au./;ateline/content/2005/s1444603.htm (accessed 12 February 2008).

Lucy, Niall & Steve Mickler (2006) *The War on Democracy.* Perth, University of Western Australia Press.

Manne, Robert (2001) *The Barren Years.* Melbourne, Text Publishing Company.

Marr, David & Marian Wilkinson (2003) *Dark Victory.* Sydney, Allen & Unwin.

McCalman, Janet (1993) *Journeyings: The Biography of a Middle Class Generation.* Carlton, Melbourne University Press.

Miller, Pavla (1986) *Long Division: State Schooling in South Australian Society.* Adelaide, Wakefield Press.

Musgrave, Peter (1979) *Society and the Curriculum in Australia.* Sydney, George Allen & Unwin.

Osler, Audrey & Hugh Starkey (2003) Learning for cosmopolitan citizenship: Theoretical debates and young people's experiences, *Educational Review,* 55(3), pp. 243–254.

Parker, Walter C (2006) Public discourses in schools: Purposes, problems, possibilities, *Educational Researcher,* 35(8), pp. 11–18.

Pettman, Jan Jindy (1996) Second-class citizens? Nationalism, identity and difference in Australia, in Barbara Sullivan & Gillian Whitehouse (eds.) *Gender, Politics and Citizenship in the 1990s.* Sydney, University of New South Wales Press. pp. 2–25.

Pinar, William (2006) *The Synoptic Text Today and Other Essays: Curriculum Development after the Reconceptualization.* New York, Peter Lang.

Print, Murray (1996) The new civics education: An integrated approach for Australian schools, *Social Education,* 60(7), pp. 443–447.

Reid, Alan (2002) Public education and democracy: A changing relationship in a globalising world, *Journal of Education Policy,* 17(5), pp. 571–585.

Sears, Alan & Emory Hyslop-Margison (2007) Crisis as a vehicle for educational reform: The case of citizenship education, *Journal of Educational Thought,* 41(1), pp. 43–62.

Senate Select Committee on Employment, Education and Training (1989) *Education for Active Citizenship in Australian Schools and Youth Organisations.* Canberra, Australian Government Printing Service.

———. (1991) *Education Citizenship Education Revisited.* Canberra, Australian Government Printing Service.

Tyack, David & William Tobin (1994) The grammar of schooling: Why has it been so hard to change? *American Educational Research Journal,* 31(3), pp. 453–480.

Urry, John (1998) Contemporary transformations of time and space, in Peter Scott (ed.) *The Globalization of Higher Education.* Balmoor, Open University Press, pp. 1–17.

Young, Iris Marion (2002) *Inclusion and Democracy.* Oxford, Oxford University Press.

3   Education, Citizenship and the Construction of a New Democracy in Brazil

Tristan McCowan and Cleonice Puggian

INTRODUCTION

Brazil is, in many ways, a highly democratic country. The Constitution of 1988 guarantees extensive civil and social rights, and electoral participation is almost universal on account of compulsory voting laws and an efficient electronic voting system. Nevertheless, these formal aspects hide significant political marginalisation in practice. Brazil has amongst the highest rates of socio-economic inequality in the world, the income of the richest 10 percent of the population being 51.3 times that of the poorest 10 percent (UNDP 2008). The severe poverty of a large portion of the population, combined with deeply ingrained privilege and abuse of power on the part of local and national elites, has put limits on effective participation in political affairs.

In this chapter we will explore the development of citizenship education in Brazil in the past twenty-five years, in the light of the political context outlined above. We begin by focusing on the structure of the educational system, exploring how the culture and processes of schools, as well as representations of civics and citizenship in the curriculum, have been determined by power asymmetries and policies regulated by international interests in a national scenario of political instability and influences of globalisation. Whilst showing the pervasive inequalities, we also highlight advances in policy and practice, indicating how they may contribute to the consolidation of a participatory democracy. Considering the contemporary political and educational context, the chapter also provides empirical evidence of programmes implemented by grass roots groups and local governments, showing how they have strengthened opposition to dominant paradigms and created viable alternatives to meet the challenges of a new democracy. We conclude by exploring the distinctive characteristics and complexities of Brazilian initiatives relating to education and democracy in the global context.

EDUCATION AND CITIZENSHIP IN THE NEW BRAZILIAN REPUBLIC

The late 1970s and early 1980s were a time of unrest in the Brazilian political scene. There was a national call for democracy and for the democratisation of education, culminating in the end of the dictatorship after twenty-one years of military rule (1964–1985). The year 1985 marks the beginning of a new era in Brazilian history, known as the Democratic Transition or the New Republic (1985–present). It was a period of intense social mobilisation, animated by debates regarding the destiny of the regained democracy. Civil society organisations (grass roots movements, non-governmental organisations, unions and left-wing sections of the Catholic Church) were able to influence the new constitution, established in 1988, as well as new legislation, such as the Statute of the Child and the Adolescent (1990). The democratic euphoria underlying the campaign for presidential elections (called *Diretas Já*) also intensified the debates between the left and right regarding the design of the new educational laws and programmes. Education became a contested field as different groups engaged in disputes to defend their particular interests.

However, both the transitional government of Sarney (1985–1990) and the first elected government of Collor and Franco (1990–1995) failed to deliver the reforms necessary for economic and social growth after the return of democracy. Collor's programmes were guided by neo-liberal policies, characterised by a gradual reduction of state intervention in the market, associated with increased privatisation and limited investment in social sectors. This approach far from guaranteed the political and social rights laid out by the new constitution, especially in the field of education. According to Burton (2008), the main obstacles for the implementation of educational reforms during this initial decade were the political inheritance received from the military regime; the instability of the first governments, with Fernando Collor resigning to avoid corruption charges in 1992; the decentralisation of political institutions; and 'the development of the education sector as an increasingly politicised arena of contestation, which would persist into the reform period after 1995' (Burton 2008, p. 2). In the process of (re)discovering democracy, little improvement was made in the educational system. In the 1980s more than 25 percent of young people between seven and fourteen years old were still out of school. On average, 50 percent of all pupils were retained in first grade and 32 percent dropped out before completing fourth grade. Furthermore, about 25.9 percent of the population over five years old was illiterate (Mattos 1992). By 1988 completion rates had increased slightly to 35 percent, but other problems such as grade repetition and dropping out continued to perpetuate the social and educational exclusion of working-class children (Patto 1999).

Citizenship education during this time was marked by competing approaches to democracy, national identity, political participation and civil rights. While military policies were conservative and presented democracy within the constraints of the 'Revolution', a number of new programmes emerged, inspired by the ideas of Paulo Freire (1972, 1974, 1976) and supported by grass roots movements and local left-wing governments, aiming for the liberation of the oppressed through dialogic action and democratic participation.

One controversial development in citizenship education during this decade was Moral and Civic Education. This subject was implemented by the law no. 869 of 12 September 1969, and remained in the curriculum until 1993. According to Rezende (2001), Moral and Civic Education was created to legitimate the actions of the dictatorship, emphasising its contribution to the maintenance of a democratic state. The subject allowed the government to publicise the overall values and aims of the 'Revolution', seeking recognition and support from people in diverse social classes. Overall, it was intended to transmit the military ideology, enforcing its legitimacy (Abreu & Filho 2006; Amaral 2007; Nunes & Rezende 2008; Rodrigues 2004).

The guiding concepts for the subject were 'the nation', 'the homeland', 'national integration', 'tradition', 'law', 'work' and 'heroes' (Fonseca 1993). These ideas, besides constituting the core of Moral and Civic Education, were also supposed to guide the work of teachers and students in all disciplines (e.g. history, Portuguese and geography) inside and outside the classroom (e.g. civic ceremonies). In addition, teachers were expected to assist students in the construction of Educational Civic Centres, allowing them to learn about their civic obligations through political participation within the school community. However, in spite of the tight military control over civilian activities, documents have shown that Moral and Civic Education ended up allowing critical teachers to engage in counter-ideological work, as they used the curriculum to challenge the military regime and the ideas advocated by the 'Revolution'. Resistance was also engendered by students within Educational Civic Centres, which became arenas of contestation and political activism for young people (Abreu & Filho 2006). These facts, however, remain largely unexplored in the literature and more research is needed to clarify their contribution to the Brazilian democratic transition.

After the end of the military regime the maintenance of Moral and Civic Education in the curriculum became a controversial issue (Amaral 2007). On the one hand, members of the parliament emphasised its links with the dictatorship and the need to remove it; on the other hand, left-wing activists argued that it should be maintained, as it allowed teachers and students to engage in political debate within schools. In spite of the controversy, the subject was removed from the curriculum in June 1993. However, Amaral (2007) has noted that between 1997 and 2006 members of the parliament presented about thirteen proposals to reintroduce 'a discipline that encompasses ethics and citizenship, seeking to restore values that have supposedly been lost by society' (p. 351). While these proposals reveal divergent understandings of morality and politics by conservative and progressive segments of Brazilian society, they also show a persistent claim for the inclusion of citizenship education in the national curriculum.

Overall, the discipline of Moral and Civic Education illustrates instabilities in government policy during the first decade of the New Republic;

it is an example of the country's unconvincing transition to democracy. Indeed, policies and practices inherited from the military regime (e.g. law 5692/71)—as well as the instability of the transitional government of José Sarney and the clumsy start of Fernando Collor—failed to increase educational opportunities and to improve the quality of state-funded schools. As a result, this period became known as the 'lost decade' (Barros, Henriques & Mendonça 2002).

The Centre-Right Government of Fernando Henrique Cardoso (1995–2003)

In 1994, former finance minister Fernando Henrique Cardoso was elected president and continued the reforms begun by Itamar Franco (1992–1995). Neo-liberal policies were prevalent during Cardoso's centre-right government (which lasted until 2003, with his re-election in 1998). One of the most indicative changes was the adoption, through the Ministry of Education, of a pedagogical orientation adjusted to the interests of international business and organisations. At the core of education policy during his government were reforms aimed at making schools efficient and effective. These reforms followed, firstly, the new constitution (1988) and later the Law of Directives and Bases of National Education—the LDB (law No. 9,394/96), which was approved in December 1996.

After the LDB was passed, the structure of the educational system was redivided into basic education (comprising early childhood, primary and secondary education) and higher education (undergraduate and postgraduate levels). Within basic education, early childhood education included day care (zero to three years) and preschools (four to six years); primary education (seven to fourteen years) accounted for compulsory education, corresponding to grades one to eight; and secondary education (fifteen to seventeen years), although not compulsory, was expected to gradually include all students. During Cardoso's government there was also the creation of the Fund for the Development of Fundamental Education and Enhancement of the Teaching Profession (FUNDEF) and the launch of a ten-year Education Plan, which mandated, among other things, the achievement of universal access to fundamental education and the training of all teachers in undergraduate programmes. These goals were partially achieved during his administration. Indeed, in 1999 about 97 percent of all school-age children between seven and fourteen years old were enrolled in primary education. The main advancement in citizenship education was the publication of the National Curriculum Parameters (NCPs), which established a common curricular basis for primary and secondary education, as will be discussed in the next section.

While Cardoso's government was marked by the universalisation of basic education, large inequalities remained after his term as president. As a result, Brazil began the new millennium having to confront serious problems, such as: (a) limited access to secondary and higher education, (b) low 'quality' of educational provision in state-funded schools, (c) persistence of grade retention and (d) low completion rates in basic education. By and large, the inconclusive democratic transition of the 1980s, the instability of Collor's government, Itamar's adoption of international economic policies and the consolidation of the neo-liberal approach during Cardoso's government were key to maintaining educational inequalities during the 1990s, and they constrained further developments in citizenship education.

The Centre-Left government of Lula (2003–present)

In a political scenario of disillusionment, the election of Luiz Inácio Lula da Silva in 2002 brought high hopes for educational and social change. However, in his first term as president, little was modified in the educational field (Frigotto 2007). One significant alteration was the consolidation of various benefit payments into a single cash transfer programme, now the basis of Brazil's reformed social protection system (Schwartz & Abreu 2007). Yet, this initiative was highly criticised for reducing the emphasis on school attendance of the original *Bolsa Escola* (school grant) and diverting attention from the initial aim of keeping children in school, increasing educational attainment and breaking the cycle of poverty among working-class families (Buarque 2007).

Despite criticisms, in 2006 Lula was re-elected for a second presidential term. Soon after his re-election, as a result of international pressure and national demands for the improvement of the state education system, the Ministry of Education launched a Programme for the Development of Education (PDE), which aimed at 'increasing the quality of state funded schools, addressing the problems of achievement, attendance and completion' (MEC 2007, p. 3). This initiative was part of the Programme for Acceleration of Growth (PAC), released in January 2007, which intended to remove obstacles to development through an investment of 503 billion *reais* (approximately US$240 billion) in various areas, such as education, infrastructure and agriculture.

The PDE holds a conception of education that emphasises, on the one hand, individual autonomy, critical thinking and citizenship and, on the other, the need to build a systemic approach to education in articulation with socio-economic development. According to Saviani (2007), while the plan represents an organisational advancement, it continues to be based on a type of 'results pedagogy' or 'competencies pedagogy', underpinned by the idea of 'quality control'. In this sense, the educational process must be externally controlled in order to maintain its quality and efficiency. New assessment tools were created, such as the Index of Development of Basic Education (IDEB), which now produce a national league table for Brazilian schools. This overemphasis on assessment, however, has reduced students' and teachers' opportunities for critical engagement and democratic participation, inhibiting developments in citizenship education. An initiative entitled Ethics and Citizenship (*Ética e Cidadania*) was launched in 2003, in order to enhance the attention given to moral and political values in the curriculum, but it remains an optional programme, and the extent of the impact on schools remains unclear.

In recent years Lula's government has also promoted targeted policies to improve the quality of schools in underprivileged areas; increased the duration of compulsory schooling from eight to nine years; extended investments in secondary education through the creation of the Fund for the Development of Basic Education (FUNDEB); and increased access of working-class students to higher education by implementing financing programmes such as the University for All (PROUNI). These governmental actions may be seen as responses to the growing pressure of international and national organisations to increase the quality and competitiveness of Brazilian education. On the other hand, they may also represent a genuine effort on the part of the Brazilian government to promote equality in basic and higher education. In any case, there seems to be a clash between the democratic aims of citizenship education and the emphasis on the contrasting conception of educational quality and assessment adopted by the new reforms.

In this section we have seen how the establishment of the new democratic state in Brazil shaped the conceptualisation and implementation of initiatives in citizenship education. In contrast to countries such as the United Kingdom, there was no national curriculum. As a result, the Brazilian approach to citizenship education has largely been developed in the peripheries of power through programmes sponsored by local governments, community and church groups, social movements and NGOs. In order to understand the nature of citizenship education in the country, therefore, it is essential to learn about these experiences, which form the focus of the next section.

CONTEMPORARY CITIZENSHIP EDUCATION INITIATIVES IN BRAZIL

This section will assess the diverse landscape of current citizenship education provision in Brazil. As stated above, given the highly decentralised nature of the education (and political) systems, it is important to assess provision at the state and municipal, as well as federal, levels. In addition, a number of non-state actors have been influential in this field, sometimes within the formal school system. This section will therefore consist of four parts, outlining the National Curricular Parameters; the Voter of the Future initiative promoted by the judicial branch of the federal government;

programmes at the municipal level; and the work of social movements within the public education system.

The National Curriculum Parameters

One important development of the Cardoso era was the publication in 1997–1998 of the NCPs, intended to provide a common base for the curriculum across the country. As previously stated, Brazil has a high degree of decentralisation, so the NCPs are far from representing a national curriculum. Nevertheless, they aim to provide a national reference point, as stipulated by the LDB, which undertook to guarantee to all 'the indispensable common education for the exercising of citizenship' (Candau 2001, p. 14).

There are separate sets of parameters for grades one to four and five to eight of primary school, as well as for secondary level. Schools are supposed to create their curricula on the basis of the NCPs, taking into account the particularities of each context. The primary school parameters feature the customary subject disciplines, but also a set of transversal themes—ethics, environment, health, cultural plurality, work, sexual orientation and consumer issues—together making up the overarching aim of promoting democratic citizenship. The moral and political values on which the notion of citizenship in the NCPs is based are the dignity of the human being, equality of rights, participation and co-responsibility for social life (Teixeira 2000). These values are uncontroversial perhaps, following the shared bases of international declarations of rights. One distinguishing factor is the NCPs' constructivist nature. It is stated, for example, that 'to be a citizen is to participate in a society, having the right to have rights, as well as constructing new rights and reviewing the existing ones' (MEC 1997, p. 54). In addition, there is some support for civic action:

> To live together democratically means to have awareness that the role of people is not only to obey and repeat the laws, but to contribute to their reformulation, adaptation and to the elaboration of new laws. (MEC 1997, p. 79)

Some commentators (e.g. Lopes 2004, 2006; Moraes 2003; Moreira 1996; Santos 2002) see the NCPs as part of an essentially neo-liberal approach to citizenship, in the sense of it being 'a strategy for improving society within the current model, without questioning it' (Candau 2001, p. 24). However, it is debatable whether the vision put forward in the ethics theme, for example, can be described as 'neo-liberal', since it explicitly criticises consumerist individualism and values the public sphere, collective decision making and respect for universal rights. Nevertheless, the statements are made at a somewhat unchallenging level, general enough to gain wide consensus, but without forcing any real and difficult change.

Whatever its orientation, there is no guarantee that the NCPs are actually being implemented. While there may be subtle ways of ensuring adoption of the parameters (Teixeira 2000), the central government is unable to verify if and how the national guidelines have been adopted. In any event, many educators consider that it would be undesirable to move further along the road of national standardisation. Despite the existence of a clear orientation towards citizenship in the NCPs, therefore, its materialisation in the taught curriculum depends on a range of other agents, organisations and initiatives.

Voter of the Future

Another distinctive initiative emerging from the federal government is the Voter of the Future programme (*Eleitor do Futuro*). This programme is characterised by focusing primarily on elections and in having its motivating force outside the education system, in the judiciary. The legal origins of the programme have a strong influence on the educational orientations and understanding of citizenship.

This ongoing programme was designed initially by the Supreme Electoral Tribunal (TSE) in November 2002, for implementation by the Regional Electoral Tribunals (TREs), one in each state of the Federation. The main aim of the initiative is to develop young people's abilities to be responsible and effective citizens in a liberal democracy. In Brazil, voting is obligatory for adults aged eighteen to seventy, with financial penalties for those who fail to do so. Those aged sixteen and seventeen are allowed to vote but are not obliged to. TSE statistics from 2000 show that the voting rate amongst this age-group was under 50 percent in most states, and only 13.5 percent in the Federal District. UNICEF's (2002) research project on Brazilian youth showed that a staggering 41.3 percent of sixteen- and seventeen-year-olds were not even aware that they were entitled to vote. Nevertheless, many of this age-group considered politics (even in the form of party politics) to be important and a number were politically active or involved in local community groups.

The initiative is intended to be a partnership between different sectors of society, particularly: officials of the electoral system, officials of the child and adolescent justice system, schoolteachers, NGOs, human rights activists and volunteers (TSE 2003, p. 6). There is significant difference in the uptake of the initiative by the individual states, with substantial activities in some, and only a token acknowledgment in others. The most prominent activity in schools is the mock election, either paralleling national or local elections, or used for choosing school officers. Through this, the pupils are supposed to develop skills of scrutinising candidates and their manifestos. There are also lectures, essay-writing competitions and visits to local institutions such as the municipal assembly.

Empirical research (e.g. McCowan 2008, 2009), however, has shown implementation to be problematic. Firstly, coming from outside the education system, the initiative has not engaged sufficiently with local education departments or with schools. There is normally only one teacher involved in each school, meaning that the activities are not incorporated across the curriculum as a whole. In addition, the uptake has been mainly by institutions that already have initiatives in the area of citizenship, with little attempt to reach the most disadvantaged schools, the ones in which these initiatives are most needed. Lastly, the programme does not engage in the democratisation of the school itself, through which it could provide meaningful experiences of participation for pupils. Some students who were highly active in the political sphere outside school were apathetic towards the initiative as they felt it failed to engage with their understandings and forms of political participation.

Local Government Initiatives

Since the end of the military dictatorship, there have been a number of experiments in democratic local government, many emerging from the early and more radical period of the Workers' Party (*Partido dos Trabalhadores*, PT). One important innovation has been the participatory budget, made famous in Porto Alegre, but extended to a number of other municipalities (Abers 2000; Navarro 2003). There have also been significant innovations in education policy, stretching back to Paulo Freire's spell as secretary of education of São Paulo from 1989 to 1991, and to earlier experiments (Lima 1999). These initiatives have been characterised by attempts to develop citizenship not through a civics element in the curriculum, but through an enhancement of pupil participation in the school and community participation in school management.

One of the best known of the municipal initiatives in education has been the Citizen School of Porto Alegre, developed during the PT local government of 1988–2004. Here, a process of collective policy making (*Consituinte Escolar*) was initiated, involving an investigation of the main issues affecting schools, followed by a series of debates in schools and regional assemblies. From these discussions, the main axes of policy emerged, with democratisation of the school being addressed in three dimensions: management, access and knowledge (Azevedo 2002; Gandin & Apple 2002). Democratisation of management involved measures such as the direct elections of head teachers and of school councils. An important aspect of the approach to access was the implementation of new grade structures so as to bring down the high levels of repetition and drop-out (Azevedo 2002; Mainardes 2007). The third form of democratisation involved the incorporation of local and minority ethnic knowledge as a valued part of the curriculum (Gandin & Apple 2002). The Porto Alegre reforms were reflected elsewhere in the state of Rio Grande do Sul, in the municipality of Pelotas, 2000–2004 (McCowan 2006), and in other parts of the country (e.g. Ghanem 1996).

One prominent initiative in a similar vein is the Plural School, initiated in the 1990s in the city of Belo Horizonte. The central principle around which the Plural School orients itself is inclusion. The traditional school is seen to exclude sections of the community in a number of ways: through its choice of valued knowledge, its assessment procedures, the structure of the school day and the teacher–student relationship. The framework, therefore, represents an opening of this rigid system to a plurality of individuals, groups and cultures, giving each equal value and opportunity (McCowan 2009). The underlying principles of the framework are well expressed by Castro:

> Initially, 'school failure' seemed to reveal the inadequacy of pupils in school, which ended up legitimising their social exclusion . . . It was understood that it was necessary to construct a new order of school capable of ensuring the inclusion of all, particularly those sections of the population that were systematically excluded and/or marginalized, guaranteeing them not only access to formal education, but above all the possibility of participating in the construction of new knowledge and the acquisition of knowledge produced throughout the history of humanity. (2000, p. 3)

The distinctive feature of the Plural School, therefore, is its recognition that the realisation of the right to education can be a form of exclusion if attention is not paid to processes within the school.

While the Plural School emerged as a grass roots movement of teachers, since being adopted as government policy it has encountered a significant degree of resistance from other sections of the teaching body. Implementation has also been made difficult by a lack of understanding of and resistance to the shake-up of traditional school practices on the part of parents and pupils (Dalben 2000a, 2000b; Glória & Mafra 2004; Soares 2002). Nevertheless, local initiatives like this one represent important new approaches to citizenship education, seeing the key task as the embedding of democratic and inclusive values across the whole curriculum and in school management, rather than relying on a fragmented teaching of citizenship as a subject.

The Landless Movement

However, there are other important players in citizenship education at an even greater distance from the central government. A number of NGOs, trades unions and social movements do important work in developing citizenship through non-formal education programmes (e.g. Fischer & Hannah 2002; Ghanem 1998; King-Calnek 2006). In addition, there are cases of non-state providers functioning within the formal education system. A notable instance here is the Landless Movement, which, despite being radically opposed to the state, runs a large network of schools with public funding.

The Movement of Landless Rural Workers or Landless Movement (MST[1]) is widely recognised as the largest and most influential social movement in Latin America. The movement was officially founded in 1984 and functioned initially in the south of the country, although now it has spread to all regions. While the central objectives are agrarian reform and responding to severe inequalities of land ownership in Brazil, it is also engaged in wider social struggles such as those relating to worker exploitation and gender equality.

In the first co-operative communities run by the movement, some fledgling primary schools emerged, along with adult literacy classes, staffed mainly by those few members of the community who had completed school. After struggles with local authorities, communities managed to have their schools officially recognised, and thereby gained state funding and provision of teachers and materials. Today there exists a network of approximately fifteen hundred schools,[2] which have provided for 160,000 children, as well as many thousands of students in youth and adult education, and provision in early years education, technical secondary courses and other higher education courses in partnership with established universities (MST 2004).

The MST is concerned not only with providing access to formal education, but also with transforming its fundamental nature. Central to this reconceptualisation are citizenship and political participation, understood along broadly Freirean lines. As stated in MST (1999, pp. 16–17):

> Education is always a political practice, in that it locates itself within a project of transformation or social conservation. But for a long time people tried to believe that education and politics should not mix. That politics was something for politicians and should not contaminate the minds and hearts of our children and young people. This is, in truth, an intentional and perverse attempt to alienate people, so that they think that nothing could be different in the society in which they live.

Political education here goes beyond lesson content, in that 'to consider democracy a pedagogical principle means . . . that it is not enough for students to study or discuss it; it is also necessary . . . to experience a space of democratic participation' (MST 1999, p. 20). Central to all MST activity is the *mística*, a term referring to ceremonial activities which engage the heart and the imagination of those engaged in the struggle. Another key element is collective work, with pupils engaging in work teams to develop agricultural and other skills, as well as co-operative values. The emphasis on the collective is also seen in the notion of *dialogue*. In the Freirean sense, this involves a radical alteration of the relations between teacher and student, and of the process of knowledge construction and acquisition. Participatory organisation of schools is also a key tenet of the MST. However, the

MST is distinctive in its encouragement not just of involvement in school affairs but also students' political activity at local and national levels. Examples of this form of activity are participation in land occupations, the establishment of co-operative camps and participation in protest marches (McCowan 2009).

The MST faces significant challenges in realising its vision of education. Yet, like the radical local government initiatives, the movement is providing an innovative model of citizenship education that contrasts strongly with the disembedded approaches of many national-level initiatives, involving a rooting of democracy in the curriculum and school management, and the linking of political spheres and action within and outside of the school.

CONCLUSION

This brief overview of contemporary initiatives shows the complexity of current provision in Brazil. Despite the influence of supranational organisations on macroeconomic policy since the end of the dictatorship, federal initiatives have emphasised the civic, as well as economic, spheres in the educational development of individuals—albeit without encouraging a real challenge to the *status quo*. At the same time, in the wake of the re-establishment of democracy, a number of local government and civil society initiatives have created radical new forms of education for participatory democracy.

As a consequence of the historical trajectory outlined at the start, the dilemmas faced by Brazil in relation to citizenship are quite distinct from those of many other countries. Its principal challenge relates not to identity but to political participation. While Brazil is still far from ensuring that the perspectives and histories of all groups are adequately reflected in the curriculum more broadly, the priority in citizenship education is not so much to create a version of national identity that is inclusive of minorities, but to allow all citizens into the sphere of political influence. As has been mentioned before, the country has a highly inauspicious history in terms of democratic participation, and despite the considerable advances since the return of multiparty democracy in 1985, there are still significant obstacles to universal participation. The education system, therefore, is left with the not inconsiderable task of both informing young people of their formal rights and empowering them to exercise those rights in the face of the barriers of socio-economic disadvantage, entrenched privilege and abuse of power.

Much of the considerable volume of literature on citizenship education published in recent years has emerged from countries—the United States, United Kingdom, Australia, etc.—which share a number of common features: well-established legal rights for citizens, significant immigrant populations with diverse ethnic and religious affiliations and an active engagement in processes of globalisation. Brazil shares little of this context. Civil and political rights were guaranteed only recently, with over half the population disenfranchised as late as 1946 on account of their being illiterate. Social rights have now been formally enshrined in the Constitution of 1988, but are rarely upheld in practice. In relation to the second element, Brazil is indeed a highly diverse country in terms of its ethnic origins. Yet, in the five centuries since the Portuguese colonisation, the country has developed a surprising degree of homogeneity in terms of language and culture, aided of late by the mass media. While Brazil is certainly inserted in the global capitalist system, it has a degree of protection particularly from the cultural aspects of globalisation through its size (giving it a degree of self-sufficiency) and its almost exclusive use of the Portuguese language. In spite of the undeniable global influences, therefore, citizenship education initiatives have been created primarily in response to local and national concerns, such as political participation, equal distribution of land and the protection of human and social rights, rather than focusing on multi- and supranational aspects of citizenship and civic action.

In spite of the challenges facing the country, Brazil also has at its disposal a powerful array of political and pedagogical movements that are making a forceful challenge to current injustices. Both within the sphere of formal politics and at the grass roots, these movements are creating new forms of policy and political relations. In education, innovative forms of school governance, curricular integration and transformative pedagogy are, in small but nonetheless significant ways, helping to turn the mighty ship around. This new and radical paradigm is fundamental not only for the future of Brazil, but for the reinvigoration of democracy in countries across the globe.

NOTES

1. Movimento dos Trabalhadores Rurais Sem Terra.
2. Only two hundred of these, however, have the complete eight grades of primary school, and only twenty have secondary provision (MST 2004).

REFERENCES

Abers, Rebecca N (2000) *Inventing Local Democracy: Grassroots Politics in Brazil*. London, Lynne Rienner.
Abreu, Vanessa Kern de & Geraldo Inácio Filho (2006) A educacao moral e civica: doutrina, disciplina e pratica educativa, Revista HISTEDBR Online, 24, pp. 125–134, www.histedbr.unicamp.br/art11_24.pdf (accessed 20 February 2009).
Amaral, Daniela Patti do (2007) *Etica, moral e civismo: difícil consenso, Cadernos de Pesquisa*, 37(131), pp. 351–369.
Azevedo, José Clóvis de (2002) A Escola Cidadã: A experiência de Porto Alegre, in Hélgio Trindade & Jean-Michel Blanquer (eds.) *Os Desafios da Educação na América Latina*. Petrópolis, Vozes, pp. 238–253.
Barros, Ricardo Paes de, Ricardo Henriques & Rosane Mendonça (2002) *Pelo fim das Decadas Perdidas: Educaçao e Desenvolvimento Sustentado no Brasil*. Rio de Janeiro, IPEA.

Buarque, Cristovam (2007) Sou Insensato. Rio de Janeiro, Garamond.

Burton, Guy (2008) Brazil's 'lost decade' in education, 1985–94: How to account for the lack of reform in the New Republic? Paper presented at the BRASA IX Congress, Tulane University, New Orleans, 27–29 March.

Candau, Vera (2001) Experiências de Educação em Direitos Humanos na América Latina: o Caso Brasileiro, (Cadernos Novamerica, No. 10). Rio de Janeiro, Novamerica.

Castro, Maria Céres Pimenta Spínola (2000) Escola Plural: a Função de uma Utopia. Paper presented at the 23rd Annual Meeting of the National Association of Educational Research and Graduate Studies (ANPED), Caxambu, Brazil, 24–28 September.

Dalben, Ângela Imaculada Loureiro de Freitas (ed.) (2000a) Avaliaçao da Implementação do Projeto Político-Pedagógico Escola Plural. Belo Horizonte, GAME/FaE/UFMG.

———. (ed.) (2000b) Singular ou Plural? Eis a Escola em Questão! Belo Horizonte, GAME/FaE/UFMG.

Fischer, Maria Clara Beuno & Janet Hannah (2002) [Re]constructing citizenship: The Programa Integrar of the Brazilian Metalworkers' Union, in Michele Schweisfurth, Lynn Davies & Clive Harber (eds.) Learning Democracy and Citizenship: International Experiences. Oxford, Symposium, pp. 95–106.

Fonseca, Selma Guimarães (1993) Caminhos da historia ensinada 5th edition. Campinas: Papirus.

Freire, Paulo (1972) Pedagogy of the Oppressed. Harmondsworth, Penguin Education.

———. (1974) Education for Critical Consciousness. London, Sheed & Ward.

———. (1976) Education, the Practice of Freedom. London, Writers and Readers Publishing Cooperative.

Frigotto, Gaudêncio (2007) A relação da educação profissional e tecnológica com a universalização da educação básica, Educação e Sociedade, 28(100), pp. 1129–1152.

Gandin, Luis Armando & Michael W. Apple (2002) Challenging neo-liberalism, building democracy: Creating the citizen school in Porto Alegre, Brazil, Journal of Education Policy, 17(2), pp. 259–279.

Ghanem, Elie (1996) Participação popular na gestão escolar: três casos de políticas de democratização, Revista Brasileira de Educação, 3, pp. 31–63.

———. (1998) Social movements in Brazil and their educational work, International Review of Education, 44(2–3), pp. 77–189.

Glória, Dília Maria A & Leila A. de Mafra (2004) A prática da não-retenção escolar na narrativa de professores do ensino fundamental: dificuldades e avanços na busca do sucesso escolar, Educação e Pesquisa, 30(2), pp. 231–250.

King-Calnek, Judith E. (2006) Education for citizenship: Interethnic pedagogy and formal education at Escola Criativa Olodum, Urban Review, 38(2), pp. 145–164.

Lima, Licínio C. (1999) Organização Escolar e Democracia Radical: Paulo Freire e a Governação Democrática da Escola Pública. São Paulo, Cortez.

Lopes, Alice Casimiro (2004) Políticas curriculares: continuidade ou mudança de rumos? Revista Brasileira de Educaçao, 26, pp. 109–118.

———. (2006) Discursos nas politicas de curriculo, Curriculo sem Fronteiras, 6(2), pp. 33–52.

Mainardes, Jefferson (2007) Reinterpretando os Ciclos de Aprendizagem. São Paulo, Cortez.

Mattos, Carmen Lúcia Guimarães de (1992) Picturing School Failure: A Study of Diversity in Explanations of Education Difficulties among Rural and Urban Youth in Brazil. Ann Arbor, MI, UMI Bell & Howell.

McCowan, Tristan (2006) Educating citizens for participatory democracy: A case study of local government education policy in Pelotas, Brazil, International Journal of Educational Development, 26(5), pp. 456–470.

————. (2008) Curricular transposition in citizenship education, *Theory and Research in Education*, 6(2), pp. 153–172.

————. (2009) *Rethinking Citizenship Education: A Curriculum for Participatory Democracy*. London, Continuum.

MEC (Ministério da Educação e do Desporto) (1997) *Parâmetros Curriculares Nacionais*. Brasília, MEC/SEF.

MEC (Ministério da Educação) (2007) *O Plano de Desenvolvimento da Educação: razões, princípios e programas*. Brasília, Governo Federal.

Moraes, Silvia Elizabeth (2003) In search of a vision: How Brazil is struggling to envision citizenship for its public schools, in William F. Pinar (ed.) *International Handbook of Curriculum Research*. Mahwah, NJ, Lawrence Erlbaum Associates, pp. 205–219.

Moreira, Antonio Flávio (1996) Os Parâmetros Curriculares Nacionais em questão, *Educação & Realidade*, 21(1), pp. 9–23.

MST (1999) *Princípios da Educação no MST* (Caderno de Educação no. 8). São Paulo, MST Setor de Educação.

————. (2004) *Educação no MST: Balanço 20 Anos* (Boletim da Educação no. 9). São Paulo, MST Setor de Educação.

Navarro, Zander (2003) O 'Orçamento Participativo' de Porto Alegre (1989–2002): um conciso comentário crítico, in Leonardo Avritzer & Zander Navarro (eds.) *Inovações Democráticas no Brasil* (O Caso do Orçamento Participativo). São Paulo, Cortez, pp. 89–128.

Nunes, Nataly & Maria José de Rezende (2008) *O ensino da Educação Moral e Cívica durante a ditadura militar*. Paper presented at the III Simposio do Grupo de Estudos de Politica da America Latina: Lutas Sociais na America Latina, Londrina, 24–26 September.

Patto, Maria Helena Souza (1999) *A Produção do Fracasso Escola: Histórias de Submissão e Rebeldia*. São Paulo, Casa do Psicólogo.

Rezende, Maria José de (2001) *A Ditadura Militar no Brasil: Repressão e Pretensão de Legitimidade 1964–1984*. Londrina, UEL.

Rodrigues, Elaine (2004) *Reformando o ensino de História: lições de continuidade, Historia*, 23(1–2), pp. 49–68.

Santos, Lucíola Licínio de C.P. (2002) Políticas públicas para o ensino fundamental: Parâmetros Curriculares Nacionais e Sistema Nacional de Avaliação (SAEB), *Educação e Sociedade*, 23(80), pp. 346–367.

Saviani, Demerval (2007) O Plano de Desenvolvimento da Educação: análise do projeto do MEC, *Educação e Sociedade*, 28(100), pp. 1231–1255.

Schwartz, Analice & Gisleide Abreu (2007) Conditional cash transfer programs for vulnerable youth: Brazil's youth agent and youth action programs, *Journal of International Cooperation in Education*, 10(1), pp. 115–133.

Soares, Cláudia Caldeira (2002) *Reinventando a Escola: Os Ciclos de Formação na Escola Plural*. Belo Horizonte, CPP.

Teixeira, Beatriz de Basto (2000) *Parâmetros Curriculares Nacionais, Plano Nacional de Educação e a Autonomia da Escola*. Paper presented at the 23rd Annual Meeting of the National Association of Educational Research and Graduate Studies (ANPED), Caxambu, Brazil, 24–28 September.

TSE (Tribunal Superior Eleitoral) (2003) *Projeto Eleitor do Futuro: Aprendendo a Ser Cidadão*. Brasília, TSE.

UNDP (2008) Inequality in income or expenditure, 2007/2008 Human Development Report, http://hdrstats.undp.org/indicators/145.html (accessed 7 April 2009).

UNICEF (2002) *A Voz dos Adolescentes*. Brasília, UNICEF.

4 South African Post-Apartheid Realities and Citizenship Education

Kogila Moodley

INTRODUCTION

Racial segregation and apartheid fragmented South Africa's population for centuries. A common citizenship did not exist. Formal legislation legitimised racial classification, residential separation, denial of the right of some groups to landownership, segregated schooling with differential expenditure for different groups and denial of the right of all black groups to vote in national elections. In 1994, this exclusive system finally changed into an inclusive democracy with equal formal rights for everyone. However, the legacy of racial domination continues, both in the everyday unequal existence as well as in the minds of most people. How education for active, participatory citizenship can transform this historical reality into a new better life for liberated people has defied solutions so far. Increasing evidence suggests that new non-racial injustices are even harder to combat than the morally discredited previous racial system.

As could be expected in the South African context, the emphases in political education under the apartheid system had been diametrically opposed to that of the liberated post-apartheid order. The former was ethnically based authoritarian indoctrination for compliance with imposed group identities while the latter promotes constitutional values of nation-building in an inclusive democracy. However, the progressive visions of an anti-racist curriculum notwithstanding, citizenship education in South Africa is undermined by a public discourse on corruption, crime and morality that contradicts the values taught in schools. Well-intentioned educational initiatives are overshadowed by contrary government practices that frequently defy the very ideals that a progressive constitution espouses. Problematic policies on HIV/AIDS, responses to human rights abuses in Zimbabwe and violations of accountability and transparency 'teach' a different program. This 'public curriculum' impacts more deeply with the political consciousness of students than formal civics lessons. The public curriculum contrasts with the school syllabus and triggers cynicism and alienation from politics instead of active engagement. Political interest and participation in civil society has declined. In one of the most unequal societies, issues of democratic governance are relegated to the luxury of a privileged elite, but hardly concern most of the impoverished and marginalised majority. Their identification with democracy depends on delivery of employment, safety, housing and other preconditions of a normal life, which is taken for granted in established Western democracies.

POLITICAL LITERACY AS THE GOAL
OF CITIZENSHIP EDUCATION

The goal of citizenship education in a globalised world can best be described as political literacy. Political literacy eschews parochialism and fosters a cosmopolitan outlook. Political literacy should not be confused with the accumulation of historical facts or socio-political data. Although based on such elementary knowledge, political literacy comprises a considered interpretation of well-known events. Political literacy explores the causes of current problems and weighs contested solutions impartially and realistically. It focuses on the relationship between local and global developments. With a thorough understanding of international affairs, politically literate students understand what is feasible in a globalised context. They can reliably spot trends and calculate risks.

However, how can concern with the world at large, with rejection of injustice wherever it occurs and with empathy for victims thrive in an environment where the majority struggle for survival? When most school-leavers cannot find regular employment, imagining world citizenship ranks low. Other global issues, such as environmental concerns, climate change or the causes of global recession remain abstractions that are overshadowed by more immediate needs.

Take understanding the HIV/AIDS pandemic beyond condom use or abstention as an example for an informed South African citizen. It is estimated that 360,000 persons died unnecessarily of AIDS-related illnesses between 2000 and 2005, because the government refused to make antiretrovirals available. HIV/AIDS denialism constitutes the most severe policy failure in a country that is ravaged with one of the highest HIV infection rates in the world, yet has endured government indifference, if not obstructionism, when early preventive measures could have relieved a silent genocide. At the International AIDS conference in Toronto in August 2006, the UN special envoy on AIDS, Stephen Lewis, castigated South Africa as the only country in Africa whose government was still 'obtuse, dilatory and negligent about rolling out treatment'. Lewis labelled the South African theories 'more worthy of a lunatic fringe than of a concerned and passionate state'. Only recently has this life-saving controversy been taught in South African schools, let alone the even more sensitive causes of the epidemic.

Compared to other countries, the most striking aspect is not the well-known high HIV infection rate in South Africa, but its differential spread in different population groups. In Cape Town, six times more Africans (19.9 percent) are stricken than coloured people (3.2 percent) and forty times more than whites (0.5 percent) in the same (fifteen to forty-nine) age-group, according to the 2005 representative survey (Shisana et al. 2005). Neither poverty nor the number of partners account for the difference. Multiple partners for what has been labelled 'survival sex' or the provision of luxuries ('consumer sex') do not explain the ethnic difference. Analysts of the survey, such as Chris Kenyon and Motasim Badri (*Cape Times*, 23 February 2009) conclude: 'There was no tendency for richer or poorer persons (men or women) in any ethnic group to have more partners'. Multiple partnerships are flaunted in the South African media among whites and blacks, from writer André Brink's four wives, or hotel magnate Sol Kerzner's many liaisons, to President Jacob Zuma's six marriages and many concubines.

The crucial variable is the *concurrent* versus the *serial* sexual relationships. With many more simultaneous partnerships, Africans are locked into infectious networks that put them at much higher risk. Everywhere the multiplying concurrency combined with the lack of awareness of the concomitant risks fuel the striking ethnic difference. Yet a change of attitude along Uganda's successful 'zero-grazing' mobilisation is hardly triggered when the revered political leaders themselves proudly practise polygamy in the name of traditional culture. Real African men, so the image suggests, keep a string of simultaneous girlfriends. The Zimbabwean journalist Busani Bafana (*Mail & Guardian*, 20 March 2009) suggests that in Africa mistresses are part of a successful man's CV, 'having a mistress is rather like wearing a badge of honour, adding to the man's social standing'. In South Africa marriage rates in the same age-group also differ substantially according to ethnicity. More than double the percentage of white people (67 percent) between twenty-five and thirty-four are married or living together, compared with 31 percent of black people. The reasons for this discrepancy are unclear, but probably result from the greater poverty and the migratory labour system which fractured African society. The disempowered women turn out to be the main victims of male promiscuity. They are disproportionally infected at a younger age because they are seldom in a position to insist on safe sex. It is, therefore, not reinforcing racist stereotypes to blame such cultural practices for women's vulnerability.

Upholding universally accepted ethical values of good governance and corporate responsibility, the politically educated South African has nevertheless been sensitised to the cultural particularities of his or her environment. Politically conscious persons have internalised required qualities such as respect for difference, tolerance and acceptance of adversaries within agreed-upon rules, accountability, transparency and negotiating skills towards democratic decision making. Politically literate persons never impose their values autocratically, but seek to persuade and reason with evidence at all times.

In short, political literacy results in active citizenship. In rapidly changing polities, responsible citizens view themselves not as passive recipients of decisions handed down from above, but persons with a right and obligation to influence policy within their specific expertise. This requires collaborative capacities, creativity and critical thinking about alternatives to conventional wisdom. Politically literate educators know that private lives, corporate worlds and public realms are intertwined. Individual identities, corporate cultures and public institutions are all shaped by a collective discourse in which ideally all stakeholders partake. The health of a democracy depends on informed, participating, critical citizens.

Harber (1998) describes a South African school undergoing training in democratisation. All stakeholders, staff, learners and parents participated in the development of a culture of democracy and the requisite skills. Departing radically from apartheid education they developed a code of conduct built upon sixty-five core values. These included open-mindedness, respect for the beliefs and cultures of others, team-work, constructive conflict resolution, the responsible practice of freedom of speech, listening skills, compromise in arriving at a common understanding and learning appropriate channels of communication.

Civic belonging, therefore, assumes increasing importance. Political education produces people grounded in their local environment as well as secure in their identity as autonomous individuals and culminates in producing both cosmopolitan internationalists as well as locally effective reformers. These mobile professionals quickly grasp the uniqueness of a situation because they have acquired a comparative, interdisciplinary understanding of most problems they encounter in varied tasks. In addition, political education will contribute to personal fulfillment through a sense of autonomy and grasp of an often bewildering complexity of contradictory demands. With a high degree of self-respect, politically informed students and teachers will be able to make confident moral and political judgments for the benefit of their private lives as well as the common good.

SOUTH AFRICAN HUMAN RIGHTS EDUCATION

Our notion of political literacy as 'active, participatory citizenship' broadly corresponds with the consensus that has emerged from the South African debate since 1994. Curriculum 2005 (C2005), launched in March 1997, introduced outcomes-based education with eight new interdisciplinary learning areas to replace discipline-based, traditional school subjects. The participating, responsible citizen was envisaged as an important outcome, underpinning all learning programmes. However, 'democracy education' as part of the human and social sciences 'circles' has been eliminated in response to the growing criticism of C2005 in 2000. No longer is any specific space allocated to 'citizenship/civics' because of alleged overcrowding. Instead human rights education, and education for civic responsibility, is to be 'infused' throughout the curriculum, or housed in the life skills component of the curriculum. In Britain, this integrated approach is said to have failed and citizenship education as a separate subject was reintroduced in 2002. Another South African curriculum report, *Streamlining C2005: Implementation Plan*, by Linda Chisholm (2003) reverts to 'History and Geography' as separate disciplines while dropping reference to democracy education. In March 2009, reflecting on the state of education, Gillian Godsell, board chair of Parktown High School for Girls commented:

> the chaos side was fed by initial interpretations of outcome-based education. Classrooms without textbooks, relying for lessons on resources unavailable in poorer families produced little or no learning. (*Business Day*, 18 March 2009)

In contrast, she sees the new curriculum as promising progress and order:

> With the emphasis on thinking skills, analysis and writing, this curriculum could develop citizens who are able to reflect on problems and clearly explain their solution. (*Business Day*, 18 March 2009)

Various panels of historians and 'roving' working groups are supposed to 'interact' in an ongoing process to clarify the ultimate history curriculum. One of those panels advocates 'putting history back into the curriculum' as a means of nurturing critical inquiry and forming an historical consciousness. The informed awareness of the past is controversially defined as 'preventing amnesia, checking triumphalism, opposing a manipulative and instrumental use of the past, and providing a buffer against the "dumbing down" of the citizenry' (Ministry of Education 2001). In the meantime, case studies of history teachers and students in Cape Town schools conclude:

> With an open-ended interim syllabus and the freedom to innovate, individual teachers and history departments have been left to themselves to answer the question of how history should be taught. They decide how to handle the isolation or integration of their schools; how to negotiate a balance between content and skills; how to deal with the social conditions of their students; and how to go about creating curricula that meets the needs of those students. (Dryden 1999, p. 6)

Another study (Proctor 2001) at UCT on 'democracy education-in-action' set out to investigate how Student Representative Councils (SRC) functioned as sites of participatory learning and concluded:

I found that teachers dominated SRC practice through their asymmetrical power relations and discursive practice that often repressed and silenced learner voices. The SRC tended to be used as an official school voice to help staff with administrative work, out reach projects and symbolic, ceremonial rituals rather than a forum for learner's voices or acquiring democratic practice. (p. iv)

History teaching according to the personal preferences of teachers and civic practice according to an authoritarian tradition seem to be the dominant mode also in the 'new' South Africa so far.

MORAL EDUCATION, THE GOOD CITIZEN AND NATION-BUILDING

Moral education is advocated in two important policy documents from high-powered committees under the chairmanship of Wilmot James, established by the Ministry of Education: *Report on the Values and Democracy in Education* (2000) and *Manifesto on Values, Education and Democracy* (2001). The first report highlighted six qualities the education system should actively promote: equity, tolerance, multilingualism, openness, accountability and social honour. The report gives a specific definition of a 'good citizen':

A good citizen is an informed citizen, someone versed in the values and principles of the Constitution and Bill of Rights, the history of South Africa and what it means to exercise democratic freedom with the restraint of personal moral character. The well-rounded South African of the future is someone with a historical consciousness, an open and inquiring mind, is trilingual, and has a healthy respect for the obligations of citizenship. (Ministry of Education 2000, p. 13)

Couched in the language of nation-building, the authors speak of those values as 'determining the quality of national character to which we as a people in a democracy aspire' (p. 6), while the minister of education wants 'to craft a new identity that defines us a nation' (p. 5). Public education, he asserts 'cannot be value-free' and is 'an indispensable adjunct of nation building' (p. 4).

In as far as the success of nation-building can be measured in attitude surveys about identification with subgroups versus the common state, a common identity has been adopted by an overwhelming majority of citizens, in addition to a wide range of subgroup identities, coexisting with a feeling of belonging to an overarching political entity called 'South Africa'. A 1997 IDASA survey (Mattes, Yul & Africa 2000) reports that 94 percent of respondents expressed pride in being South African and more than 80 percent said people should stop thinking in group terms. Obviously simultaneous multiple identities parallel the conviction that one united South African nation is possible and desirable. This is hardly surprising considering the assimilationist agenda of the majority of schools (Carrim 1998; Zafar 1998). Furthermore, while the virtues of diversity are extolled, little attention is given to examining the structures which perpetuate old divisions. The South African Human Rights Commission Report, which studied ninety desegregated schools, revealed the entrenched nature of racism in schools (Vally & Dalamba 1999). These tendencies are also reflected in the growing xenophobia toward other African immigrants and refugees.

However, there is also a lively debate as to how far the national project should go, particularly in promoting English as a national language at the expense of minority languages. Particularly some Afrikaner academics warn about the danger of marginalising Afrikaans as a public language and as a medium of higher education. The South African moral philosopher Johan Degenaar (1994, p. 26) advises the promotion of democratic values rather than insisting on a national consensus:

> the use of nationalist terminology is dangerous since it feeds on the myth of a collective personality and creates wrong expectations in the minds of citizens while not preparing them to accept the difficult challenges to create a democratic culture which accommodates individuality and plurality.

Degenaar dismisses a national project as 'Jacobin', calling it a modernist discourse in a postmodernist age which imposes uniformity instead of acknowledging diversity. Likewise, the historian Hermann Giliomee has cautioned against teaching an official history, as suggested by some members of the Truth and Reconciliation Commission. The latter insist that in a divided society people need an agreed-upon common story—for example, history as human rights abuses—to heal the wounds and divisions of the past.

Critics on the political left have inveighed against defining citizenship as part of nation-building for different reasons. They suspect that an uncritical consensus is demanded that demonises and discredits dissent:

> This reduces the space for debate and contestation about possible outcomes of the transition and the nature of South African democracy. The creation of such 'national unity' perpetuates and masks continuing inequality, and thus constitutes a very real threat to the consolidation of democracy. (Barchiesi & Huyssteen 2001, p. 2)

Nation-building has implied to a large degree, Marais (1998, pp. 5, 245) argues, 'the perpetuation of values, institutions, systems and practices of the past', which leads to the 'legitimation of social inequalities'. The left critics are correct that debate has been stifled; however, not in order to maintain national unity, but to maintain ruling party cohesion. The demand for party loyalty, with threats of heavy penalties for public dissent, has largely silenced internal party democracy.

The 2001 *Manifesto on Values*, published after an international *Saamtrek* ('pulling together') conference in Cape Town, further explores constitutional ideals by elaborating on social justice, non-racism and non-sexism, *ubuntu* ('human dignity and solidarity'), responsibility, the rule of law, respect and reconciliation. It also outlines educational strategies, predicated on the notion that values cannot be legislated, but merely promoted through the educational system (Ministry of Education 2001).

AND CITIZENSHIP EDUCATION?

Citizenship education in South Africa means basically advocating the constitution. 'How the Constitution can be taught, as part of the curriculum and brought to life in the classroom, as well as practically applied by educators, administrators, governing bodies and officials' (Ministry of Education 2001, p. iii) is defined as the crucial challenge in all debates. 'The Constitution expresses South African's shared aspirations, and the moral and ethical direction they have set for the future' (Ministry of Education 2001, p. iv). Indeed, the South African constitution, modeled after exhaustive studies of several liberal Western democracies, is universally hailed as a state-of-the-art document. Its impressive preamble embodies the new spirit and is worth quoting:

> We, the people of South Africa, recognise the injustices of our past; honour those who suffered for justice and freedom in our land; respect those who have worked to build and develop our country; and believe that South Africa belongs to all who live in it, united in our diversity. We therefore, through our freely elected representatives, adopt this constitution as the supreme law of the Republic so as to—Heal the divisions of the past and establish a society based on democratic values, social justice and fundamental human rights;
>
> Lay the foundations for a democratic and open society in which government is based on the will of the people and every citizen is equally protected by law;
>
> Improve the quality of life of all citizens and free the potential of each person; and
>
> Build a united and democratic South Africa able to take its rightful place as a sovereign state in the family of nations. May God protect our people.

THE DISCREPANCY BETWEEN THEORY AND PRACTICE

The educational policy documents recognise the discrepancy between theory and reality. 'As a vision of a society based on equity, justice and freedom for all it is less a description of a society as it exists than a document that compels transformation' (Ministry of Education 2001, p. iv). However, none of the documents spell out how transformation is to be achieved. They postulate ideals in an unobtainable dream-world. It perpetuates illusions to assume that a country with South Africa's authoritarian and racist past, current lawlessness, vast unemployment, spreading HIV pandemic and huge illiteracy rates can be transformed by curriculum changes. Critics have wondered whether the utopian discourse:

> is not shooting policy and its implementation in the foot. Policy documents should establish achievable, defined concepts rather than further turning controversial terms, such as "democratic" and "literate, creative and critical citizens" into rhetorical buzzwords or "magic-bullets", that lose their distinctive meaning through their close proximity with what must realistically remain the rhetorical use of "social hope poetry". (Proctor 2001, p. 5)

In short, the idealised account of the critical citizen itself lacks the critical edge by glossing over a contrary reality.

To support these appealing but abstract virtues of democracy, effective citizenship education would require concrete contextual analysis. Only through a critical exploration of how democracy functions in the everyday reality of the political community in which learners live—by comparing the ideals with the practice—can we hope to motivate students to narrow the gap and become active, engaged citizens.

Students would therefore need to be exposed to competing discourses about the meaning of democracy. After the end of the Cold War, virtually all factions across the political spectrum celebrated 'democracy' as the alternative to the discredited authoritarian master narratives of communism and apartheid racism. This facilitated a negotiated settlement by invoking a shared moral universe of nation-building, reconciliation and non-racialism. As long as the meaning of this 'democracy' remained abstract, people could unite around democracy building. However, as soon as the 'the will of the people' had to be concretised, deep divisions emerged. How do you determine the 'will of the people'? When are elections 'free and fair'? What rights should be accorded to minorities? How much opposition should be tolerated? As the heated debate about the 2002 Zimbabwean elections has demonstrated, no universal consensus exists on these vital questions. Even among black Africans, notions of an 'African Democracy' clashed with Western visions of a liberal democracy. Prominent Africanists in South Africa and elsewhere warned against imposing 'extraneous criteria' of a foreign 'Western' ideology on different cultural traditions. Proponents of a one-party state or a 'people's democracy' in several African countries consider multi-party democracies as an invisible form of Western imperialism.

The ANC 'Freedom Charter' of 1955, the inspiring precursor of the celebrated post-apartheid constitution, pronounced 'The people shall govern'. *Amandla awethu* (power to the people) echoed from all anti-apartheid rallies. In the meantime, a debate has even arisen about the question: 'who are the people?' When Mandela, as admired president, referred to 'my people', it was not always clear whether he meant all South African citizens, all formerly disenfranchised (including coloureds and Indians), only black Africans or only ANC voters. When in 2002 President Mbeki reminded the sports-obsessed country that it should expect its national cricket and rugby teams to lose for a few years in the higher interest of transformation until 'our people' are fairly represented, it was clear that he excluded other citizens from the definition of his 'people'.

In short, of the little political education that takes place in South African schools, a decontextualised teaching of citizenship and the institutions of democracy characterises democracy education in South Africa. It is argued that problematising the contested issues in the context of current debates makes for more relevant and effective learning about democracy than the abstract and idealised exposition of democratic values. Furthermore, implementation seems to have been given short shrift in new education policies. In a scathing study, Sayed and Jansen (2001, p. 274) go so far as to assert that 'dramatic policy announcements and sophisticated policy documents continue to make no or little reference to the modalities of implementation'. Sayed and Jansen (2001, p. 275), arguably, maintain that in most cases 'implementation was never on the agenda at all' and that the syllabus revision was mainly about:

> achieving a symbolic and visible purging of the apartheid curriculum in order to establish legitimacy for an ANC-led government under unprecedented criticism for its failure to deliver in education. (p. 275)

Such a failure would be another case of public pronouncements breeding cynicism and paralysis in reality.

CONCLUSIONS

Educators are familiar with the importance of the hidden curriculum of invisible expectations, assumptions and practices that often counteract the official curriculum. Like this unspoken curriculum, the spoken, public practice of politics also shapes the attitude of learners. This public curriculum—how politics is conducted and communicated—may reinforce or contradict the desired civic attitudes. More than the teaching in schools, the public curriculum may either turn students off politics or encourage active involvement.

South Africa's noble constitutional values are undermined by a political culture that often practises the opposite of what it allegedly promotes in civic education. Essential democratic values, such as accountability, transparency, free debate, non-racism and non-sexism, and even the right of life itself, are sometimes so blatantly disregarded that cynicism rather than commitment results. My focus group discussions among student teachers at the University of Cape Town and learners alike revealed an alienation from politics that is not so much grounded in ignorance, but in disillusionment. Active citizenship is discouraged as long as government policy ostracises legitimate dissent, rewards sycophants and turns a blind eye to the suffering of millions of citizens.

Perhaps nothing can better illustrate the 'squandering of liberation' than the rampant corruption among political and corporate leaders as well as the connected crime and abuse culture (see Johnson 2009 for further elaboration). When President Zuma is tainted with massive corruption charges and yet tries to avoid a trial to clear his name, it is little wonder that South African democracy has acquired a dubious reputation. One of the highest murder rates in the world has contributed to this demise from a once shining example of peacemaking.

The doyen of South African journalists, Allister Sparks ('Crime's become a routine part of life', *Cape Times*, 4 February 2007) has rightly connected the persistent high crime rate with 'the ethical erosion, the rampant self-enrichment culture' that has corrupted the political process at every level. When 77 percent of sixteen- to twenty-five-year-olds say that their main ambition in life is to make more money; when there is hardly any struggle hero left who has not become a multimillion Rand tycoon through dubious black empowerment deals in a very short time; when the conspicuous consumption and obscene high life of this black and white elite is celebrated by the media ad nauseam, it is not surprising that the relatively deprived also desire to grab a share through robbery. In his article, Sparks reiterates an old sociological insight that—contrary to conventional wisdom and government rhetoric—crime waves do not result from poverty and unemployment. 'The really poor don't carry out cash-in-transit heists, big hold ups or the blowing up of ATMs. Nor do they shoot the project manager of Business Against Crime'. The homeless on all street corners beg the drivers of fancy cars, but do not hijack their vehicles. Most shack dwellers in ever-expanding slums merely feel abandoned. Most fatalistically strive for survival and meaning through some simplistic religion or other addictive hallucinations.

Yet out of the anomie and destruction of community springs organised crime. The abandoned are easy recruits for well-heeled syndicates. With the social fabric of caring families long destroyed, gangs form as emotional substitutes. Some gang members are no longer shamed by traditional values, but governed by the new value system of greed and instant wealth. The illegal robbery by mafia-type gangsterism corresponds to the legal enrichment by well-connected state agents, including a poorly paid, poorly trained and corrupt police. Therefore, putting more police on the beat will not necessarily decrease crime, although the professionalisation of law enforcement and a reform of a dysfunctional justice system would help.

Gang members who tasted the good life are also not deterred by stricter laws or mandatory sentencing. The overcrowded prison system does not rehabilitate, but merely toughens hardcore deviants. Nor would the death penalty—which 80 percent of South Africans advocate—lower the murder rate, though it would save the state some prison costs. Blaming an indulgent human rights culture for the malaise misses the point of the much deeper erosion of the social fabric and value system. Unqualified teachers who casually neglect their socialising duty in many township schools contribute to the root causes of crime. An authoritarian school system that richly rewards a few winners but abandons many more losers to low self-esteem, conditions criminals to succeed outside overvalued credentials. If the losers cannot receive the public recognition that the class of the new rich has allocated itself in abundance, not even symbolically by the party that claims to be their representative, then many will steal the dream by force.

These social conditions are mirrored in increasing violence in South African schools (BBC World News, 12 March 2008, 'Violence rife in SA schools'). Forty percent of children interviewed reported that they had been victims of crime at school. AN HRC study cited seven-year-olds playing a game called 'rape me, rape me'. The 2008 South African Catholic Bishops Conference quotes 'gangs, weapons, sexual violence, assault, theft, robbery, vandalism as part of daily reality of our schools'. According to a 2008 South African Institute of Race Relations survey (SAIRR), only 23 percent of South African pupils said they felt 'safe at school', a ranking 20 percent points below the worldwide country average of 43 percent who claimed a 'high degree of safety' at school. A 2003 South African Medical Research Centre Survey reports that 17 percent carried weapons, 14 percent belonged to gangs, 15 percent were forced to have sex (often by teachers) and 41 percent said they were bullied. This profile, of course, applies almost exclusively to township schools, while the private and former Model C schools with their high fees are as safe as any institution in a Western democracy. Class not only deprives the majority of educational quality, but also of physical safety. It goes without saying that no children of the liberation leadership, together with most of the offspring of the burgeoning black middle class of civil servants, attend township schools. Democracy education was designed for these privileged sections; for the rest, taught by many unqualified and uninterested teachers, citizenship and democracy remain abstractions.

Such deficits in political sophistication disadvantage South Africa in the globalised competition for skills and resources. Foreign investment does not flow into a country that cheers Mugabe, tolerates official corruption, threatens independent judges or glorifies political violence, such as when a popular ANC youth leader pronounces readiness to 'kill for Zuma!' Citizenship education should immunise against populism and authoritarianism and instill readiness to defend the rule of law. Current attitudes indicate the reverse among the minority of politicised students: an uncritical and passionate inclination to follow popular leaders with mere lip service to the rule of law. Unless a substantial shift of political consciousness at both leadership and grass roots levels takes place, South Africa will not take its rightful place among true democracies for whom human rights trump expediency in a globalised comparison.

In this vein, South Africa also needs to strengthen its critical understanding of the impact of globalisation. The adoption of neo-liberal economic policies has acquired a sense of inevitability. The meager social security net has been shortchanged. The international arms industry induced unnecessary military expenditure. Global sport interests insisted on the construction of expensive new stadiums for the 2010 Soccer World Cup instead of eliminating urban slums. Finally, at the cultural level, the blind embrace of English at the expense of indigenous languages further disadvantages African learners forced to compete in a second language, and also spells the demise of local languages.

In short, the legacy of apartheid lingers on, but should not exempt the new power-holders from responsibility. At the same time, civic education of a new generation endowed with political literacy remains the main hope of overcoming the current malaise.

REFERENCES

Barchiesi, F., and van Huyssteen, E. (2001, June), Constitutionalism and social citizenship in the South African democratic tradition. Paper presented at the *International Institute for the Sociology of Law*, Onati, Spain.

Carrim, Nazir (1998) Anti-racism and the 'new' South African educational order, *Cambridge Journal of Education*, 28(3), pp. 301–320.

Chisholm, Linda (2003) *Streamlining C2005: Implementation Plan*. Pretoria, Ministry of Education.

Degenaar, Johan (1994) Beware of nation-building, in Nic Rhoodie & Ian Liebenberg (eds.) *Democratic Nation-Building in South Africa*. Pretoria, HSRC, pp. 23–30.

Dryden, Sarah (1999) Mirror of a nation in transition. MA dissertation in Education, University of Cape Town.

Harber, Clive (1998) Desegregation, racial conflict and education for democracy in the New South Africa: A case study of institutional change, *International Review of Education*, 44(6), pp. 569–582.

Johnson, R.W. (2009) *South Africa's Brave New World*. London, Allen Lane.

Marais, Hein (1998) *South Africa: Limits to Change*. Cape Town, Oxford University Press.

Mattes, Robert, Yul Derek Davids & Cherrel Africa (2000) Citizen's commitment to democracy, in Wilmot James & Moira Levy (eds.) *Pulse: Passages in Democracy-Building: Assessing South Africa's Transition*. Cape Town, Idasa, p.35.

Ministry of Education (2000) *Report of the Values and Democracy in Education.* Pretoria, Department of Education.

———. (2001) *Manifesto on Values, Education and Democracy.* Pretoria, Department of Education.

Proctor, Elspeth (2001) Talking democracy in grade 7. MA dissertation in Education, University of Cape Town.

Sayed, Yusuf & Jonathan Jansen (eds.) (2001) *Implementing Education Policies.* Cape Town, University of Cape Town Press.

Shisana, Olive, Thomas Rehle, Leickness Simbayi, Walter Parker, K. Zuma, A. Bhana, C. Connolly, S. Jooste & V. Pillay (2005) *South African National HIV Prevalence, HIV Incidence, Behaviour and Communication Survey 2005.* Pretoria, HSRC Press.

Vally, Salim & Yolisa Dalamba (1999) *Racism, Racial Integration and Desegregation in South African Public High Schools. A Report on a Study by the South African Human Rights Commission (SAHRC).* Johannesburg, SAHRC.

Zafar, Samiera (1998) *School-Based Initiatives to Address Racial and Cultural Diversity in Newly Integrating Public Schools.* Durban, Educational Policy Unit, University of Natal.

5 Citizenship Education in Pakistan
Changing Policies and Practices in Changing Social-Political Contexts

Bernadette Dean

INTRODUCTION

Citizenship education has been an aim of education since the creation of Pakistan but its conception and practice of have changed with each successive government. This chapter begins by exploring how Pakistani governments have understood the challenges facing Pakistani society and how these understandings have influenced policies and approaches to citizenship education in Pakistani schools. In doing this it shows how citizenship education has been conceptualised to serve the particular government's versions of what it means to be a Pakistani citizen. It also documents the change in policy from an inclusive to a more exclusive conception of citizenship so that citizenship education has become synonymous with Islamic education. It then demonstrates how the structure of schools, the curriculum and the culture and process of schooling serve to promote the exclusivist conception of citizenship and delineate the problems that have arisen. Finally, it suggests education policy and practice to promote a more inclusive, democratic citizenship.

THE HISTORICAL CONTEXT: CHANGING GOVERNMENT POLICIES AND PRACTICES TO CITIZENSHIP EDUCATION IN CHANGING SOCIO-POLITICAL CONTEXTS

In 1947 when Pakistan was created as a separate state for the Muslims of India, the founder of Pakistan, Muhammad Ali Jinnah, made it clear that Pakistan was not to be an Islamic theocratic state but a secular democratic state in which there would be civic equality regardless of the religious identity of its citizens. Addressing members of the first constituent assembly on 11 August 1947, he said:

> We are starting with the fundamental principle that we are all citizens and equal citizens of one state . . . Now I think we should keep that in front of us as our ideal, and you would find in due course of

time Hindus would cease to be Hindus and Muslims would cease to be Muslims, not in the religious sense, because that is the personal faith of each individual, but in the political sense as citizens of the state . . . You may belong to any religion, caste or creed—that has nothing to do with the business of the state. (quoted in Rashid 1985, p. 81)

Recognising the importance of education for nation-building and formation of a national identity, the government of the newly independent state of Pakistan held an education conference to reconstruct and reorient the colonial system of education to serve these ends. In his inaugural address to the Education Conference, the then education minister Fazlur Rehman stated that Pakistan was created not as a 'theocratic state' in which the ruler is a 'vice-regent of God on earth' and the government a 'sacerdotal class deriving its authority from God' but as 'a modern democratic state' based on the Islamic principles of the 'universal brotherhood of man [sic], social democracy and social justice'. In such a state, 'ruler and the ruled alike are equal, [the ruler is] but a representative of the people who have chosen him to serve them' (Ministry of the Interior, Education Division 1947, p. 6). He then made it clear that the task of the education system was the 'building of a modern democratic state' in which all members of the body politic, 'no matter what political, religious or provincial label' they possessed were citizens of Pakistan. Education for democracy, he suggested, should include vocational, social or political, spiritual and physical elements. He attached the highest importance to the spiritual element because it helped 'purge men's minds of barbarianism and turn them to humanitarian purposes' and to do this it needed to be universal in outlook and 'must eschew sectarian and narrow doctrinal lines'. The socio-political element entailed 'training for citizenship'. In his words, citizenship education was important because:

> The possession of a vote by a person ignorant of the privileges and responsibilities of citizenship . . . is responsible for endless corruption and political instability. Our education must . . . [teach] the fundamental maxim of democracy, that the price of liberty is eternal vigilance and it must aim at cultivating the civil virtues of discipline, integrity and unselfish public service. (Ministry of the Interior, Education Division 1947, p. 8)

He identified major problems that could hinder the realisation of the vision and identified ways to address them. Illiteracy was seen as a 'grave menace' in a democratic state and therefore it was the duty of the state to provide 'boys and girls universal, compulsory and free basic education . . . in the shortest period of time' and promote 'adult education'; and he proposed the improvement of university and technical education to raise the intellectual and moral tone of society and promote industrial development.

However, with the difficulties of trying to administer a country separated spatially and temperamentally, deal with divisive ethnic and provincial forces and stabilise the government (Ziring 1997), little attention was paid to education. Schools continued to be structured as before and the curriculum and text-books of pre-partition India were used, albeit with only a few necessary changes.

In 1958, just eleven years after independence, martial law was imposed in Pakistan. President and Chief Martial Law Administrator (CMLA) General Ayub Khan was determined to reconstruct Pakistan as a modern society. He conceived of a political order without political parties but with a form of grass roots government called 'Basic Democracies' in which representatives elected to local councils were responsible for addressing public needs. He established the National Reconstruction Bureau to encourage traditional power groups such as ethnic nationalists, feudal lords, tribal leaders and religious fundamentalists to give up their vested interests to help in the creation of a civil society and build the nation. At the same time, he embarked upon a programme of industrialisation and modernisation, new industries were set up and the Muslim Family Law Ordinance 1961 was introduced to give greater protection and more rights to women.

The government also set up an education commission to evolve a national education system that would contribute to national development and assist in the creation of a modern, democratic society. The commission recognised the importance of education for all citizens noting that:

> Such universal education is normally a concomitant to parliamentary democracy. A democracy requires that its citizens can distinguish between the claims of rival political parties, can interpret news intelligently and critically and are willing to serve on local bodies, committees and councils. (Ministry of Education 1959, p. 11)

However, in making its recommendations the commission eschewed free basic universal education and proposed the development of quality tertiary education, which, it held, would result in economic development, the benefits of which would 'trickle down' to the poor. Similarly, the commission proposed that citizenship education serve to prepare a small cadre of knowledgeable and skilled citizens who would be able to take up future leadership positions and also develop the masses as good human beings and loyal and patriotic citizens. There were two major implications of the recommendations of the commission. Firstly, it gave rise to class-based education that differentially socialised children to fit into perceived future class positions thus allowing the elite to continue to govern and control the masses (Saigol 1993). Secondly, rather than the preparation of informed and responsible citizens willing to participate actively in the public sphere, character education led to citizenship being seen as personal development with action in the private sphere.

The lack of a fair distribution of wealth created by the economic development of the country, the perceived oppression of different ethnic nationalities due to the amalgamation of the provinces into 'One Unit' and the lack of people's participation in decision making led to the people demanding an end to military rule. The political crises forced General Ayub Khan to hand over power to General Yahya Khan who at once abolished the One Unit and reconstituted the provinces and held general elections on the basis of population. Reluctance to allow the party with the majority vote to form the government led to a civil war and the secession of East Pakistan to form a new country, Bangladesh.

In 1973, Zulfiqar Ali Bhutto, head of the Pakistan Peoples Party (PPP) that had won the majority vote in what was now Pakistan, took over power as president and CMLA. This dual and interrelated role gave him absolute power. Bhutto had won the election on the PPP manifesto that merged Islam, socialist ideas and liberal democratic values. In line with the manifesto he immediately nationalised banks, industries, schools and colleges. He announced land reforms that reduced land holdings and distributed the resumed land to landless farmers. In 1973, the constituent assembly unanimously adopted a new constitution, making Pakistan an Islamic Republic with a parliamentary form of government. The provinces were given greater autonomy and the people a number of rights guaranteed by the constitution.

Having lost half the country and facing separatist movements in the part that now constituted Pakistan, the new civilian government saw education as a means of building national cohesion, achieving social justice and increasing the people's participation in decision making (Ministry of Education 1972). To achieve these aims the government nationalised schools and colleges to provide free and universal education and started an adult education programme. The power of education to convey the government's ideology to the people was recognised and the National Curriculum Board was established, and curriculum, hitherto a provincial subject, was made a federal one. A complete revision of the curriculum was undertaken to emphasise the learning of concepts and skills and encourage exploration, experimentation and creative expression. A new subject, Pakistan studies, was added to the high school curriculum with the aim of developing patriotism and promoting national cohesion. Furthermore, active participation of all in national development was encouraged through the setting up of the National Literacy Corps and the National Service Corps.

The Bhutto government was quite successful in developing patriotism and promoting national cohesion. The working class was empowered and people participated in decision making through their representatives in parliament. Within a few years, however, Bhutto's commitment to his party's ideals of social justice succumbed to the creation of a personality cult. The 1977 general elections were followed by claims they had been rigged and demands by a united opposition for fresh elections. In response to massive protests that turned violent, the military staged a coup and General Zia-ul-Haq became the president and CMLA. The geopolitical context, the demand by the opposition parties for *Nizam-e-Mustafa* (rule of the Prophet) and Zia's own devout observance of Islamic tradition and his conviction that Islam was the only force that could bind Pakistanis together led him to begin converting Pakistan into an Islamic theocratic state.

He instituted Islamic banking and made the payment of *zakat* (a proportion of wealth to be given in alms) compulsory. He issued the *Hudood* Ordinance (punishments prescribed in the Quran and Sunnah) enforcing the Islamic code of behaviour and harsh punishments for infringements. He set up *Qazi* courts (courts headed by a religious judge) and imposed Islamic laws such as *qisas* (the right of pre-emption) and *diyat* (the Islamic law of evidence which equates the evidence of two women with that of one man). Politically he formed the *Majlis-i-Shura* (consultative assembly) of selected people to perform the task of the legislature without the powers associated with it (Haque 1985).

In keeping with the government's ideology, the main aim of the National Education Policy and Implementation Program (1979) was the conversion of Pakistan into an Islamic theocratic state. Hence, it sought to develop in 'the people of Pakistan in general and students in particular a deep and abiding loyalty to Islam and Pakistan'; to inculcate in accordance with the Quran and Sunnah, the character, conduct and motivation expected of true Muslims; and produce citizens 'that feel proud of their heritage and display firm faith in the future of the country as an Islamic state' (Ministry of Education 1979, pp. 1–2). To ensure implementation, the 'highest priority' was given to the revision of school curricula so that 'Islamic ideology permeates the thinking of the younger generation' and society is refashioned according to Islamic tenets (p. 2). Separate institutions were to be opened and curricula prepared for female education related to the traditional role assigned women in Islamic society. *Islamiyat* (the study of Islam) and Pakistan studies were made compulsory up to the undergraduate level. For the first time, a chapter on 'Education of the Citizen' was included in the policy document. It called for the use of the media to ensure all citizens were 'impart[ed] the teachings of Islam' to prepare them for a clean, purposeful and productive life. Citizenship education now became synonymous with Islamic education.

Islamisation of the state led to over 3 percent of the population being declared minorities and to their being denied equal citizenship by having them vote under a separate electoral system. It also led to a growing lack of respect for members of minority groups within Islam and to greater gender inequality as women were both legally and socially ostracised. These divisions and lack of respect were further entrenched by a citizenship education programme that used both conventional and non-conventional means to achieve its aims and by the use of the coercive apparatus of the state.

From 1988 to 1999 Pakistan had four civilian governments. The Benazir Bhutto governments did little to develop an education policy, but the Nawaz Sharif governments announced education policies in both terms in office. The 1992 policy continued in the same vein as the 1979 National Education Policy. The 1998 policy shifted emphasis from fundamentalist Islam to Islam for social reconstruction and egalitarianism. In addition to preparing devout Muslims, education was to produce a scientific and technologically educated workforce who would 'become productive and useful citizens' and 'contribute to the social and economic development of the country and the *Ummah*' (Ministry of Education 1998, p. 11). To realise its aims, the policy called for universalising education by encouraging the private sector to establish schools. The emphasis on education as an industry was entrenched in the class-based education system, increasing class divisions rather than erasing them. No change was proposed in the curriculum and text-books and citizenship education continued as before and citizenship education as Islamic education was further strengthened.

In 1999 Pakistan came under military rule once again. On taking over the Chief of Army Staff, General Pervez Musharraf promised to work towards national integration, economic development and the establishment of a secular democratic state. In early 2002 he held a referendum that made him the president for five years. Having secured his position he sought to gain legitimacy by holding general elections in which the major political parties headed by Benazir Bhutto and Nawaz Sharif were debarred, resulting in fundamentalist religious parties gaining ground. Thus, instead of creating a secular democracy he ended up strengthening the Islamists. At about this time Pakistan became a frontline state in the war on terror. The government and the people of Pakistan believed that this was not their war. However, at the time of writing this chapter, terrorism perpetrated by Islamist groups such as the Taliban against the state have led to the government and the people of Pakistan recognising the threat they pose to the survival of the state and the need to challenge the ideology that gave rise to them. Moreover, the need for the re-creation of a secular democratic Pakistan as envisioned by the founder of Pakistan, Muhammad Ali Jinnah, is also being realised.

The Musharraf government continued with the 1998 education policy. It was only in 2005 that work began to develop a new education policy and a new curriculum. Drafts of the policy have recognised the importance of education for citizenship; however, the policy is not clear about the nature of and approaches to citizenship education. In the curriculum, social studies aimed at citizenship education has been replaced by general knowledge in grades one through three and history and geography in grades six through eight, thus greatly reducing the already little citizenship education young people receive.

The Musharraf government was brought down by the people under the leadership of the lawyers protesting the sacking of the chief justice of

Pakistan in March 2007 and the proclamation of emergency in November 2007. Elections in 2008 once again brought in a civilian government. It is yet to be seen how this government envisions citizenship and how this vision is to be reflected in education policy and practice.

The changing socio-political context of Pakistan has given rise to different conceptions of citizenship and citizenship education. In the early years the civil and military bureaucracy and the emerging capitalists served as modernising forces, promoting science and technology and the values of questioning, critical inquiry and entrepreneurship (Saigol 1993) aimed at developing a modern, democratic state. At this time all citizens enjoyed equal rights and fulfilled the responsibilities of a member of the state. Since the late 1970s the military regimes, civil bureaucrats, the Islamists and the feudal classes have worked together towards the Islamisation of society (Jalal 1995). These groups have promoted extremist interpretations of Islam and traditional feudal values such as obedience, deference to authority, submission and subordination to serve the creation of an Islamic, theocratic state. Citizenship is conceived as being exclusively Muslim. Thus, a good citizen must be a practising Muslim living the teachings of Islam in both the private and public spheres of life and working for the good of the Muslim *ummah* in and beyond the boundaries of the state. This conception not only excludes religious minorities from citizenship but also excludes women, as their roles in extremist interpretations of Islam are confined to the private sphere.

CITIZENSHIP EDUCATION IN SCHOOLS

Since the late 1970s citizenship education has become synonymous with Islamic education. This is reflected in the organisation of the education system, the structure of schools, the citizenship education curriculum and the culture and processes of schools.

The Structure of Schools

Unlike most countries Pakistan does not have free, compulsory and universal education although it is a constitutional right. All education policies have recognised the right of citizens to education and have set targets to ensure it. They have, however, all failed to meet the targets so that even today many children of school age are not in school. The inability of the state to provide education has led to the privatisation of education so that education in Pakistan has become a commodity with the quality of education determined by the price one is willing to pay for it. Thus, in Pakistan, a number of school systems cater to the different socio-economic classes. There is the International Baccalaureate (IB), the American system, the British system of O and A levels, the Matriculation system and the religious madrassas. The international school system caters largely to a small cadre of students belonging to the elite. The largest number of students study in the Matriculation system. Religious madrassas have historically provided education to a small cadre of students; however, since the late 1970s they have grown in number, catering to about 7 percent of the student body today. With the exception of schools in the Matriculation system, all the other school systems (including many in the Matriculation system) are in the private sector, giving this sector a share of around 36 percent in education (Ministry of Education, 2009).

Although the private sector plays a major role in the provision of education, it has no role in education policy formulation. Education policy is developed by civil bureaucrats in the Ministry of Education, Islamabad. The policy determines the aims and objectives of education and outlines plans for their realisation. The aims and objectives of education are translated into a national curriculum. The development of the national curriculum is also centralised. The curriculum is then translated into text-books, the writing and publishing of which are tightly controlled by the Provincial Textbook Boards. Only text-books prepared and published under the board's authority and approved by the Ministry of Education can be used in schools. The centralised system of curriculum and text-books development ensures that only 'official knowledge' gets legitimated and enters the classroom (Apple 1993, 1996, 1999).

Schools in Pakistan are organised hierarchically and managed in a highly authoritarian style. Clearly defined rules and regulations are made by the provincial department of education in the case of government schools and added to by boards of directors in the case of private schools. Generally, principals of schools have little or no decision-making power, rather they are expected to execute faithfully government (and in the case of private schools, the board's) decisions. Teachers in the classrooms have even less autonomy, being expected to teach the prescribed text-book and ensure students memorise it so that they do well on tests and examinations.

The Curriculum and Text-Books

In Pakistan, the goal of social studies/Pakistan studies is citizenship education. Citizenship concepts and values thus form part of the curriculum. Since the late 1970s citizenship concepts and values have also been included in the curriculum and text-books of Urdu, English and Islamiyat. Numerous analytical studies of the content of the citizenship curriculum and text-books have shown that instead of drawing on the knowledge base of the social sciences for curriculum development, a narrow body of instructional content is selected to serve ideological ends (Ahmad 2008, 2004; Ali 1986; Aziz 1992; Dean 2007, 2005, 2000; Future Youth Group 2003; Nayyar & Salim 2004; Rehman 1999; Saigol 1993). Following from the curriculum, the social studies/Pakistan studies text-books include facts that are carefully selected and woven into narratives to reflect the government ideology. Since the Islamisation of education in the 1970s, text-books have provided a particular view of the struggle for, creation, existence and future of the Pakistani nation.

The pre-independence period is depicted as a time when Muslims suffered great cruelty and injustice at the hands of the Hindus and the British (who sided with the Hindus against the Muslims), making it impossible for Muslims and Hindus to live together. This led to the conception of the two nation theory (Hindus and Muslims are two separate nations), the Muslims demand and struggle for their own country and ultimately their success with the division of the Indian subcontinent into Pakistan and India. This account of the struggle for and creation of Pakistan ignores the rule of the Mughals over India from the beginning of the sixteenth century to the mid-nineteenth century. Moreover, the role of non-Muslims in the long struggle for self-rule that presaged the struggle for Pakistan is ignored.

Text-books depict India as hegemonic, hostile and aggressive towards Pakistan, and caution vigilance on the part of citizens towards India. To counter this threat the text-books promote a militarised state by promoting hatred towards India and Hindus and encouraging the use of force and even war (Aziz 1992; Nayyar & Salim 2004; Saigol 1993). The text-books discuss the three wars Pakistan has fought with India, describing vividly the glorious victories won in the battle-field and eulogising military heroes.

These text-books repeatedly define national identity in a manner that excludes non-Muslims and extends nationalism to the Muslim *ummah* (Dean 2007, 2008). The idea of Pakistan as an Islamic state rather than a Muslim majority country and Pakistani citizens as Muslims has been developed (Nayyar & Salim 2004). Further, national unity is promoted through the depiction of Pakistan as a culturally homogenous society with Pakistanis having one religion, one language and one way of life. In order to preserve national unity, Pakistanis must be loyal, desist from questioning the government on issues of national importance or working against national interests and be willing to sacrifice their life for the defence of their country and Islam. Thus, text-books ignore the religious and cultural diversity of Pakistan, encourage prejudice and discrimination against religious minorities and render suspect the patriotism of those who challenge these narratives and the aims to which they are directed (Nayyar & Salim 2004).

The texts promote gender apartheid in Pakistan. The texts show men active in social, political and economic life and confine women to the domestic sphere in the caring and nurturing roles of mother and home-maker. When women go out to work, their work as teachers, nurses and social workers is seen as an extension of the caring and nurturing role they are best suited to play. Thus the text-books foster gender stereotypes, entrench biases against women and relegate women to a secondary status. In so doing they deny women equal citizenship.

Pakistan's constitution envisions it as a parliamentary democracy. Creation of a democratic society requires citizens to be knowledgeable about democracy and the role of citizens in it. However, the complex political, social, cultural and religious history of Pakistan has resulted in the curriculum and text-books drawing on both Islamic and conventional democratic theory to present concepts such as democracy, citizenship, rights and responsibilities of citizens, freedom and participation in civic life. However, rather than analysing the commonalities and differences in the way these concepts are understood in Islam and conventional democratic theory, the concepts are discussed in contradictory and ambiguous terms, resulting in teachers and students having contradictory and ambiguous understandings.

Democratic societies require students who are skilled at gathering information, able to think independently and critically and who can solve problems and make decisions in the interest of the common good. Unfortunately these skills are absent from the curriculum. Furthermore, for democracy to flourish, values such as equality, justice and pluralism are required. Rather than helping students develop these values, the curriculum and text-books seek to inculcate in students the values of respect for and obedience to those in authority, discipline and sense of duty and alms-giving and filial piety. The lack of appropriate content and the ignoring of the development of skills and values important for the creation of a democratic society result in the promotion of a passive rather than active citizenry.

The Culture and Processes of Schools

Most Pakistani schools begin the day with an assembly. During the assembly students stand in straight lines to listen to the recitation of verses from the Quran and a *Naat* (poetry recited in praise of Prophet Muhammad) following which they sing the national anthem at which time the national flag is raised. The assembly is also used to teach students discipline, inculcate values and celebrate success in various inter-school competitions. In keeping with the focus on discipline and inculcation of values, students who arrive late must either return home or wait at the school gate until the assembly is over. Teachers or student monitors censure latecomers and encourage them to be punctual in the future. As students walk to their classrooms they are checked to ensure they are wearing the prescribed uniform and that it is neat and clean.

The hierarchical and authoritarian organisation of the school is reflected in the classroom. The teacher is positioned at the front of the class, often on a raised platform or behind a podium. Teaching generally follows an algorithm of read-lecture-question. Content from the text-book is read, followed by a lecture in which the teacher simply paraphrases the text. Occasionally the teachers' explanations go beyond the text-book to include examples from the local context or their personal experiences. Less frequently are students asked to provide examples or share their own experiences. On completion of the lecture, the teacher asks students to answer questions which require them to repeat text-book content. Lessons end with teachers giving students text-based homework such as reading the next section or completing end-of-chapter exercises. The complete dependence of the teacher and student on the text-book ensures students learn not only text-book facts but are also indoctrinated into the world-view of the government in power.

Classroom teaching is inclined towards authoritarianism. The teachers' attitude and behaviour is one of domination and control over students. As learning largely depends on students listening to the teacher, teachers expect students to sit quietly and attentively for the duration of the lesson. Most students do sit quietly and attentively, those who do not are ordered to be quiet and pay attention, verbally humiliated and sometimes even physically punished. There is no teacher–student interaction other than students responding to the teachers' instructions and questions. There is even less student–student interaction as none is permitted in most classrooms. Furthermore, rather than empowering students, the organisation and conduct of teaching disempowers them by instilling in them the values of passivity and obedience to and respect for authority of the teacher and the text.

In addition to teaching and learning in the classroom, schools also offer students the opportunity to engage in co-curricular activities such as celebration of national days and Muslim religious festivals and participation in various inter-school competitions. On national days students make speeches highlighting the significance of the day, dramatise the event and sing national songs. *Milads* and *naat khawni* are held to celebrate *Eid-i-Milad-un-Nabi* (the birthday of Prophet Muhammad). Only a few students most likely to perform well are chosen to represent the school in sports competitions, debate and science fairs.

A few schools provide opportunities for students to join the Girl Guides/Boy Scouts, be members of the student council and engage in community service. The literature on citizenship education suggests that such activities are important as they prepare students with the knowledge, skills and dispositions required for informed, responsible and active citizenship. Girl Guides/Boy Scouts are especially encouraged as students learn the importance of helping others, are better prepared to solve daily life problems, have an increased understanding of the local and national context and become more patriotic and nationalistic. Membership of student councils is thought to facilitate citizenship education as they involve student participation in elections and engagement in processes similar to those of elected government officials. In most Pakistani schools members of the student council are generally chosen by teachers. In others, only a few active and intelligent students are encouraged to participate in the elections. Once elected, members are usually assigned tasks related to maintaining discipline and organising school events, such as a fair to raise money, they are, however, excluded from decision making regarding discipline policy or how to spend the money raised. Students are also encouraged to engage in community service such as visiting sick children in a hospital, teaching out-of-school children, planting trees and raising funds for various causes. There is, however, little discussion of why so many children are out of school or the nature of the human activities contributing to global warning.

The structure of schools, the curriculum, the text-books and the teaching and learning experiences of students in schools have a number of implications for the construction of citizenship. The hierarchical and authoritarian structure of the school and classroom teach students to be passive and obedient and to unquestioningly respect authority. The essence of democracy is the acceptance of diversity but this is lost as the curriculum and text-books present a single point of view encouraging students to view the world in 'black and white' and 'us versus them' terms, developing exclusivist rather than inclusivist mindsets (Social Policy and Development Centre 2003). Teaching and learning that focuses on transmission and memorisation of text-books result in the belief that knowledge is to be found in text-books and the words of teachers and that one's own experiences and realities are insignificant. Such teaching and learning is said to produce 'parrots' (Hoodbhoy 1998) and 'educated slaves' (Aziz 1992) rather than informed, responsible and active citizens. The focus on knowledge means that students acquire considerable information but not the skills of how to use it to obtain their rights, take and defend positions on issues or solve problems. Furthermore, rather than encouraging students to choose and develop their values, values like knowledge are transmitted through lectures. Little wonder then that Pakistani educators are critical of teaching and learning in Pakistani classrooms. They point out that:

> The existing teaching practice is contributing to the socialization of obedient, passive citizens who lack critical thinking, questioning, decision-making and problem solving skills, who are closed minded followers rather than responsible and independent citizens. (Kizilbash 1986, p. 168)

CREATING AND SUSTAINING DEMOCRACY: THE CITIZENSHIP EDUCATION PROGRAMME

As in other countries a key goal of education in Pakistan is citizenship education. At the time of writing this chapter, Pakistan once again has a representative government in power, the result of a valiant struggle waged by the people of Pakistan to unseat a powerful military dictator. Pakistani people expect their government to work towards institutionalising parliamentary democracy and expanding democracy to all realms of social life. They want civic equality, greater socio-economic justice, a significant expansion of participation in decision making in matters that affect them, a celebration of the diversity of Pakistan, a desire to be informed through an independent and responsible media and the institutionalisation of an independent judiciary. This vision suggests comprehensive changes in the political, social, economic and educational context.

I now turn to describing the citizenship education programme that will contribute to realising this vision. The citizenship education programme must have as its aims and objectives the preparation of young people to realise the conception of democracy articulated earlier. Central to realising the aims and objectives are the production and dissemination of curriculum and teaching and learning materials without the limitations research has shown to exist in the present versions. It is imperative that the curriculum sets clear standards and outcomes in not only the knowledge domain but also skills and values. Skills such as inquiry, critical thinking, decision making and problem-solving and values such as social justice, equality and diversity must be included as these are important to citizenship education. Rather than being prescriptive, the curriculum should illustrate effective teaching and assessment practices, allowing teachers the autonomy of deciding how best to attain the outcomes. This flexibility would recognise the variations in contexts and acknowledge teacher professionalism.

To implement the curriculum in letter and spirit will require the education of teachers. Presently teachers are not viewed as professionals able to make decisions about what to teach and how to teach; rather they are seen as implementers of other people's ideas. They are encouraged to transmit faithfully not only text-book knowledge but also the values inhered in the text. In such circumstances it is important that teachers acquire knowledge of different ideologies, critically reflect on their own and the conception of the work of the teacher formed through it. Teacher education is required to: (a) improve teachers' content knowledge, ensuring a substantive understanding of prevalent political systems and regimes, especially democracy, and of citizenship and citizen rights and responsibilities, as well as an understanding of the local, national and global contexts with their persistent and current issues and (b) facilitate the acquisition of skills, especially the skill of learning how to learn so that they can continue to learn independently. This approach would involve introducing teachers to pedagogies that are more dialogical, co-operative and inquiring. It would also involve providing teachers opportunities to use these in the real classroom with support until they become part of their pedagogical repertoire. To facilitate the use of these pedagogies will require teachers to learn and use assessment practices that assess not only knowledge but skills and values. It also requires that they be encouraged to reflect on and research their practice so as to better understand and improve their practice to make it more democratic. Teacher education should itself become more democratic, including prospective and in-service teachers in making decisions regarding the curriculum of their program. Teacher educators must also model and encourage teachers to engage in critical reflection, collaborate with others, have a questioning and inquiring stance, be open to learning and participate actively and responsibly in the society.

Restructuring schools as sites for preparation of democratic citizens will require that schools be structured democratically and use democratic processes at all levels. This requires that those directly involved in schools—head teachers, teachers, students and parents—be involved in making policy decisions and in governance guided by democratic values (Apple & Beane 2007). There are already structures, such as the School Management Committees and student councils, which must be made more democratic and whose participants must be taught how to engage in democratic decision making. In schools, teachers must be involved in curriculum design and decisions regarding teaching and learning, and in the classroom teachers must involve students in deciding what to learn, how to learn and in the assessment of learning. Schools must provide opportunities for all students to participate in co-curricular activities and encourage preparation for and reflection on them. To enlarge possibilities for democracy they must both draw on and support the efforts of civil society organisations working towards the same.

CONCLUSION

A new democratic government is in place and a new education policy is in the making. If Pakistan is to create and sustain itself as a democracy it must ensure the preparation of democratic citizens through setting educational goals directed towards this end and committing to realisation of the goals. This should include the introduction of citizenship education as a statutory subject; a participatory approach to citizenship education curriculum development; provision of a wide range of quality teaching and learning materials to support the curriculum; and teaching, learning and assessment practices that facilitate realisation of the goals. Given the existential threat to Pakistan, the government cannot afford to lose the opportunity—it must act now.

REFERENCES

Ahmad, Ifitikhar (2004) Islam, democracy and citizenship education: An examination of the social studies curriculum in Pakistan, *Current Issues in Comparative Education*, 7(1), pp. 39–50.
———. (2008) The anatomy of an Islamic model: Citizenship education in Pakistan, in David L. Grossman, Wing On Lee & Kerry J. Kennedy (eds.) *Citizenship Curriculum in Asia and the Pacific*. Hong Kong, Comparative Education Research Centre, pp. 97–109.
Ali, M. Athar (1986). *Tareekh Aur Agahi (History and Awareness)*. Lahore, Pakistan, Urdu Art Press.
Apple, Michael (1993) *Official Knowledge: Democratic Education in a Conservative Age*. New York and London, Routledge.

————. (1996) *Cultural Politics and Education.* New York and London, Teacher College Press.

————. (1999) *Power, Meaning and Identity: Essays in Critical Educational Studies.* New York, Peter Lang.

Apple, Michael & James Beane (2007) *Democratic Schools: Lessons in Powerful Education* (2nd ed.). Portsmouth, NH, Heinemann.

Aziz, Kamal (1992) *The Murder of the History of Pakistan.* Lahore, Pakistan, Vanguard.

Dean, Bernadette (2000) Islam, democracy and social studies education: A quest for possibilities. Unpublished doctoral dissertation, University of Alberta, Canada.

————. (2005) Citizenship education in Pakistani schools: Problems and possibilities, *International Journal of Citizenship and Teacher Education,* 1(2), pp. 1–17.

————. (2007) Creating gender apartheid: A critical study of an English language Pakistani textbook, in Rashida Qureshi & Jane Rarieya (eds.), *Gender and Education in Pakistan.* Karachi, Oxford University Press, pp. 116–137.

————. (2008) The changing face of citizenship education in Pakistan, in James Arthur, Ian Davies & Carole Hahn (eds.) *Handbook of Citizenship and Democracy.* London, Sage Publications, pp. 227–238.

Future Youth Group (2003) *Ideas on Democracy, Freedom and Peace in Textbooks.* Islamabad, Liberal Youth Forum.

Haque, Ziaul (1985) Islamization of society in Pakistan, in Mohammad Asghar Khan (ed.) *Islam, Politics and the State: The Pakistan Experience.* London, Zed Books, pp. 114–126.

Hoodbhoy, Pervez (1998). *Education and the State: Fifty Years of Pakistan.* Karachi, Oxford University Press.

Jalal, Ayesha (1995) *Democracy and Authoritarianism in South Asia.* Cambridge, Cambridge University Press.

Kizilbash, Hamid (1986) *Pakistan's Curriculum Jungle: An Analysis of the SAHE Consultation on the Undergraduate Curriculum in Pakistan.* Lahore, SAHE Publication.

Ministry of Education (1959) *Report of the Commission of National Education.* Islamabad, Government of Pakistan, Ministry of Education.

————. (1972) *The New Education Policy 1972–1980.* Islamabad, Government of Pakistan, Ministry of Education.

————. (1979) *National Education Policy and Implementation Programme.* Islamabad, Government of Pakistan, Ministry of Education.

————. (1998) *National Education Policy 'IQRA' 1998–2010.* Islamabad, Government of Pakistan, Ministry of Education.

————. (2009) *National Education Policy 2009.* Islamabad: Government of Pakistan, Ministry of Education.

Ministry of the Interior, Education Division (1947) *Proceedings of the Pakistan Educational Conference.* Islamabad, Government of Pakistan, Ministry of the Interior (Education Division).

Nayyar, Abdul Hameed & Ahmad Salim (2004) *The Subtle Subversion: The State of Curricula and Textbooks in Pakistan.* Islamabad, Sustainable Development Policy Institute.

Rashid, Abbas (1985) Pakistan: The ideological dimension, in Mohammad Asghar Khan (ed.) *Islam, Politics and the State: The Pakistan Experience.* London, Zed Books, pp. 69–89.

Rehman, Tariq (1999) Teaching ideology and textbooks, *Daily Dawn,* 27 September.

Saigol, Rubina (1993) *Education: Critical Perspectives.* Lahore, Pakistan, Progressive Publishers.

Social Policy and Development Centre (2003) *Annual Review of Social Development in Pakistan: The State of Education*, Karachi, Social Policy and Development Centre.

Ziring, Lawrence (1997) *Pakistan in the Twentieth Century: A Political History.* Karachi, Oxford University Press.

6   The Dilemmas of Singapore's National Education in the Global Society

Mark Baildon and Jasmine B-Y Sim

INTRODUCTION: MANAGING GLOBALISATION

Globalisation is resulting in new arrangements between nation-states, markets and citizens. In particular, nation-states are developing new strategies to manage transnational flows of people, ideas, goods, media and technologies. To remain competitive in the global economy requires responsive populations able to flexibly and quickly adapt to ever-changing circumstances. While Green (2007) contends that nation-states will not disappear into a borderless world, they are, however, increasingly challenged.

Unsurprisingly, this situation heightens anxieties over citizenship. One of the anxieties nation-states face revolves around traditional notions of national citizenship being destabilised by forces of global capitalism, popular culture and new technologies and media (Parker, Nonomiya & Cogan 1999). Citizenship education especially takes on great importance during an age of transnationality as the nation-state tries to develop the necessary affiliations for national projects identified as vital for national advantage in competitive global contexts. This poses challenges for educators and educational systems as they try to educate students in ways that will develop and promote national identities while also trying to educate students to be more cosmopolitan and global in their outlook and skills. As Mitchell and Parker (2008) note, educational systems tend to view the global cosmopolitan and the national patriot as counter identities rather than as relational entities that might be produced together. George Yeo, a government minister in Singapore, aptly captured the delicate balancing act of producing national identities that can live and work in a global society when he noted in 1989 that:

> [Singaporeans] must balance this contradiction between being cosmopolitan and being nationalistic. We cannot be a trading nation, if we are not cosmopolitan. We cannot be a nation, if we are not nationalistic. We must be both at the same time. (cited in Green 1997, p. 150)

In response to these contradictions and tensions, some civic education scholars are calling for multilevel forms of citizenship (Falk 1994) and multidimensional citizenship (Cogan, Grossman & Liu 2000). However, national education systems struggle to fully consider the implications of such forms of citizenship or implement citizenship education programmes that have more fluid and multiple notions of citizenship.

Educational reform and policy play a central role in mediating and managing the shifting relationships between state and society, and are one way governments try to address anxieties accompanying fundamental changes due to globalisation (Koh 2004). In Singapore, the government is constantly strategising how to work with globalisation to reposition Singapore in the larger scheme of capital flows. As a nation, Singapore is simply too small to function economically on its own. Tharman Shanmugaratnam (2007), then minister of education, fittingly expressed:

> Globalisation is a big plus for Singapore. We want to swim with the tide of globalisation, be part of its ripples, because that's how we will prosper. But we know that a global world brings real challenges that we have to face squarely, resolve and overcome.

So while the government works with globalisation, it also strives to inculcate civic values perceived to be eroding (Koh 2006). Tharman (2007) again:

> Our response has to rest on both economic and social strategies. As Singaporeans leave our shores to work and live overseas, as new immigrants join our Singapore family; as incomes widen; and as Singaporeans get exposed to and even bombarded with alternative views, ideologies, lifestyles, we have to work harder to keep a sense of shared identity amongst all our citizens and keep our society cohesive.

Singapore therefore provides a good case study of some of the challenges that globalisation poses for citizenship education. In this chapter we examine more fully the implications of how nations try to position themselves and their populations in the new social, cultural, economic and political realities accompanying globalisation while seeking to maintain national affinities. In particular, we examine National Education in Singapore, the latest nation-building initiative that addresses citizenship, as a case study to better understand some of the dilemmas confronting citizenship education in 'new times' (Hall 1989). After providing an overview of National Education in Singapore, we focus on the following dilemmas: (a) the challenge of managing identities; (b) the nature and limits of critical thinking; and (c) the impact of consumerism on citizenship.

CITIZENSHIP EDUCATION IN SINGAPORE

Key Contexts

A former British colony, Singapore is a multiracial society built by immigrants from China, Malaysia and Southern India. It became independent when it separated from Malaysia in 1965 and, as a tiny island with few natural resources, it faced multiple challenges to its existence from the very beginning. The threat of communism and racial riots in the early years of independence emphasised to the People's Action Party (PAP) government, which has been consistently returned to power, that for Singapore to survive nation-building and modernising the economy were urgent priorities (Chua 1995).

The themes of vulnerability and survival have been strong ideological constructs of the government in Singapore, and the 'structuring centre of reasoning and rationalisation of the policies by which Singapore has been governed since independence' (Chua 1995, p. 48). Education has been viewed in instrumental terms as a means of achieving both the development of human capital and the building of social, communitarian reflexes to bind together a highly diverse state (Gopinathan 2007). While the education system has undergone numerous changes, it has never faltered in its aim to 'support and develop the Republic as a modern industrial nation with a cohesive multiracial society' (Wilson 1978, p. 235).

Singapore's education system is centrally planned and remarkably responsive to the directives of the Ministry of Education (MoE) and its political leaders. Unsurprisingly, with the strong state presence in managing the educational needs and charting the educational future of the country, the aims of education in Singapore are inextricably linked with the political aims of the government. Similar to other developmental states, Singapore's school system is essentially an instrument of nation-building (Green 1997). In such states, the goals of national development are 'sacrosanct', 'ongoing' and are often couched in terms of 'national survival' (Sim & Print 2005, p. 60).

Similarly, strong state management of the educational system also served the pragmatic interests of the new 'administrative state' that focused on economic and social management rather than political debate about new policies (Gopinathan 2007). Technocratic solutions to social and political problems became intertwined with a narrative of national progress and able leadership. Education became 'an important legitimising instrument in sustaining the hegemony of the governing People's Action Party' (Loh 1998, p. 1) to ensure order, stability and development. An official narrative of the government providing what matters most to people—safety, security and prosperity—in exchange for economic discipline and social conformity provided the common shared national history education that helped forge the young nation.

With Singapore being a small city-state in a global economy, the PAP has consistently made the whole society well aware of potential challenges and threats in global contexts (Mok & Tan 2004). To remain globally competitive, Singapore instituted a major reform of the education system in 1997 with the launch of Thinking Schools, Learning Nation (TSLN). The vision describes 'a nation of thinking and committed citizens capable of meeting the challenges of the future, and an education system geared to the needs of the 21st century' (MoE 2009a). TSLN was partly in response to perceived economic imperatives. As Gopinathan (2007) argues, education reform in Singapore 'is primarily a way of retooling the productive capacity of the system' (p. 59). In a global context shaped by information and communication, the ability to think critically and continually learn is essential to be able to respond appropriately to rapid and complex changes. This is true particularly of the employment flexibility dictated by global economic trends.

An Overview of Citizenship Education in Singapore

As one might imagine, forging national identity, managing social cohesion and making sure people were committed to national development made citizenship education a national priority in Singapore since its inception. The focus of citizenship education has consistently been one of inculcation; the purpose is to instill the state-defined national values in students. In the early years of nationhood, citizenship was taught in an ethics course that aimed at character development and social responsibility. Civics was introduced in 1967 to teach students about the constitution, legislation and international relations while instilling the values of patriotism, loyalty and civic responsibility (Sim & Print 2005). In 1974, an education for living course combined civics, history and geography (Green 1997).

The rapid industrialisation in the 1970s and 1980s raised concerns that the adoption of science and technology and the increasing use of English were causing young Singaporeans to become too Westernised. The state perceived values in dichotomous terms. Western values appeared to emphasise individualism while Asian values emphasised communitarianism and the associated values of hard work, thrift and sacrifice (Chua 1995). This shift in values, according to the state, caused a moral decline because it was perceived to have deculturised and individualised society (Hill & Lian 1995). However, Prime Minister Lee Kuan Yew soon made a case for greater emphasis on moral values to shape citizens to be loyal and patriotic, law-abiding, ready to defend the nation, and filial, respectful, responsible and well mannered (Hill & Lian 1995). This led to the introduction of a new moral education programme 'Being and Becoming' in 1981, to:

> curb the perceived growth of western individualist values which it was
> believed would promote such social ills as a decline in the work ethic,

parents being sent off to old people's homes and corruption among bankers. (Green 1997, pp. 149–150)

'Being and Becoming' was renamed 'Civics and Moral Education' in 1992 to focus on moral and political socialisation. This was further revised after 1997 to strengthen the nation-building focus.

Social studies was also introduced in primary schools in 1981 to:

enable pupils to understand their social world and to develop the knowledge, skills and attitudes necessary to participate effectively in the society and environment in which they live. (MoE 1999, p. 1)

A continued emphasis on Asian values in social education was one way government officials hoped to make sure Singapore would remain resistant to Western social ills and competitive in the global economy, and these values can be seen in the five themes outlined by the *Shared Values White Paper* of 1991:

1. nation before community and society before self
2. family as the basis of civil society
3. regard and community support for the individual
4. consensus instead of contention
5. racial and religious harmony (Green 1997; Tan 2001)

The emphasis on values education, especially the ideals of meritocracy and Confucian values of hard work and harmony, provided the core of citizenship education in the 1980s and 1990s.

National Education

Similar to the emphasis on Asian values, what also marked TSLN reforms was the explicit recognition that globalisation and the changing economy 'will strain the loyalties and attachments of young Singaporeans' (Gopinathan 2007, p. 61). Singaporean officials have become increasingly concerned that young people might be pulled into allegiances that challenge the hold of the nation-state. Growing up amidst affluence in the cosmopolitan city, technologically savvy and highly mobile, young Singaporeans were perceived by the government to be 'footloose and fancy free'. Political leaders became concerned that many of them 'will pack their bags and take flight when our country runs into a little storm' (Goh 2001), and it was reported in the press that as many as 53 percent of Singaporean teens would consider emigrating (J. Lim 2006). Leaders were also concerned by reports that young Singaporeans had little knowledge of events surrounding Singapore's independence and expressed little interest in nation-building issues (*Straits Times* 1996). In 1997 Lee Hsien Loong, then deputy prime minister, claimed:

This ignorance will hinder our effort to develop a shared sense of nationhood. We will not acquire the right instincts to bond as one nation, or maintain the will to survive and prosper in an uncertain world. (Lee 1997)

In response to these concerns, the National Education project was launched in 1997 to develop the knowledge, values and skills deemed necessary for national citizenship in Singapore. The objectives of National Education were to develop national cohesion; foster a sense of national pride; learn 'the Singapore story' (mainly the hardships and sacrifices of the founding generation and PAP); understand Singapore's unique challenges, constraints and vulnerabilities; and instill the core values of meritocracy, harmony and good governance (MoE 2009b). Forging a national identity in the midst of globalisation was paramount, making citizenship education a continuing concern of officials.

Highlighting the continuity of citizenship education as national values, six messages were conveyed by National Education. They are:

(1) Singapore is our homeland; this is where we belong. Singapore's heritage and way of life must be preserved; (2) Racial and religious harmony must be preserved. Despite the many races, religions, languages and cultures, Singaporeans must pursue one destiny; (3) Meritocracy and incorruptibility must be upheld. This means equal opportunities for all, according to ability and effort; (4) No one owes Singapore a living. She must find her own way to survive and prosper; (5) Singaporeans themselves must defend Singapore. No one else is responsible for the country's security and well-being; (6) Singaporeans must have confidence in our future. United, determined and well prepared, Singaporeans shall build a bright future for themselves. (MoE 2009b)

The secondary social studies curriculum was launched in 2001 as a major vehicle for National Education (Sim 2008). As a compulsory and examinable subject for fifteen- and sixteen-year-olds, social studies in Singapore aims to prepare students for work in the knowledge-based global economy and develop and deepen national consciousness—a sense of belonging to and feeling for Singapore. The future-oriented aims of the secondary social studies syllabus are to enable students to:

1. Understand the issues that affect the socio-economic development, the governance and the future of Singapore.
2. Learn from experiences of other countries to build and sustain a politically viable, socially cohesive and economically vibrant Singapore.
3. Develop citizens who have empathy towards others and who will participate responsibly and sensibly in a multiethnic, multicultural and multireligious society.

4. Have a deep sense of shared destiny and national identity (MoE 2006, p. 1).

However, against the backdrop of the TSLN vision, National Education and social studies articulate a dialectical tension. While TSLN emphasised critical and creative thinking to prepare students for post-industrial forms of labour and the knowledge-based global economy, National Education and social studies promoted a notion of citizenship favoured by the government, which was inherently convergent and parochial. With National Education, Koh (2006) argues that the government 'is creating new modalities of ideological narratives to "inoculate" the Singapore body politic against the ills of globalisation' (p. 360). This could also be usefully understood as a form of governmentality, that is, techniques for constituting subjectivities according to desired norms (Foucault 1979). Consequently, citizenship education through National Education and social studies has become a complex task; the tension is between rapidly changing social, economic and political circumstances on one hand, and the PAP government's conservatism on the other. We now move to a fuller discussion of these tensions.

CONTRADICTIONS, TENSIONS AND CHALLENGES OF NATIONAL EDUCATION

As Koh (2007) notes, Singapore is an excellent example for understanding the discourses and operations of globalisation. It also provides an excellent case study for understanding the ways a national education system is trying to address some of the contradictions, tensions and challenges that nation-states face in educating national citizens who are well positioned to participate in and take advantage of new global conditions. Drawing on Perry and Maurer (2003), Koh (2007) argues that Singapore has developed a 'metapragmatics of globalisation' to manage the unpredictability of global flows and conditions. This metapragmatics consists of a 'rhetoricist position to persuade its populace to accept the implementation of certain policies' (p. 180) and strategies to shape and instrumentalise Singaporean institutions so that Singaporeans can 'live with globalisation tactically' (p. 182). Education in Singapore plays a major role in this process.

Several speeches by government officials to support National Education and the broader TSLN framework consistently placed Singapore's educational reform in the contexts of global, regional and national imperatives. For example, then deputy prime minister Lee Hsien Loong (1997), noted the dangers of Chinese chauvinism and racial politics in Singapore's elections, Indonesian haze and its effect on Singaporean air quality and financial instability in Thailand, which had both regional and global repercussions. He stressed that the next century would bring a whole new set of problems and circumstances and that TSLN needed to prepare citizens to be ever ready to adapt to new realities and problems. Then prime minister Goh Chok Tong (1997) cited the increasingly competitive global environment and how globalisation and technology were transforming the nature of work and communities. Dr. Aline Wong (2000), the former senior minister of education, made a case for social studies as a means to develop a deep sense of belonging to community and nation in the face of rapid globalisation. As Koh (2004) argues, this realignment of the educational landscape can be seen as 'a response to the trajectories of (global) economic conditions, concomitantly framed by (local) sociopolitical and cultural-ideological needs' (p. 335).

Recent reform in Singapore adopts a multifaceted, flexible, almost all-encompassing approach that draws on a diverse range of strategies. National survival itself now rests on continual, non-stop education, as Hawazi Daipi (2005), senior parliamentary secretary in the Ministries of Education and Manpower, noted in a forum on 'Achieving a Social and Moral Balance in Globalisation' in 2005. Hawazi argued that Singapore could not survive and prosper if Singaporeans did not 'make the effort to re-look, re-invent and re-vitalize' themselves. He called on all Singaporeans to:

> continue to upgrade [their] skills and capabilities, and keep an open mind. Indeed, those who are able to survive and thrive in this new borderless, global environment are those who can respond quickly to take advantage of the new opportunities and meet the challenges presented by globalisation. (Daipi 2005)

TSLN and National Education are efforts to manage the dialectical tension between preparing young people to be national citizens able to thrive in a global society. However, this tension continues to manifest itself in ways that are unique to Singapore while being representative of nation-states' attempts to manage globalisation. In particular, there are three key tensions central to preparing a national citizenry for changing global contexts: (a) the challenge of managing identities; (b) the nature and limits of critical thinking; and (c) the impact of consumerism on citizenship.

The Challenge of Managing Identities

Globalisation has created pressures on nation-states and educational systems to form allegiances and create identities amenable to national projects. National identity formation in these contexts remains a concern of Singaporean officials. Schools in Singapore have traditionally played a twofold role in the developmental state: 'to provide students with the skills required in an industrializing and modern Singapore; and to inculcate in them values that will ensure their loyalty and commitment to the nation' (Quah 2000, p. 78). However, as noted earlier, what marks new educational reform is the explicit recognition that the imagined worlds of 'the official mind and of the entrepreneurial mentality' (Appadurai 1996, p. 33) are contested and subverted by the increasing range of options available to young people through transnational flows of media, technologies, popular culture and ideas. Identities are increasingly up for grabs (Koh 2004; Tan 2007).

Also, new sets of skills to remain competitive in the global economy suggest an identity that is more cosmopolitan. Another concern for Singaporean officials is how to strategically balance the new cosmopolitan identity that globalisation and educational reform such as TSLN seem to require and promote with national identity. As Mitchell (2003) argues, there has been growing pressures for 'the creation of the tolerant, "multicultural self", a more individuated, mobile, and highly tracked . . . "strategic cosmopolitan"' (p. 387). This 'strategic cosmopolitan', however, is not motivated by ideals of national unity, but by:

> understandings of global competitiveness, and the necessity to strategically adapt as an individual to rapidly shifting personal and national contexts . . . i.e., [they are] individuals oriented to excel in ever transforming situations of global competition, either as workers, managers, or entrepreneurs. (2003, p. 387)

In other words, the flexible identity required by globalisation is a different type of identity than that required by the developmental state and may be much more difficult for nation-states to manage and hold in allegiance. This is particularly problematic for Singapore, where globalisation has made some segments of its already stratified society 'more internationally mobile, wealthier and more tolerant of diversity than others—or, in short, more cosmopolitan' (Tan 2007, p. 296). Identity and citizenship once united through notions of national identity and statehood are increasingly destabilised (Green 2007).

New technoscapes, ideoscapes and mediascapes (Appadurai 1996) make possible new imagined identities and communities. Transnational movements of ideas and media that are increasingly beyond governments' capacities to filter and control are powerful shapers of identities and pose the potential for transnational or postnational allegiances and communities. These ideas and media comprise an out-of-school curriculum and offer powerful content and pedagogies that vie with official curricula and pedagogies. Students have access to various technologies that are fundamentally social in nature and make transnational communication, expression and mobilisations possible. Young people live increasingly digital lifestyles with opportunities to develop identities and communities in gaming environments, through blogging, in online chat rooms, through popular Web sites like YouTube and through interaction in social networking Web sites such as Facebook and MySpace. They are able to create and share content that may have the potential to challenge official discourses.

Emerging technologies and media thus pose new problems for nation-states at the same time they are embraced. While new media and technology have become integral to the educational landscape, there are several negative aspects of digital content that nation-states and schools alike must deal with: students may come upon misinformation or 'malinformation' that is harmful, such as pornography or bomb making (Burbules & Callister 2000); and potential 'counter-ideologies' that challenge official narratives and knowledge. For example, with the advent of digital content not only Western values and the lure of foreign lands threaten the social fabric of Singapore; easily accessible fundamentalist ideologies pose threats as well. As Singapore's Education Minister Tharman (2007) acknowledged, 'Ideologies and events that threaten to polarize communities are now instantly spread and instantly accessed globally, via both traditional media and the Internet'. How Singapore's government will engage oppositional or alternative identities and communities represents a core challenge to the nation-state.

The Nature and Limits of Critical Thinking

The social studies teachers in a study we conducted (Baildon & Sim, forthcoming) highlighted the contradictions between the demands of globalisation (that call for greater openness, a broader range of cognitive skills and social practices and the ability to tolerate and appreciate increasing diversity and different perspectives) and the local ideological and political contexts that constrain the range of teaching and learning possibilities available to teachers and students. The teachers in the study highlighted the anxieties they experienced teaching in school cultures that emphasise curriculum coverage and examination while recognising that deep, sustained learning and the development of capacities necessary for critical thinking and innovation require certain commitments in terms of time, resources and support. They also talked about broader political-ideological contexts in Singapore by discussing the 'out-of-bounds (OB) markers' that regulate and set supposed limits to acceptable public discourse. Catherine Lim (2006), a local writer, argues that Singapore uses OB markers to set firm limits on what is acceptable while advocating critical and creative thought. Noting that OB markers shape the limits of political discourse, she argues that they are purposefully left vague to promote a 'general sense of fear, hardly definable and therefore easily challenged by the government' as non-existent (2006, p. 89). According to Lim, this results in self-censorship.

Concerns about OB markers and political contexts as inhibiting innovation and criticality make apparent the contradictions of official rhetoric which calls for greater innovation and openness while maintaining tight control and imposing restrictions (with potentially severe consequences) to limit criticality and innovation. In the contexts of TSLN and National Education, Singapore's social studies teachers receive conflicting messages about critical thinking and innovation from a state that cherishes order and stability while trying to position itself in a knowledge-based economy requiring greater innovation and risk taking. Official rhetoric calls for more innovation, creativity, critical thinking and risk taking in classroom practice while exams and other systemic constraints continue to militate against such change in classrooms.

How to reconcile what many see as the propagandistic messages of National Education and social studies education with calls for greater critical thinking and consideration of divergent perspectives is a challenge social studies teachers in Singapore face. It is a core challenge facing educators everywhere: how to prepare globally minded national citizens with the skills and understandings necessary for living in increasingly diverse and complex life-worlds. With contradictory messages of preparing students to live in global society and developing twenty-first-century skills while emphasising National Education and exam preparation and results, students and teachers find themselves in a 'double bind' (Bateson 1999). These mixed messages make it difficult to offer an education that will help young people deal with the complex shifting landscapes of knowledge and knowing that students will encounter as they move across local, global and digital landscapes.

Critical thinking in Singapore's social studies classrooms has been cast as a process of technical problem-solving requiring procedural skills such as analysing, interpreting and evaluating information rather than a criticality that questions 'the power structures and the ideological constructions of truth and belief' (Koh 2004, p. 339). To what extent this limits citizenship education remains a lingering question. As Adler and Sim suggest:

> If the Social Studies curriculum as it is enacted asks students to accept ideas uncritically, they will be capable of little more. They will be unable to grapple with the problems of the twenty-first century, not only in technology and science, but also in human interrelationships. (2008, p. 177)

The Impact of Consumerism on Citizenship

Singapore has successfully made the shift from a manufacturing economy emphasising the standardisation of goods and services and centralised state economic management to a post-industrial economy that emphasises greater decentralisation, diversification and local autonomy and initiative. It has also shifted from strong state efforts to socialise and educate obedient populations necessary for state building toward greater use of cultural and symbolic forms of control that emphasise self-regulation aligned with a broader portfolio of state interests. In response, state policies, rather than mandating prescribed sets of rules and regulations, focus more on the habitus (Bourdieu 1977) of populations by addressing education and training as well as a variety of cultural and institutional conditions, such as health, communication, leisure, recreation and sociability (Castells 1999). Accompanying these changes is greater emphasis on consumption and the development of consumer culture.

Singapore is a consumers' paradise, where Singaporean citizens seem generally disinterested in politics, deferring to the government so long as it gives them the good life. This, Cherian George (2000) argues, has prompted general acceptance of the status quo. Conceptions of citizenship (and education) are also being shaped by a cultural landscape of burgeoning consumption. In fact, in post-industrial society, consumption has become a new form of social labour:

> The labor of reading ever-shifting fashion messages, the labor of debt servicing, the labor of learning how best to manage newly complex domestic finances and the labor of acquiring knowledge in the complexities of money management. This labor is . . . directed at producing the conditions of consciousness in which *buying* can occur . . . This inculcation of the pleasure of *ephemerality* is at the heart of the disciplining of the modern consumer. (Appadurai 1996, pp. 82–83)

However, if people view themselves first and foremost as consumers, they may be more likely to cultivate allegiances, forms of identity and habits of mind aligned with consumer culture than with active citizenship. Consumers must keep abreast of the latest fads, new trends, new technologies and new services and experiences. Consumption, rather than informed civic engagement, becomes the central focus of social life.

Singapore's reforms have tried to balance flexibility with discipline (MoE 2005); however, flexible consumerism may work to erode social discipline. In other words, consumerism may not instill the kind of social discipline that will provide competitive economic advantage or civic engagement. As the social historian Christopher Lasch (1984) argued, mass consumption and rampant consumerism:

> tend to discourage initiative and self-reliance and to promote dependence, passivity, and a spectatorial state of mind both at work and at play . . . The state of mind promoted by consumerism is better described as a state of uneasiness and chronic anxiety. The promotion of commodities depends, like modern mass production, on discouraging the individual from reliance on his [sic] own resources and judgment: in this case, his judgment of what he needs in order to be healthy and happy. The individual finds himself always under observation, if not by foremen and superintendents, by market researchers and pollsters who tell him what others prefer and what he too must therefore prefer. (pp. 27–28)

When combined with the forfeiture of public decision making to the ruling elite who manage the corporate state, such consumerism may interfere with

Singaporeans capacities to innovate, create and think critically. It may challenge national identity and weaken civic engagement and responsibility. It may result in a lessening of the social discipline desired by the nation-state.

CONCLUSION: MANAGING TENSIONS BETWEEN THE NATIONAL AND GLOBAL

Since new social, organisational and educational strategies are implemented to accommodate and manage the myriad changes accompanying globalisation:

> the reform rhetoric is remarkably similar across very different education jurisdictions; all reform proposals stress the need for greater attention to processes, higher order thinking skills, better utilisation of technology in education, changes to assessment, greater devolution of power to principals, etc. (Gopinathan 2007, p. 56)

Such reforms can be seen as efforts by states to produce and manage educational systems and populations that are attractive to the shifting requisites of global capital (Ong 1999). As a result, educational reform becomes ever more critical in the never-ending drive for competitive advantage in the global innovation economy. Singapore, in particular, presents an interesting case of how education is used to promote and sustain economic development in a relentlessly changing and increasingly competitive global economy. Since its independence in 1965, Singapore has implemented educational policy and reform for nation-building purposes, to engineer consensus among diverse ethnic groups, and to promote economic growth and development. The recent suite of educational reforms initiated by Singapore in 1997 under TSLN and National Education represents an attempt by Singapore to recalibrate schooling in order to accommodate and manage the both global and national imperatives and potential consequences of globalisation.

Whether or not TSLN reforms, National Education and the implementation of the new social studies curriculum are more about attempts by governing elites to maintain power in increasingly challenged contexts (by forces such as globalisation) than a genuine concern for better educating young people (Sim & Print 2005, p. 65) is a lingering question. Official rhetoric has called for greater critical and creative thinking, innovation and openness. However, as Tan and Gopinathan have pointed out:

> The larger problem for Singapore's educational reform initiative is that Singapore's nation-building history resulted in an omnipresent state that cherishes stability and order. A desire for true innovation, creativity, experimentation, and multiple opportunities in education cannot

be realized until the state allows civil society to flourish and avoids politicizing dissent. (2000, p. 10)

Will continuing limits on dissent and civil society act as a brake on economic growth and prosperity in the new economy?

While these types of challenges with respect to identity, critical thinking and consumerism cannot easily be resolved, a broader conception of critical global citizenship might address these tensions more directly. One notion of critical global citizenship recognises that people have multiple affiliations and commitments based on racial, cultural, ethnic, linguistic, religious and national ties, and that these affiliations and commitments do not need to be surrendered. Others argue that only through a broader allegiance to shared notions of justice, reason and public deliberation can societies avoid the dangers of partisanship and sectarianism (Nussbaum 2002). As Banks and colleagues (2005, p. 24) argue, 'pride in one's own heritage can co-exist with appreciation for other traditions and loyalty to the human family'. In an interconnected world, this balanced cosmopolitan outlook is necessary. According to Nussbaum (2002), such an outlook entails an ethical commitment to understand different perspectives and experiences in order to 'recognize common aims, aspirations, and values, and enough about these common ends to see how variously they are instantiated in the many cultures and their histories' (p. 9).

Similarly, Green (1997) argues that citizenship education needs to:

> eschew narrow cultural chauvinism while seeking to promote new and more inclusive forms of civic identity based on common political commitments and understandings not divisive cultural myths . . . oriented to the future not the past. (p. 5)

He goes on to argue, 'The modern education project is to form new, more democratic societies and the citizens which sustain them—not to transmit and reproduce historic cultures and identities' (p. 5). This is one way to manage the dilemmas confronting nation-states and citizenship education in an era of rapidly accelerating globalisation.

REFERENCES

Adler, Susan A. & Jasmine B-Y Sim (2008) Secondary social studies in Singapore: Intentions and contradictions, in David L. Grossman & Joe T-Y Lo (eds.) *Social Education in the Asia-Pacific: Critical Issues and Multiple Perspectives.* Greenwich, CT, Information Age Publishing, pp. 163–182.

Appadurai, Arju (1996) *Modernity at Large: Cultural Dimensions of Globalisation.* Minneapolis, University of Minnesota Press.

Baildon, Mark & Jasmine B-Y Sim (Forthcoming) Notions of criticality: Singaporean teachers' perspectives of critical thinking in social studies, *Cambridge Journal of Education.*

Banks, James A., Cherry A.M. Banks, Carlos E. Cortes, Carole L. Hahn, Merry M. Merryfield, Kogila A. Moodley, Stephen Murphy-Shigematsu, Audrey Osler, Caryn Park & Walter C. Parker (2005) *Democracy and Diversity: Principles and Concepts for Education Citizens in a Global Age*. Seattle, Center for Multicultural Education.

Bateson, Gregory (1999) *Steps toward an Ecology of Mind*. Chicago, University of Chicago Press.

Bourdieu, Pierre (1977) *Outline of a Theory of Practice*. Cambridge, Cambridge University Press.

Burbules, Nicholas C. & Thomas Callister Jr. (2000) *Watch IT: The Promises and Risks of New Information Technologies for Education*. Boulder, CO, Westview Press.

Castells, Manuel (1999) Flows, networks, and identities: A critical theory of the informational society, in Manual Castells, Ramon Flecha & Peter McLaren (eds.) *Critical Education in the New Information Age*. Lanham, MD, Rowman & Littlefield Publishers, pp. 37–64.

Chua, Beng-Huat (1995) *Communitarian Ideology and Democracy in Singapore*. London, Routledge.

Cogan, John J., David L. Grossman & Mei-hui Liu (2000) Citizenship: The democratic imagination in a global context, *Social Education*, 64(1), pp. 48–52.

Daipi, Hawazi (2005) Achieving a social and moral balance in globalisation, http://www.moe.gov.sg/speeches/2005/sp20050831.htm (accessed 31 March 2009).

Falk, Richard (1994) The making of global citizenship, in Bart van Steenbergen (ed.) *The Condition of Citizenship*. London, Sage, pp. 127–140.

Foucault, Michel (1979) Governmentality, *Ideology and Consciousness*, 6, pp. 5–21.

George, Cherian (2000) *The Air-Conditioned Nation: Essays on the Politics of Comfort and Control 1990–2000*. Singapore, Landmark Books.

Goh, Chok Tong (1997) *Shaping our Future: Thinking Schools, Learning Nation*, http://www1.moe.edu.sg/Speeches/020697.htm (accessed 31 March 2009).

———. (2001) *Remaking Singapore: Changing Mindsets*, http://www.gov.sg/nd/ND02.htm (accessed 31 March 2009).

Gopinathan, Saravanan (2007) Globalisation, the Singapore developmental state and education policy: A thesis revisited, *Globalisation, Societies and Education*, 5(1), pp. 53–70.

Green, Andy (1997) *Education, Globalisation and the Nation State*. London, Macmillan Press.

———. (2007) Globalisation and the changing nature of the state in East Asia, *Globalisation, Societies and Education*, 5(1), pp. 23–38.

Hall, Stuart (1989) The meaning of New Times, in Stuart Hall & Martin Jacques (eds.) *New Times*. London, Lawrence & Wishart, pp. 116–133.

Hill, Michael & Kwen-Fee Lian (1995) *The Politics of Nation Building and Citizenship in Singapore*. New York, Routledge.

Koh, Aaron (2004) Singapore education in 'New Times': Global/local imperatives, *Discourse: Studies in the Cultural Politics of Education*, 25(3), pp. 335–349.

———. (2006) Working against globalisation: The role of the media and national education, *Singapore: Globalisation, Societies and Education*, 4(3), pp. 357–370.

———. (2007) Living with globalisation tactically: The metapragmatics of globalisation in Singapore, *Sojourn: Journal of Social Issues in Southeast Asia*, 22(2), pp. 179–201.

Lasch, Christopher (1984) *The Minimal Self: Psychic Survival in Troubled Times*. New York, Norton.

Lee, Hsien Loong (1997) *National Education,* http://www.moe.gov.sg/speeches/1997/170597.htm (accessed 31 March 2009).

Lim, Catherine (2006) Managing political dissent: Uniquely Singapore, in Lai Ah Eng (ed.) *Singapore Perspectives 2006. Going Glocal: Being Singaporean in a Globalised World.* Singapore, Institute of Policy Studies, pp. 87–96.

Lim, Jessica (2006) Youth seeking to uproot an 'urgent' concern, *Straits Times,* 27 July.

Loh, Kah Seng (1998) Within the Singapore story: The use and narrative of history in Singapore, *Crossroads: An Interdisciplinary Journal of Southeast Asian Studies,* 12(2), pp. 1–21.

Ministry of Education (1999) *Primary Social Studies Syllabus.* Singapore, Ministry of Education.

———. (2005) *The Next Chapter,* http://www.moe.gov.sg/bluesky/The_Next_Chapter.pdf (accessed 31 March 2009).

———. (2006) *The Combined Humanities Subject: 'O' Level, Examination Syllabuses for 2007.* Singapore, Ministry of Education.

———. (2009a) *About Us,* http://www.moe.gov.sg/about/ (accessed 31 March 2009).

———. (2009b) *National Education Website,* http://www.ne.edu.sg/ (accessed 31 March 2009).

Mitchell, Katheryne (2003) Educating the national citizen in neoliberal times: From the multicultural self to the strategic cosmopolitan, *Transactions of the Institute of British Geographers,* 28(4), pp. 387–403.

Mitchell, Katheryne & Walter Parker (2008) 'I pledge allegiance to . . . ' Flexible citizenship and shifting scales of belonging, *Teachers College Record,* 110(4), pp. 775–804.

Mok, Ka Ho & Jason Tan (2004) *Globalisation and Marketization in Education: A Comparative Analysis of Hong Kong and Singapore.* Northampton, MA, Edward Elgar Publishing.

Nussbaum, Martha C. (2002) *For Love of Country?* Boston, Beacon Press.

Ong, Aihwa (1999) *Flexible Citizenship: The Cultural Logics of Transnationality.* Durham, NC, Duke University Press.

Parker, Walter, Akira Nonomiya & John Cogan (1999) Educating world citizens: Toward multinational curriculum development, *American Educational Research Journal,* 3(2), pp. 117–146.

Perry, Richard W. & Bill Maurer (2003) Globalization and governmentality: An introduction, in Richard W. Perry & Bill Maurer (eds.) *Globalisation under Construction: Governmentality, Law, and Identity.* Minneapolis, University of Minnesota Press, pp. viii–xxi.

Quah, Jon S.T. (2000) Globalisation and Singapore's search for nationhood, in Leo Suryadinata (ed.) *Nationalism and Globalisation: East and West.* Singapore, Institute of Southeast Asian Studies, pp. 71–101.

Sim, Jasmine B-Y (2008) What does citizenship mean? Social studies teachers' understandings of citizenship in Singapore schools, *Educational Review,* 60(3), pp. 253–266.

Sim, Jasmine B-Y & Murray Print (2005) Citizenship education and social studies in Singapore: A national agenda, *International Journal of Citizenship and Teacher Education,* 1(1), pp. 58–73.

Straits Times (1996) Serious gap in the education of Singaporeans. We are ignorant of our own history, 18 July, p. 41.

Tan, Eugene (2001) Singapore shared values, http://infopedia.nl.sg/articles/SIP_542_2004-12-18.html (accessed 31 March 2009).

Tan, Jason & Saravanan Gopinathan (2000) Education reform in Singapore: Towards greater creativity and innovation? *NIRA Review,* 7(3), pp. 5–10.

Tan, Kenneth P. (2007) Singapore's National Day Rally speech: A site of ideological negotiation, *Journal of Contemporary Asia*, 37(3), pp. 292–308.

Tharman, Shanmugaratnam (2007) Speech at the *Network* conference, http://www.moe.gov.sg/media/speeches/2007/sp20080814.htm (accessed 31 March 2009).

Wilson, Harold E. (1978) *Social Engineering in Singapore*. Singapore, Singapore University Press.

Wong, Aline (2000) Address at the opening ceremony of the Primary Social Studies Symposium, York Hotel, Carlton Hall, http://www.moe.gov.sg/speeches/2000/sp13032000a.htm (accessed 31 March 2009).

7 State and Civil Society Embattled in Colonialism, Capitalism and Nationalism

Civic Education and its Politics in Hong Kong

Thomas Kwan-choi Tse

INTRODUCTION

That school is an ideological state apparatus has become sociological common sense. Many states have sought to convey their ideal of citizenship and nationhood through their public schooling systems, albeit in different ways depending on the political culture, values and ideologies that are endorsed, transmitted and practised in concrete historical contexts. In this chapter I will use a case study of civic education in Hong Kong to demonstrate this process at work, with the Gramscian concept of hegemony as my theoretical framework.

Civic education can be understood as part of a cultural-political strategy—through persuasion, instead of coercion—for the ruling groups to maintain power (Apple 1990; Gramsci 1971; Mouffe 1979; Simon 1982). This cultural hegemony rests in shifting alliances among different groups led by the state, and in the struggle on the ideological terrain through both organisational and discursive practices. Naturally different configurations of state-civil society constitute different forms of hegemony, in terms of both genesis and operation. Cultural politics involves multiple fronts of confrontation and several layers of mediation and articulation, even within a historical bloc (Wong 2002). As such, diverse groups might collaborate with some, or manoeuvre against other, groups. Hence, the state often faces multiple and sometimes contradictory pressure, requiring selective tactics which privilege some groups but marginalise or exclude others, in order to keep control. These complicated group dynamics, together with the relative autonomy of the civil society, mediate the course and outcome of hegemonic formations and make it complicated and ever changing, being the unstable equilibriums of compromises between the ruling and subordinate groups.

Hong Kong, formerly a British colony and now a Chinese Special Administrative Region (SAR), is a classic case of this process at work. In brief, Hong Kong is unusual in its combination of a number of parameters (Tse 2002):

1. the legacies of British colonial rule for one and a half century
2. a coastal city playing an important role in the global division of labour within capitalism

3. a predominantly Chinese community close to Mainland China
4. the heavy involvement of civil society in providing public education

In addition, Hong Kong's belated decolonialisation, the strained progress of democratisation, the designated return of Hong Kong from Britain to China in 1997 and its special international position have constituted a peculiar path of citizenship. The wave of globalisation and anti-globalisation in recent years further complicates the ongoing struggles of citizenship empowerment against state paternalism and tyrannical capitalism in a budding democracy.

Civic education in Hong Kong has mirrored these broader characteristics. In the course of its development, there have been fierce contests between official and alternative camps concerning the meanings and direction of citizenship. As a British colony or a Chinese SAR, Hong Kong's autonomy has always been based upon external political forces. Civic education in this special city thus differs significantly from those countries which have a conventional unitary model of national citizenship.

The chapter starts with a brief discussion of the socio-political context of Hong Kong, before focusing on the recent past and the contemporary period. After a brief review of the characteristics of civil society–state relations in Hong Kong, the following two sections will explore civic education in Hong Kong, using the heuristic of the three modalities of schooling outlined in the introductory chapter: viz., the structure of schooling, the formal representations of civics and citizenship in the curriculum and the culture and processes of schools. This account of the changes and continuities in civic education from the colonial era to the present also provides the background for some concluding comments about possible future directions.

THE COLONIAL ERA: CIVIC EDUCATION WITHOUT NATIONAL EDUCATION

The Context

After WWII, political power in British Hong Kong was largely monopolised by the governor, career civil servants and a small group of co-opted elites. For the period between the 1950s and the late 1970s, alongside a secluded and autocratic bureaucratic polity, a loosely organised Chinese immigrant society and substantive economic growth, was a 'parochial and subject political culture' characterised by an acceptance of colonial rule, a pervasive sense of political powerlessness and political inefficacy and a low level of political participation (Lau & Kuan 1988). During this period, the colonial state tried to maintain the status quo and the subject political culture, being half-hearted about initiating civic education and unenthusiastic about a participatory civic education programme.

The socio-political situation changed after the serious challenges of the riots in 1966 and 1967. The colonial state gradually opened its political structure and played a more active role in regulating economic and social affairs and in providing public services to the community. With the introduction of political reforms towards a representative democracy system, Sino-British talks on Hong Kong's future intensified and as the handover approached, in the final years of colonial rule from 1982 to 1997 more and more people became concerned about social and political affairs. The Tiananmen Massacre in June 1989 shocked the people of Hong Kong and triggered local concern over China's situation as well as human rights protection in Hong Kong after 1997. Despite these factors becoming catalysts for a civic education campaign on the part of the civil society (Bray & Lee 1993), there was a lukewarm and passive approach to promoting civic education on the part of the colonial state, with the publication of two sets of official guidelines on civic education in schools in 1985 and 1996, respectively (Curriculum Development Committee 1985, 1996). Meanwhile, a relatively vibrant civil society, coupled with school-based practices, prompted a mushrooming of civic education and political activities by various non-government organisations. Thus, during the last years of the colonial era, notions of citizenship and civic education policies were hotly contested between different social forces, often from very different political and ideological positions. These differences were reflected in the controversies and debates regarding the purposes and practices of civic education in the past two decades (Lee 1999; Lee & Sweeting 2001).

The following will give a brief account of three modalities of schooling during the colonial era.

The Structure of Schooling

As a result of a variety of historical and cultural factors, colonial Hong Kong had a peculiarly complex educational system, divided by various cultural, political and historical distinctions, and reinforced by the government's educational policy which evolved over 150 years (Luk 2000; Sweeting 2004). No sooner had Hong Kong become a British colony in 1841, than a Western-style educational system was transplanted into the territory, side by side with the Chinese schools that were styled on those from Mainland China. At the very beginning, there was a dual education system distinguished by both the medium of instruction and the course of study. The post–World War II era witnessed fundamental changes to this structure. These changes included the expansion of educational opportunities for the rising population of secondary school students as a result of an increase in schooling provision; the establishment of a tripartite secondary school system with grammar school as the dominant stream; the dominance of Anglo-Chinese secondary schools over the Chinese middle schools; and the rise and fall of the private sector in educational provision.

The differentiation of schools at the secondary level in terms of curriculum, finance and the medium of instruction, as well as the existence of historical factors, resulted in a hierarchy of schools and of students even within the same level of the secondary school system, where a small group of renowned schools enjoyed popularity.

This rapid growth of education in the post-war era was partly attributed to economic growth over several decades. As a consequence, education was expanded in stages through the growth of primary education in the 1950s and secondary education in 1960s and 1970s; the introduction of the nine-year (six years of primary education and three years of junior secondary) free and compulsory education in 1978; and the rapid development of tertiary education in the 1990s. Also, the educational system was characterised by continuous selection and assessment, mainly in the form of public examinations. Accordingly, the mainstream curriculum had a strong academic orientation.

After years of spectacular expansion, the great majority of school places from primary school upwards were provided either free or at highly subsidised rates in the public sector (government and aided schools), and only a few private schools operated entirely on their own. The colonial state directly managed only a small proportion of primary and secondary schools while most were run by religious, business, charitable or other voluntary organisations on a non-profit-making basis through public funds. These aided schools received recurrent financial assistance from public funding and operated under a variety of sponsoring bodies. The colonial state, through the arms of the Education Department, exercised strict and centralised control over all schools, especially in areas of funding, curriculum, qualification of teachers and allocation of students.

After the implementation of nine years of compulsory education in 1978, school quality and school effectiveness emerged as prominent themes in education policy discourse in Hong Kong. From that time, the colonial state began to introduce a number of managerialist strategies and quasi market mechanisms into the educational sector.

The Curriculum

In Hong Kong, the terms *civics*, *civic education* and *citizenship education* have been commonly used interchangeably with one another for years. But civics was actually a special school subject about the communities in which students lived, while civic education and citizenship education refer to broader concerns with education about one's connections with the communities, inside or outside schools. And people differ in their normative expectations of good citizenship, and also in their understanding of the proper goals and practices contributing to good citizenship. From the 1950s to the mid-1980s, the colonial government tightly controlled the educational system through the prohibition of political activities in schools and the imposition of officially approved text-books and model syllabuses (Tsang 1984, 1998; Morris & Sweeting 1991; Morris 1992; Tse 1998). To counterbalance and marginalise the political influence from Mainland China and Taiwan, the government was particularly suspicious of political issues in education and evaded political education as an explicit educational objective. From the 1950s to the 1970s, subjects like 'Social Studies' (1953–1996) at the primary level and 'Civics' (1942–1965—later to become Economic and Public Affairs) at the junior secondary level avoided sensitive political topics, such as Hong Kong's colonial status, Hong Kong's links and relationships with Mainland China and issues concerning contemporary China (Wong 1981). Before 1997, the colonial government deliberately downplayed political affairs and civic education, which led to political apathy and a lack of human rights awareness among the general public (Fok 2001). There was no formal human rights education in schools and topics like basic human rights, anti-discrimination, gender equality and freedom of speech and expression were rarely or superficially covered in the school syllabuses. The content of democratic education was also constrained by incomplete curricular objectives and contents; limited learning opportunities; and the distorted, biased, formalistic and non-critical presentation of the teaching materials (Cheung & Leung 1998; Lo 2005; Po & Fang 2000; Yip 2000; Tse 2000; Ho 2004; Choi 1997).

In line with the official syllabuses, the text-books were characterised by a large coverage of self- and group-related values, with non-political topics outweighing political topics and factual knowledge overriding skills and attitudes. The text-books merely provided a bunch of discrete topics dealing with economic and public affairs or historical facts showing no direct relevance to any reflective or critical citizenship education. Relevant political topics concerning local and national communities were omitted, oversimplified, trivialised or marginalised. The composite image of citizenship conveyed was also incomplete, distorted and parochial in its oversimplification and poor treatment of democratic orientations. The knowledge and political messages transmitted conformed to the mode of citizenship transmission, while little was devoted to discussion of political principles, in particular those relating to democracy and civic liberties. Instead, the text-books entailed a strong moralised notion of citizenship, teaching students to be good and compliant citizens. The citizen's power to influence government was not given equal emphasis with that of the citizen's duties.

The text-books also misrepresented the realities of the social and political systems by portraying a harmonious relationship between the government and the people and exaggerating the government's contributions to the citizens' welfare. By depicting a highly administrative and functional conception of government and a favourable and beneficial image of the Hong Kong government, the text-books served to foster a positive but unrealistic attitude towards government performance and induce in students a faith and trust in government; hence legitimising the existing socio-economic arrangements. Finally, questions and exercises in the text-books and work-books emphasised memorisation but did not give students sufficient practice in developing critical and analytical abilities.

The Culture and Processes of Schools

Apart from problematic syllabuses and teaching materials, the teaching of citizenship through social science subjects was severely undermined by the prevalence of conventional instructional practices and expository methods of teaching, arising from examination and competition pressures, large class sizes and authoritarian class climate (Tse 1997). The teaching of political topics was characterised by a spoon-feeding mode, with recitation, notes, examinations and tests pervasive in a majority of lessons. Students were given little opportunity to discuss issues or practice critical thinking, action skills and value analysis.

Being a custodial institution concerned with order and discipline, the shaping of the political environment within the school also detached the students from involvement in daily school policies and affairs. For teachers and students in Hong Kong secondary schools, many aspects were characterised by dominant–subordinate relationships, both in terms of learning activities and behavioural control, with teachers usually playing the role of authority figure and students being excluded from decision making in school affairs. Indeed, much of the so-called civic education in schools was concerned with moral education, particularly compliance with rules and standards of conduct.

Many schools emphasised obedience and compliance rather than active participation in decision making. There was little participation by students in school governance, extra-curricular activities and political activities, such as school elections, clubs, societies and service and community groups. Quite a number of secondary schools did not set up their student unions or student associations, and where they did exist, they were tightly controlled and usually small in scale with inactive position-holders and limited activities. In short, students received limited democratic and self-governance experience in their schooling.

Owing to legal constraints over political activities in schools, political education for national and state identities was rare except in a small number of partisan schools. Consequently, civic education in this period was 'a-nationalistic', conformist and depoliticised in nature, detaching students from their indigenous nationality and local politics and moulding them into residents or subjects, rather than citizens, in a colony (Morris 1992; Tsang 1998). As such, civic education in this period served to contain the challenges of nationalism and, in turn, to consolidate colonialism.

A unique system of 'state-civil society' was established during Hong Kong's colonial era. There co-existed a soft-authoritarian foreign coloniser and a pluralistic civil society that blended with traditional Chinese communities and Western volunteering organisations (Ip 1997; Lui et al. 2005; Lam & Tong 2007). The colonial state strongly depended on the provision of education and social welfare by various non-governmental organisations—with the result that the establishment was unchallenged. After decades, an apoliticised civic education evolved, focusing on community service rather than active political participation. Love and care towards other citizens were encouraged through civic education activities, but political awareness was barely touched.

However, from the beginning of the transitional period the nature of politics in Hong Kong began to change. And this has had an impact on the development of civics education in post-colonial Hong Kong.

THE POST-COLONIAL ERA: NATIONAL EDUCATION OVERRIDES CIVIC EDUCATION

The Context

1997 was a turning point in Hong Kong's history. Ironically, China's policy towards post-colonial Hong Kong is to keep its original political configuration largely intact. Hong Kong is ideally positioned as an economy city under Chinese rule, contributing to the Mainland's project of economic modernisation and national unification. With the handover of sovereignty and the imperatives of national sovereignty and nationalism, the present political order as conceived by the Beijing leaders takes precedence over democratisation and human rights. The signs of democratic regression and threats to the rule of law and human rights in Hong Kong raise doubts about the level of autonomy that the SAR will have, in practice, under the principle of 'one country, two systems' (Wong 2004). There are also worries about individual freedom and rights being jeopardised and local identity being suppressed.

The deepening economic integration of Hong Kong and China and the economic and political crises in the aftermath of 1997 caused the new administration to introduce nationalism or patriotism to China as a new official ideology (Lau 2007). Consistent with the domesticating stance of the Beijing government has been an emphasis on national or patriotic education, with the dual purposes of diluting anti-communist sentiments and taming the defiance of the Beijing government, as well as controlling the quest for growing democratisation or potential separatism in Hong Kong. Besides, with very much concern over the crisis of Hong Kong's competitive advantages in a period of economic restructuring prompted by the Asian financial crisis, the emergence of a knowledge-based economy and the further opening of China to the world, local senior officials have been eager to position Hong Kong as an Asian world city, or a gateway to Mainland China, serving the purposes of maintaining Hong Kong's vitality in a globalised economy.

Meanwhile, the SAR government still adopts a strategy of elite co-optation, but with changes in the relations between the local government and different groups in the civil society under the new master. The new administration has forged a new alliance with the pro-Beijing camp, in tandem with the Chinese Communist Party's United Front policy towards Hong Kong (Lau 2007).

With official endorsement and support from the post-colonial government and the central government, the national education project has displaced other competing discourses and practices (Tse 2007a). Under the guidance of the central government and pressure of the local pro-Beijing camp, the chief executives Tung Chee-hwa and Donald Tsang, together with other high-ranking officials, have been articulating a new cultural hegemony project in tandem with national reunification and nation-building in the new era—with an extraordinary emphasis on national identity and patriotism, and strengthening the teaching of the Basic Law and the concept of 'one country, two systems', as evident in their public speeches on many occasions.

The realities of non-democratic politics in post-colonial Hong Kong and its new master China dictate that civic education is oriented towards a 'patriotic and compliant subject and enterprising individual in a competitive globe' (Ku & Pun 2004). Blending political paternalism with economic neo-liberalism, the new official programme endorses a collective-oriented national subject juxtaposed with an individual economic being. A brief review of three modalities of schooling during the post-colonial era follows.

The Structure of Schooling

The sweeping education reforms since 1998 onwards have changed the ecology of the education sector. The reforms, in the name of quality education, can be seen in the first place as a response to concerns about the consequences of the nine-year compulsory education policy. Against the background of a sharp increase in public expenditure on education in recent years, and after the financial turmoil and economic recession of 1997, these reforms were also fuelled by very specific concerns about Hong Kong's educational standards and future economic competitiveness vis-à-vis its key regional competitors, as well as financial considerations rooted in recent public sector reform. To these ends, the government has further strengthened and expanded a vast array of management-led and market-oriented strategies and mechanisms in the school sector (Choi 2005; Tse 2005).

In addition, the education system has been the subject of a comprehensive review undertaken by the Education Commission. Again, the quest for quality education was a central tenet of the reform package. The overall objective was to put in place an education system that will develop the abilities and attitude of students for lifelong learning so that they may meet the challenges in the new millennium. The new aims of education include an emphasis on four key areas: students should enjoy and love learning and be capable of self-learning; be able to communicate effectively in both Chinese and English; be creative and able to think independently and critically; and be willing to take responsibility for themselves and have commitment to their families, society, nation and the world at large (Education Commission 2000). The review was completed in 2000 with a number of proposals about the academic structure, curricula, assessment mechanisms and the interface between different stages of education.

Taken together, these reforms not only have a deep impact on teachers and the work of schools, but also redefine the meanings and values of school education, disseminating an ideology of economic rationalism centred on efficiency, productivity, accountability and an encouragement of consumerism and competition. Accordingly, education is redefined as being in the service of developing human capital, and the roles of parents and students as being clients and customers—often at the expense of equality and citizenship.

The Curriculum

Patriotism was formally placed on the education reform agenda after 1997. The national education program, inside and outside the school education system, has been promoted and implemented in a high-profile manner through a number of measures over the past eleven years.

It was first manifest in the new aims of education, promulgated by the Education Commission when reviewing the education system for Hong Kong. In tandem with this was a wholesale revision of school syllabuses, subjects and text-books across all levels, which placed a specific emphasis on Chinese elements, relationships between Hong Kong and China and the Basic Law (Hughes & Stone 1999; Ho 2007; Leung 1999; Wong 1999). The national language, Putonghua, has been increasingly used as the medium of instruction in schools. Also, whereas the former 1996 guidelines were shelved shortly after the handover, a promotion of moral and civic education was highlighted as a key task to carry out and to put national identity, responsibility, commitment and perseverance as priority values for the years 2001–2006 (Curriculum Development Council 2001, 2002). To fulfill their obligations as Chinese nationals following Hong Kong's reversion to the sovereign state, and to take advantage of the new business opportunities on the Mainland brought by China's openness to the world, young people in Hong Kong are expected to possess the knowledge, abilities and attitude for interacting with their fellow Chinese on the Mainland, and for facing international competition in an era of increasing global interdependence. In the fashion of parochial ethnocultural nationalism, young people are told that they have to find their roots, take pride in their Chinese heritage and identify themselves with the interests of China. The recurring themes of the official discourse are the promotion of traditional Confucian values and virtues, a focus on the obligations and responsibilities of individuals towards the community and their 'fatherland', a stress on social cohesion and harmony, *de facto* diluting political issues (Morris & Morris 2000a, 2000b; Morris, Kan & Morris 2000; Leung & Ng 2004). However, the ideas of democracy and human rights are accorded a low priority.

Recent studies also confirm the prevalence of passivity, partiality and ambiguity about citizenship in local junior secondary text-books written for the subject Economic and Public Affairs (So 2007). Some are hoping that the new senior secondary compulsory subject, Liberal Studies, implemented in 2009 will promote human rights. But although human rights is mentioned, since there is little emphasis on action for personal and social transformation, it may be at best a form of 'action-poor' human rights education (Leung 2008), not adequately cultivating a universal human rights culture. The incomplete curricular objectives and topics of the syllabuses of relevant social subjects undermine the potential of democratic education.

As a matter of fact, global dimension has long been a part of citizenship learning in Hong Kong. Situated in a Cold War milieu, there has been a strong emphasis on Hong Kong as an international and cosmopolitan city—with strong geographical, cultural and economic ties with many other countries—in the syllabuses and text-books during the colonial era. For years, Hong Kong has been depicted as a successful economic metropolis changing from an entrepôt to a major industrial centre, and recently, to an international financial centre. Associated with these images was a favourable treatment of foreign countries and people. Stepping into the post-colonial era, for economic or other considerations stated earlier, the relevant primary and secondary school syllabuses also heighten the global elements in citizenship such as generic skills, global awareness, intercultural understanding, information technology and environmental concerns, as well as the universal human values like human rights, though in an implicit and permeated manner (Lee 2008).

The Culture and Processes of Schools

In view of the fact that the relevant courses in many schools are taught primarily in a rote learning style—in contrast to the stated purposes of civic education—there have been attempts to promote student-centred and interactive pedagogies (Curriculum Development Council 2001, 2002). Curriculum designers are trying to bridge the gap between knowledge and action, with a view to encouraging students to think in a reflective and critical way, as well as encouraging participation in public life. But there are sharp contrasts between the intended curriculum and the enacted curriculum in classrooms. A common observation is that classroom teaching or the actual schooling practices of civic education are still transmissive (Leung 1997; Lee & Leung 1999; Chung 2000; Morris & Morris 2001). The participation of student unions in school affairs is limited and provocative discussions on politics are discouraged (Lee & Yuen 2003; Lai & Wu 2003, 2004). A survey conducted in 2008 of 1,028 youth, aged five to twenty-nine, showed that 67.9 percent of the interviewees disagreed that their schools encouraged them to conduct study on school policies and school rules (Breakthrough 2008); and 65.3 percent disagreed that their schools encouraged them to question school policies and school rules in light of critical thinking. The lack of an open classroom climate means that students prefer social to political activities (Lee, 2004).

Other factors have hindered the implementation of civics education, including the emphasis of recent education reforms on competition; the apolitical orientation of subject teachers; insufficient resource support; inflexible time-tabling; the physical constraints of classroom settings; and the examination-oriented education system (Tang 2001; Wai 2003; Ng & Leung 2004). Congruent with earlier findings on the implementation of civic education in Hong Kong schools (Leung 1997), the kind of civic education provided in schools are thus depoliticised, close to promoting conformity and responsibility, but ineffective in helping pupils become autonomous citizens with abilities in critical thinking and problem-solving. Such components of political education in the curriculum as political ideology and political participation are not emphasised. This learning environment is not favourable to the development of creative thinking and problem-solving.

Since 1997, the focus has been on patriotic rituals designed to arouse students' awareness of their national identity. This includes a number of ritualistic activities, such as displaying the national flag, singing the national anthem and participating in many cultural and educational activities for National Day Celebration. The practice of displaying the national flag has been implemented and regulated by legislation and through administrative measures to ensure that due respect is given to the national flag. Starting in 2003, the government launched a series of territory-wide national celebration activities called China Fortnight, with exhibitions, talks and experience-sharing seminars on the promotion of national education in primary and secondary schools. In June 2004 the government issued a circular to government schools requesting an increase in school flag-raising activities and greater uniformity in the format of flag-raising.

Over the years more and more schools in Hong Kong have celebrated the anniversary of the People's Republic of China, and have held commemorative activities. In 2004, even music programmes were designed to convey national education, with a Web site dedicated to fifteen nationalistic songs for learning; and kindergarten children are now learning to sing the national anthem, 'The March of the Volunteers'. Collective identity is bound up with rituals. Participation in rituals in effect is a continual reminder of nationhood (Billing 1995). These mass ceremonies and festivals, usually with flags, anthems and parades, aim to sustain the process of national imagination and to consolidate a shared sense of community. Resembling religion-sacredness, the rituals and ceremonies are put in place to evoke one's deep feelings towards the collective. Even more didactic and coercive, these ritualistic activities are endowed with the symbolic power and collective pressure of the participants which command uniformity and conformity. To a certain extent, observing the rituals and performances is a forced patriotism requiring belief internalisation, self-regulation, emotion management and a docile body.

Outside schools, a series of national education programmes has been launched and a range of promotional activities and publicity materials organised by the Committee on the Promotion of Civic Education, the Commission on Youth and the Home Affairs Bureau. The post-colonial state, through the Quality Education Fund and the Chinese Cultural Projects Incentive Award Scheme, has poured in tens of millions of dollars yearly into schools and non-governmental organisations, offering national education programmes or activities such as cultural exchange activities, trips and study tours to the Chinese mainland to boost nationalism and a sense of social responsibility among Hong Kong's teenagers.

CONCLUSIONS: CHANGING HEGEMONY AS UNFINISHED STRUGGLES

In summary, at policy level, civic education in the colonial era took the form of a denationalised and depoliticised one; in the transitional period from 1982 to 1997, a new civic education campaign characterised with diversities and eclecticism was triggered by the retreat of colonialism and a demand of national reintegration; and following the resumption of Chinese sovereignty in the present post-colonial era, civic education has been shifted to national education, mainly for purposes of building nationalism and patriotism. As such, the recent nationalisation process of civic education is paradoxically accompanied with perpetual domestication.

Despite the changes in the socio-political milieu and in government education policy since the mid-1980s, the current practices of civic education in Hong Kong have exhibited a striking continuity with the stunted version of citizenry that existed in the colonial era. What is transmitted to students is still conformist in nature, detaching students from the 'real politics' of the society and the school. Similar to the colonial era, current civics education programmes—and the structures and processes of schools—reflect a mode of 'citizenship transmission' which is mainly concerned with developing the good and co-operative citizen, rather than a reflective and critical participant in political life. Paying attention to political and economic considerations such as disseminating nationalistic propaganda and developing human resources in a global competitive world runs the risk of fulfilling political and economic imperatives instead of humanistic and democratic concerns. Paradoxically the nationalisation of civic education is contradictory to a concern for developing the sorts of critical thinking and analysis skills that the current education and curriculum reforms are intended to achieve (Curriculum Development Council 2001). As such, it could serve better to prepare Hong Kong's younger generation for national integration and global competition than the further development of self-governance in Hong Kong and social transformation on the part of its people.

Similar to the social milieu at large, despite being marginalised by the post-colonial state and the pro-Beijing sector, some individuals and groups within the civil society, small in number, weak in strength and fragmented in organisation, have been persistent proponents of alternative civic education for democracy, human rights, rule of law and global citizenship (Wong, Yuen & Cheng 1999). And there are also contests between different fractions of the civil society, along the lines of different and sometimes conflicting ideologies. This vibrant civil society allows a hybridisation and cross-cutting of multiple civic education discourses and practices running in parallel with the state project, either in a compatible or competitive way alongside different geographical levels—global, national and local (Tse 2007b).

To a certain extent, the pro-Beijing camp and pan-democratic camp have been engaged in a tug of war against the backdrop of colonialism, capitalism and nationalism. These contestations over citizenship education exhibit the inherent tension of the present socio-political configuration of Hong Kong. While the governing coalition seeks to maintain its hegemony, the quest for democratisation in the form of civil society movement is alive and active, particularly when governance or credibility crises occur in Hong Kong and Mainland China. By making use of opportunities arising during these crises, those wanting to contest the prevailing hegemony can offer competing or challenging interpretations about citizenship and civic education through the continuous discursive and organisational articulation.

ACKNOWLEDGMENTS

Work on this chapter was funded by a grant from the Research Grants Council of Hong Kong (project no. 4675/06H). The author wishes to thank Ms. Anais So for her kind research and editorial assistance. Of course, any omissions or deficiencies remain the author's responsibilities.

REFERENCES

Apple, Michael (1990) *Ideology and the Curriculum* (2nd ed.). London, Routledge.
Billig, Michael (1995) *Banal Nationalism*. London, Sage.
Bray, Mark & Wing-On Lee (1993) Education, democracy and colonial transition: The case of Hong Kong, *International Review of Education*, 39(6), pp. 541–560.

Breakthrough (2008) *A Study of Educational Settings and Civic Participation.* Hong Kong, Breakthrough.

Cheung, Chi-Kim & Margaret Leung (1998) From civic education to general studies: The implementation of political education into the primary curriculum, *Compare*, 28(1), pp. 47–56.

Choi, Ming-Fai (1997) The changes of political culture reflected in textbooks: A content analysis of EPA textbooks in the transitional period of Hong Kong. Unpublished master thesis, The Chinese University of Hong Kong.

Choi, Po-King (2005) A critical evaluation of education reforms in Hong Kong: Counting our losses to economic globalization, *International Studies in Sociology of Education*, 15(3), pp. 237–256.

Chung, Man-Kin (2000) School-based civic education in Hong Kong: Case study of three schools. Unpublished master thesis, The Chinese University of Hong Kong.

Curriculum Development Committee (1985) *Guidelines on Civic Education in Schools.* Hong Kong, Government Printer.

———. (1996) *Guidelines on Civic Education in Schools.* Hong Kong, Government Printer.

———. (2001) *Learning to Learn: The Way Forward in Curriculum Development.* Hong Kong, CDC.

———. (2002) *The Basic Education Curriculum Guide—Building on Strengths.* Hong Kong, CDC.

Education Commission (2000) *Learning for Life, Learning through Life: Reform Proposals for the Education System in Hong Kong.* Hong Kong, Education Commission.

Fok, Shui-Chi (2001) Meeting the challenge of human rights education: The case of Hong Kong, *Asia Pacific Education Review*, 2(1), pp. 56–65.

Gramsci, Antonio (1971) *Prison Notebook.* London, Lawrence & Wishart.

Ho, Pui-Hung (2004) Constructing modern citizen: Civic education in postwar Hong Kong. master thesis, Department of Sociology, The Chinese University of Hong Kong.

Ho, Wai-Chung (2007) Politics, culture and school curriculum: The struggles in Hong Kong, *Discourse: Studies in the Cultural Politics of Education*, 28(2), pp. 139–157.

Hughes, Christopher & Robert Stone (1999) Nation-building and curriculum reform in Hong Kong and Taiwan, *China Quarterly*, 160, pp. 977–992.

Ip, Po-Keung (1997) Development of civil society in Hong Kong: Constraints, problems, and risks, in Pang-Kwon Li (ed.) *Political Order and Power Transition in Hong Kong.* Hong Kong, The Chinese University Press, pp. 159–186.

Ku, Agnes & Ngai Pun (eds.) (2004) *Re-Making Citizenship in Hong Kong: Community, Nation and the Global City.* London, RoutledgeCurzon.

Lai, Pak-sang & Siu-wai Wu (2003) Democratic citizenship and school civic education: A case study on civic learning through school students' association activities, *Journal of Youth Studies*, 6(1) pp. 158–165.

———. (2004) School civic education in Hong Kong: Student citizens' participatory learning and reflection, *Hong Kong Teachers' Centre Journal*, 3, pp. 155–161.

Lam, Wai-Man & Irene Lik-Kay Tong (2007) Civil society and NGOs, in Lam Wai-Man, Percy L.T. Lui, Wilson W.H. Wong & Ian Holliday (eds.) *Contemporary Hong Kong Politics: Governance in the Post-1997 Era.* Hong Kong, Hong Kong University Press. pp. 135–154.

Lau, Siu-Kai (2007) In search of a new political order, in Yeung Yue-Man (ed.) *The First Decade: The Hong Kong SAR in Retrospective and Introspective Perspectives.* Hong Kong, The Chinese University Press, pp. 139–159.

Lau, Siu-Kai & Hsin-Chi Kuan (1988) *The Ethos of the Hong Kong Chinese.* Hong Kong, The Chinese University Press.

Lee, Angela Ngai-Kam & Mary Mei-Yin Yuen (2003) Promoting human rights education in Hong Kong secondary schools, in *Human Rights Education in Asian Schools*, 2, Osaka, HURIGHTS OSAKA, http://www.hurights.or.jp/hreas/2/10.htm (accessed on 30 June 2008).

Lee, Wing-On (1999) Controversies of civic education in political transition, in Judith Torney-Purta, John Schwile & Jo-Ann Amadeo (eds.) *Civic Education across Countries: Twenty-Four National Case Studies from the IEA Civic Education Project*. Amsterdam, IEA, pp. 313–340.

———. (2004) Students' concepts and attitudes toward citizenship: The case of Hong Kong, *International Journal of Educational Research*, 39(6), pp. 591–607.

———. (2008) The development of citizenship education curriculum in Hong Kong after 1997: Tensions between national identity and global citizenship, in David Grossman, Wing-On Lee & Kerry Kennedy (eds.) *Citizenship Curriculum in Asia and the Pacific*. Dordrecht, Springer/Hong Kong: Comparative Education Research Centre, pp. 29–42.

Lee, Wing-On & Sai-Wing Leung (1999) Institutional constraints on promoting civic education in Hong Kong secondary schools: Insight from the IEA data, in *Occasional Paper Series No. 8*. The Hong Kong Polytechnic University, Hong Kong.

Lee, Wing-On & Anthony Sweeting (2001) Controversies in Hong Kong's political transition: Nationalism versus liberalism, in Mark Bray & Wing-On Lee (eds.) *Education and Political Transition: Themes and Experiences in East Asia* (2nd ed.). Hong Kong, Comparative Education Research Centre, University of Hong Kong, pp.101–121.

Leung, Lai-Yung (1999) Value orientations in junior secondary social studies curriculum. Unpublished master thesis, University of Hong Kong.

Leung, Sai-wing (1997) *The Making of an Alienated Generation: The Political Socialization of Secondary School Students in Transitional Hong Kong*. Aldershot, Ashgate.

Leung, Yan-Wing (2008) An 'action-poor' human rights education: A critical review of the development of human rights education in the context of civic education in Hong Kong, *Intercultural Education*, 19(3), pp. 231–242.

Leung, Yan-Wing & Shun-Wing Ng (2004) Back to square one: The re-depoliticizing of civic education in Hong Kong, *Asia Pacific Journal of Education*, 24(1), pp. 43–60.

Lo, Tin-yau Joe (2005) Continuity and change in the meanings of citizenship: A case study of the primary education curriculum in Hong Kong, 1967–2002, *Pacific-Asian Education*, 17(1), pp. 54–68.

Lui, Tai-Lok, Hsin-Chi Kuan, Kin-Man Chan & Sunny Cheuk-Wah Chan (2005) Friends and critics of the State: The case of Hong Kong, in Robert P. Weller (ed.) *Civil Society, Globalization and Political Change in Asia: Organizing between Family and State*. New York, Routledge, pp. 58–75.

Luk, Bernard Hung-Kay (2000) *A History of Education in Hong Kong*. Hong Kong, Lord Wilson Heritage Trust.

Morris, Paul (1992) Preparing pupils as citizens of the special administrative region: Curriculum change and control during the transitional period, in Gerard A. Postiglione (ed.) *Education and Society in Hong Kong: Toward One Country and Two Systems*. Hong Kong, Hong Kong University Press, pp. 117–145.

Morris, Paul, Flora Kan & Esther Morris (2000) Education, civic participation and identity, *Cambridge Journal of Education*, 30(2), pp. 243–262.

Morris, Paul & Esther Morris (2000a) Civic education in Hong Kong: From depoliticisation to Chinese values, *International Journal of Social Education*, 14(1), pp.1–18.

Morris, Paul & Esther Morris (2000b) Constructing the good citizen in Hong Kong: Values promoted in the school curriculum, *Asia Pacific Journal of Education*, 20(1), pp. 36–52.

———. (2001) Becoming civil in Hong Kong: A tale of two schools, *International Journal of Educational Research*, 35(1), pp. 11–27.

Morris, Paul & Anthony Sweeting (1991) Education and politics: The case of Hong Kong from an historical perspective, *Oxford Review of Education*, 17(3), pp. 249–267.

Mouffe, Chantal (1979) Hegemony and ideology in Gramsci, in Chantal Mouffe (ed.) *Gramsci and Marxist Theory*. London, Verso, pp. 168–204.

Ng, Shun-Win & Yan-Wing Leung (2004) A survey on implementation of civic education in junior secondary schools in Hong Kong, *Journal of Hong Kong Teachers' Centre*, 3, pp. 72–84.

Po, Sum-Cho & Jun Fang (2000) The changing concept of social education in the primary school curriculum, in Y.C. Cheng, K.W. Chow & K. Tsui (eds.) *School Curriculum Change and Development in Hong Kong*. Hong Kong, Institute of Education, pp. 571–591.

Simon, Roger (1982) *Gramsci's Political Thought: An Introduction*. London, Lawrence & Wishart.

So, Anais Wai-Chun (2007) Continuation of crippled citizenship: Civic virtues are for social responsibility or for political participation? *Educational Research Journal*, 22(2), pp. 201–228.

Sweeting, Anthony (2004) *Education in Hong Kong, 1941 to 2001: Visions and Revisions*. Hong Kong, Hong Kong University Press.

Tang, Sze-Ho (2001) Evaluating the implementation of the new civic education curriculum: A case study of a Hong Kong secondary school. Unpublished master thesis, Hong Kong University.

Tsang, Wing-Kwong (1984) Review and prospect of the political education in Hong Kong, *Hong Kong Economic Journal*, 8(5), pp. 34–40.

———. (1998) Patronage, domestification or empowerment? Citizenship development and citizenship education in Hong Kong, in O. Ichilov (ed.) *Citizenship and Education in a Changing World*. London, Woburn Press, pp. 221–252.

Tse, Kin-Lop (1998) The denationalization and depoliticization of education in Hong Kong, 1945–92. PhD thesis, University of Wisconsin-Madison.

Tse, Thomas Kwan-Choi (1997) Preparing students for Citizenship? Civic education in Hong Kong secondary schools. Unpublished PhD dissertation, Department of Sociology, University of Warwick.

———. (2000) Deformed citizenship: A critique of the junior secondary Economic and Public Affairs syllabus and textbooks in Hong Kong, *Pedagogy, Culture and Society*, 8(1), pp. 93–110.

———. (2002) Hong Kong society in a historical perspective, in Kwun-choi Tse (ed.) *Our Place, Our Time: A New Introduction to Hong Kong Society*. Hong Kong, Oxford University Press, pp. 2–38.

———. (2005) Quality education in Hong Kong: The anomalies of managerialism and marketisation, in Lok-Sang Ho, Paul Morris & Yue-Ping Chung (eds.) *Education Reform and the Quest for Excellence: The Hong Kong Story*. Hong Kong, Hong Kong University Press, pp. 99–123.

———. (2007a) Remaking Chinese identity: Hegemonic struggles over national education in post-colonial Hong Kong, *International Studies in Sociology of Education*, 17(3), pp. 231–248.

———. (2007b) Whose citizenship education? Hong Kong from a spatial and cultural politics perspective, *Discourse: Studies in the Cultural Politics of Education*, 28(2), pp. 159–177.

Wai, Anita Kit-Lan (2003) Citizenship education in a Hong Kong secondary school. Unpublished master thesis, University of Hong Kong.

Wong, Caroline Pui-Ching (1999) Change of value orientations in the junior secondary economic and public affairs (EPA) curriculum in Hong Kong. Unpublished master thesis, University of Hong Kong.

Wong, Paul Chi-Wai, Mary Mee-yin Yuen & Yuk-yin Carl Cheng (1999) Christian organizations, civil society and civic education, in Murray Print, James Ellickson-Brown & Abdul Razak Baginda (eds.) *Civic Education for Civil Society.* London, ASEAN Academic Press, pp. 175–192.

Wong, Ping-Man (1981) The civic education and the curriculum of the subject Economic and Public Affairs in Hong Kong after World War II: A comparative perspective. Unpublished master Thesis, Faculty of Education, The Chinese University of Hong Kong.

Wong, Ting-Hong (2002) *Hegemonies Compared: State Formation and Chinese School Politics in Postwar Singapore and Hong Kong.* New York, Routledge.

Wong, Yiu-Chung (2004) One country, two systems, in Wong Yiu-Chung (ed.) *Crisis: Hong Kong's Transformation since the Handover.* Lanham, MD, Lexington Books, pp. 9–34.

Yip, Amy Ah-May (2000) Curriculum change and pedagogy shift of primary social studies, in Y.C. Cheng, K.W. Chow & K.T. Tsui (eds.) *School Curriculum Change and Development in Hong Kong.* Hong Kong, Institute of Education, pp. 539555.

8   England
Searching for Citizenship

Ian Davies

CONTEXT

Civics and citizenship education are principally concerned with developing knowledge, skills and dispositions that develop the capacity of individuals and groups to understand and become involved in contemporary democratic society as well as to contribute to its further development. Of course all education, directly or indirectly, is relevant to these ambitions but it is in the particular connection with democracy in public contexts that citizenship education becomes most obviously significant. Definitions or characterisations of citizenship education are notoriously contested. The new Labour government in 1997, concerned about civic disengagement, commissioned Sir Bernard Crick to chair a committee that would clarify the meaning of citizenship. The resulting report came to be seen as a seminal document and would lay the ground for the introduction of the National Curriculum in citizenship. The report includes the following:

> So what do we mean by 'effective education for citizenship'? We mean three things, related to each other, mutually dependent on each other, but each needing a somewhat different place and treatment in the curriculum: social and moral responsibility; community involvement and political literacy. Firstly, children learning from the very beginning self confidence and socially and morally responsible behaviour both in and beyond the classroom, both towards those in authority and towards each other . . . Secondly, learning about and becoming helpfully involved in the life and concerns of their communities, including learning through community involvement and service to the community . . . Thirdly, pupils learning about and how to make themselves effective in public life through knowledge skills and values—what can be called 'political literacy' searching for a term that is wider than political knowledge alone. (Crick Report 1998, pp. 11–13)

In this chapter I review what has happened in citizenship education in England in the past and then in the present (and including some discussion of the future), and raise some issues about the structure of schooling, relevant processes of learning and curriculum frameworks. The chapter ends with some overarching reflections on the challenges for citizenship education and those who teach and learn it.

THE PAST

Prior to 1969, when the Politics Association was established with Bernard Crick as its founding president and Derek Heater as its chair, little or nothing was provided in the form of explicit education about, through and for citizenship. Even in 1969 the focus was not on civics and citizenship but on what was called 'political education and political literacy' (Crick & Porter 1978). Heater (1977, p. 62) has cited four key factors to explain the neglect of educating young people about and for democracy: a lack of tradition in schools; few teachers who were professionally committed to it; a belief that politics was solely an adult domain; and a fear of indoctrination. This attitude led to political education being taught (if at all, in an explicit sense) as civics which 'may have been utopian, quietist, simplistic, indoctrinating as well as class based, hardly meriting the description of "education"' (Entwistle 1973, p. 7). The key reports and policy documents on education during most of the twentieth century were either silent on the topic of civics and citizenship education or negative about it. The 1944 act did include a clause favourable to political education but this was never implemented (Brennan 1981, p. 40). The 1949 pamphlet *Citizens Growing Up* (Ministry of Education 1949/1961) suggested that a 'healthy democratic society' can be encouraged if schools develop 'the old and simple virtues of humility, service, restraint and respect for personality' (p. 41). Although there was some interest in times of crisis, such as 1918, 1930 and 1939–1945 (Stradling 1987), those who were advocating such forms of education (e.g. Gollancz & Somervell 1914) attracted little attention at times of relative security.

There was some activity that aimed positively at the development of democratic understanding and action and it was, of course, possible to draw from relevant work whether it was from the fields of philosophy (e.g. Oakshott 1956), education (e.g. Dewey 1916/1966), political socialisation (e.g. Greenstein 1969) or curriculum development (e.g. the Humanities Curriculum Project of the 1970s). The Programme for Political Education in the mid-1970s pushed the agenda into new areas, arguing for something that should be issue focused, using a broad concept of politics (rather than a narrower constitutional focus), emphasising procedural values (such as toleration and respect for truth and reasoning) and promoting skills as well as knowledge and understanding (Lister 1987). This growth of interest in the 1970s seemed to be caused by a variety of interlinking factors. The lowering of the age of majority from twenty-one to eighteen in 1970 meant that at least some school students would be able to vote. Arguments about the need to keep politics out of education systems seemed in such a context to be not only disingenuous (politics is always present) but more straightforwardly unhelpful when young people had a pressing and immediate need to understand key issues. Given that young people were aware of political issues but understood them imperfectly, there was a need to educate more effectively (Stradling 1977). Although crises are less frequent than might initially be imagined (see Sears & Hyslop-Margison 2007) the sense of emergency during the mid-1970s, which saw the rise of unemployment, a national bailout by the International Monetary Fund and the increased influence of the far right, led to an acceptance of the need for a form of civic education. The need for political literacy was accepted by some in all political parties but there was perhaps a more ready formal level of support from the Labour governments that were in power during the period 1974–1979. Finally, the growing democratisation of the school system, which saw a shift from the tripartite structure of grammar, secondary modern and technical schools allowing selective entrance on the basis of age, ability and aptitude, to a more egalitarian comprehensive school movement. In this new system with a large school-age population of the children of post-war 'baby boomers', the new and larger schools staffed by relatively young teachers were the places in which new ideas about educating for involvement in society would thrive.

These early proponents of political education were, however, to be disappointed. By the end of the 1970s, despite the support of some high-profile politicians and Her Majesty's Inspectorate (HMI), political literacy had been supplanted by the so-called 'new educations' which focused variously and in a rather fragmented and wide-ranging manner on peace, gender and other social and political matters. These educations were both more obviously politically connected and affectively oriented. The members of the peace education movement of the 1980s which attempted to secure arms reductions and the removal of American service personnel from the U.K. were at times the same people who argued for the reorientation of the curriculum so that questions that related to international relations could be pursued in particular ways. Further, the nature of 'peace' was not limited to questions of possible nuclear annihilation but also included identity, tolerance and personal relationships. Such issues related less to the public contexts that had been the focus of the political educators and more to a sense of inner harmony that led to opponents characterising it as a politically motivated and indoctrinatory secular religion (Scruton 1985).

By the late 1980s and beginning of the 1990s the attention of the Conservative governments, who had been in power since 1979, had turned from the economy and international relations to the nature of education that would be needed for the new post–Cold War order. Fullan (1991) argued that change was a process but in education policy there were also many events. The Inner London Education Authority (ILEA) was abolished, HMI was privatised, many local education authority advisers were made redundant and others were refashioned as inspectors, funds for in-service education were moved to be under the control of individual schools who had tighter budgets and university departments of education were, by means of circular 9/92, forced to transfer money and staff as schools were now said to be 'in the lead' in relation to initial teacher education. These matters were the result—and an expression—of new understandings of citizenship. The power of central government was strengthened, education was discussed more explicitly in relation to political parties and the professions were seen as unreliable. The National Curriculum, which had been the province of the political left who emphasised an entitlement to knowledge, became a Conservative reality with subjects drawn from high-status traditional contexts. There was no space for citizenship education as a separate subject; it instead became a cross-curricular theme inspired by the need to remind young people of their 'voluntary obligations' (Hurd 1988). Young people could not be forced to volunteer (the so-called fourth dimension of the 1990 report from the Speaker's Commission), but they could, so it was argued, be encouraged to see the necessity for such action at a time when a tier of civil society was being removed. When Kenneth Baker, as secretary of state, was asked what would replace local authorities which had acted as the spokes of the educational 'wheel', he replied that central government and schools would be linked by circulars and other policy announcements from his office. While the 1990 document outlining curriculum guidance in education for citizenship was seen as open to wide interpretation, it became merely a vehicle for inaction. In an increasingly competitive environment where examination results became the principal ways in which schools were compared, few cared about what was going on in relation to the five cross-curricular themes (Whitty, Rowe & Aggleton 1994) and education for citizenship was seen as the least important.

A significant choice had been made by the 1990s: citizenship, not political education or human rights education, was the new characterisation of educating about and for a democratic society. Positively, citizenship can through its connection with national legal status provide the means by which rights can become a reality. Whereas the global educators are seen by some to be limited by the absence of a polity, citizenship educators can with dramatic effect relate to the existence of legally enshrined rights. However, the use of citizenship as the key concept for a democratic society may also restrict. At a time when refugees and asylum seekers are high on the political agenda, educators are not encouraged to focus on human rights but rather to identify more clearly who 'belongs'. Citizens can be identified very clearly and this is not always comfortable for those who seek to promote inclusive democratic engagement.

Perhaps the most important academic figure in the recent development of citizenship has been T.H. Marshall. His essay 'Citizenship and Social Class' argued the compatibility of modified capitalist enterprise and collectivist social policies, postulating that a free economic market contributed to the enhancement and creation of welfare (Marshall 1963). Given this search for a dynamic concept, citizenship could be useful to politicians and policy makers with different objectives. I noted earlier how it had been seen by the Conservatives as a means by which individual responsibility could be strengthened at a time of centralism. It was also straightforward for President Clinton in the United States and then Prime Minister Blair in the United Kingdom to take the agenda of citizenship into a new direction that would be congruent with their notions of communitarianism. In England, after the election of Blair in 1997, citizenship would be the means by which communities would be regenerated giving expression to the 'third way' that lay beyond right and left in the absence of any realistic alternative to capitalism and the need for meaningful democratic dialogue (Giddens 1998). Two versions of the National Curriculum have so far been introduced: the first for implementation from September 2002 and the current version by September 2008. The initial version focused on three interlinked areas of knowledge and understanding, skills of inquiry and communication and skills of participation and responsible action. The current version with expanded guidance and requirements on assessment and a clearer focus on conceptual underpinnings of citizenship has the three key areas for study and action: democracy and justice; rights and responsibilities; and identities and diversity, living together in the U.K. It is this version of citizenship education that will be examined most closely in the remaining sections of this chapter.

THE PRESENT AND FUTURE

The Structure of Schooling

Ninety percent of young people in England are educated in state schools but, according to the Training and Development Agency for Schools (2009) (a government agency responsible for the training and development of the school workforce), 'There is no such thing as a typical school in England'. This variety of provision can be illustrated by reference to the School Standards and Framework Act of 1998 in which four main categories of state-maintained schools exist: community, foundation, voluntary controlled and voluntary aided. These schools differ according to who is the employer of staff, the owner of the school grounds and the nature of any religious affiliation. More recently Trust Schools which can set their own admissions criteria have been recognised. Other state schools include specialist schools, academies, City Technology Colleges (CTCs), community and foundation special schools, church and faith schools, pupil referral units, grammar schools and maintained boarding schools.

What does this variety mean? The 2005 Queen's Speech, which was seen as a means of driving forward the Labour government's agenda, promised more choice for parents. In November 2006, the Economic and Social Research Council organised two seminars to explore issues of choice. Among the variety of views put forward at those seminars there were some who suggested that this form of choice was not helpful to democratic citizenship. Those who express similar reservations include Reay and colleagues (2008, p. 239), who suggest, 'What has increasingly been marginalized in white middle class identity formation is civic commitment and a sense of communal responsibility'. In other words, choice means a greater concern with one's own priorities. But choice also means the failure to achieve those preferences. Curtis and Lipsett (2009) reveal that although 81 percent of parents do get their first choice of school, the remainder (i.e. over one hundred thousand families) do not. Six percent of local authorities are now using a lottery system to allocate places and attempts are being made to reduce the complexity associated with admissions, which some have suggested is providing a smoke-screen for the use of selection which is illegal for certain types of schools. What seems to be happening in relation to school selection is reflective of a particular approach to participatory citizenship. A general call for increased engagement has perhaps led to the decline of macro-participation and the rise of micro-participation. Whereas the former emphasises collective action through, for example, voting, trade union membership and community associations, the latter in a context influenced by declining levels of deference allows for individual action in a range of areas including health, education and local planning. The potential dangers associated with micro-involvement are that the market becomes the mechanism by which scarce goods are distributed, with success being achieved by those who are best able to exert influence. Although there are too many issues in relation to broad issues of education and the market (e.g. see Ball 2007), the potential of communitarian citizenship, when applied to the structure of schooling, to fragment society by dividing groups and favouring those who already enjoy disposable income, high levels of education and above-average health is clear.

The Culture and Processes of Schools

The preceding comments about the structure of schooling are clearly relevant to any consideration of culture and process. The competitive nature of schooling contributes to the sort of environment that is experienced by teachers and students. The importance of the resulting school and classroom ethos or climate has long been asserted by those who wish to promote forms of citizenship education (e.g. Ehman 1980; Hahn 1998; John & Osborn 1992). It would seem a contradiction to expect appropriate forms of civic knowledge, understanding and action to emerge from a closed and negative environment. Importantly, data from the largest survey of young people's views and experiences showed consistently (e.g. Malak-Minkiewicz 2005; Campbell 2008) that there was a positive correlation between an open classroom where student voice could be heard and positive civic outcomes. This of course does not mean that there is no place for formal teaching. The crucial distinction between those teachers who are authoritarian and who would damage citizenship education and those who work more positively by being authoritative should be remembered (Kakos 2007). In those distinctions the connections between what teachers and students are expected to do by inspectors and the publicists of academic league tables are clear. It is never possible in such a sensitive area that relates so strongly to values to be sanguine about what is intended or actually experienced. However, there are a number of very positive indicators about the possibilities for citizenship education in England. The National Curriculum (2009) explicitly outlines three processes that should be in place when teaching and learning citizenship. Firstly, in relation to critical thinking and inquiry, pupils should be able to engage with controversial issues, research inquiries and analyse sources. Secondly, pupils are expected to learn about and how to practise advocacy and representation in which they will express their own opinions, communicate and justify their arguments and represent the views of others, including those with whom they disagree. Finally, they are expected to take informed and responsible action individually and with others. It is extremely important that in relation to action pupils are expected to analyse the impact of what they have done (locally and/or globally), reflect on progress, assess learning, identify any difficulties encountered and determine what might be done differently. This means that there is a clear intention not to encourage actionless thought or thoughtless action. Rather this requirement for pupils to think about what they have achieved will help avoid the situation in which volunteering is promoted without proper consideration of why action needs to be taken and what it might lead to.

But the preceding has dealt with assertions about the need for an appropriate classroom climate and policy recommendations for its achievement. We need to know more about what is actually happening in classrooms. There are mixed signals about the progress of citizenship in schools. Ofsted, the schools inspection service, has claimed that there are significant problems (Meikle 2006) and this is supported by a range of evidence (although perhaps some of these commentators, for example, Biesta, Lawy & Kelly 2009, are seeking to draw attention to how it can be improved through recharacterisation rather than to see it as something that is exclusively the preserve of schools or irreparably flawed).

The National Foundation for Educational Research (NFER), as part of their longitudinal evaluation of citizenship education, has reported several positive features to the House of Commons Select Committee on citizenship education (Kerr 2007). The NFER suggests staff view school as an institution that is moderately democratic.

> [Although] there is a traditional teaching and learning environment, where note taking and listening while the teacher/tutor talks are more

prevalent than more active discursive approaches there is also a positive classroom climate (i.e. students feel free to express their opinions and bring up issues for discussion). (Kerr 2007, ev. 257)

In addition, the report notes that:

> there are signs that school experiences can have an influence on students' conceptions of citizenship, their civic knowledge and on their sense of efficacy and empowerment. (Kerr 2007, ev. 257)

The NFER evidence is certainly not enough to suggest that schools have suddenly become sites in which democratic discourse is the norm. The report may be phrased so positively in an effort to help achieve the goal of the Crick committee to establish citizenship education. It may need to be contextualised by clarifying the expectations on—and by—schools and teachers. I am not sure whether to regard the following quotation from the report as necessary pragmatism or as something more worrying about what happens when teaching for democracy is introduced into a non-democratic context: 'the idealism of citizenship as involving equal democratic participation of everyone in a school is giving way to an acceptance that there are limits to participation and democracy in schools' (ev. 258).

Formal Representations of Civics and Citizenship in the Curriculum

Much has already been written about the nature of the citizenship curriculum. Its key concepts and key processes have already been mentioned. The range and content (e.g. political and human rights, the environment, law and justice, changing nature of a diverse U.K. society and the U.K.'s relations with the European Union, Commonwealth and wider world) and curriculum opportunities (through classroom, school and community-based activities) are perhaps what might be expected in their coverage of a wide range of local, national and global issues. I will comment further, briefly, about these areas of content and suggestions about implementation in this section of the chapter and will return again to curricular issues in the final concluding remarks. Debates about the nature of the citizenship curriculum are usually framed by discussions over its characterisation as a National Curriculum subject. The NFER evaluation (Kerr 2007) suggests that schools are at rather different stages in their development work. Figure 8.1 shows the four categories that have been used to classify schools (each type is found equally across the national sample of schools).

Ofsted, the inspection service, has expressed a preference for specialist teaching of citizenship together with assessment through course work and examination at GCSE level (taken by students aged sixteen years) although there are those who continue to explore the potential for work through other subjects and in beyond-school contexts.

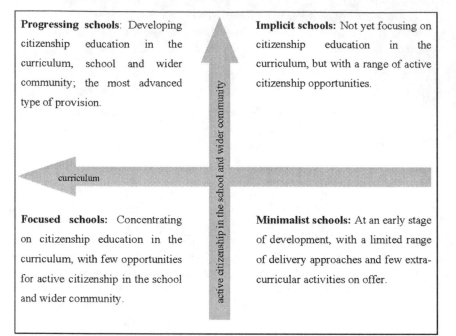

Progressing schools: Developing citizenship education in the curriculum, school and wider community; the most advanced type of provision.

Implicit schools: Not yet focusing on citizenship education in the curriculum, but with a range of active citizenship opportunities.

curriculum

Focused schools: Concentrating on citizenship education in the curriculum, with few opportunities for active citizenship in the school and wider community.

Minimalist schools: At an early stage of development, with a limited range of delivery approaches and few extra-curricular activities on offer.

active citizenship in the school and wider community

Figure 8.1 Four approaches to citizenship education. Adapted from Kerr (2005, p. 79).

CONCLUDING REMARKS

I have attempted to provide some historical background and to comment on the structure of schooling, the culture and processes that relate to citizenship education and to curricular matters. In order to further probe these matters that have been thus far presented separately, I highlight in the following some of the overarching key issues in the form of questions that may need to be considered in an evaluation of whether citizenship education in England is appropriately positioned for the future.

Characterising Citizenship Education: Subject or Something Broader?

The decision to make citizenship a National Curriculum subject had the benefit of providing status and coherence associated within established frameworks as well as allowing for other extra-curricular contributions to be made to the life of a school. However, there are also several disadvantages associated with such dynamism and there needs to be continuing efforts to resolve these issues. The curriculum is always overcrowded and citizenship competes with (or at times is lost within) personal and social education programmes. Citizenship, as something that all are expected to know about, is often being taught by anyone with space on their time-table and occupies a small and neglected part of the teaching week. Characterising the term 'citizen' to mean the same as 'person' and citizenship as the preferred outcome of all schooling leads to a significant difficulty. The dangers of this position are neatly summed up by Audigier (1998), who has suggested that:

> Since the citizen is an informed and responsible person, capable of taking part in public debate and making choices, nothing of what is human should be unfamiliar to him [sic], nothing of what is experienced in society should be foreign to democratic citizenship. (p. 13)

If these vague and hugely ambitious positions are maintained then little or nothing will be achieved. But, of course, schools are expected to solve all society's problems. Schools generally and citizenship education in particular are now also expected to take on the need to promote well-being through the wide-ranging new government policy of 'every child matters' as well as meeting the requirement to contribute to community cohesion. These wide-ranging ambitions are both necessary and hugely problematic.

Identity and Citizenship: Private and Public Issues

Identity is an extremely broad label but it is used here principally to allow for reflections on the extent to which citizenship should be regarded as a public or private matter. In light of the historical rather quietist tradition of citizens' involvement in British democracy (Jefferys 2007), the determination of Crick as a political scientist to focus on *public* matters and the support from official government bodies such as Ofsted to insist on the differences between citizenship education and personal and social education is useful but, nevertheless, the relationships between the public and the private, the individual and the community, have still not been resolved.

More precisely there are difficulties in creating meaningful characterisations of identity and diversity. The Crick Report took a broad approach to social justice, emphasising, for example, the need for tolerance. This position led to accusations by a few individuals that the report was an example of institutional racism (Osler 2003). Kiwan (2008) has more subtly and convincingly shown the need for a more explicit approach to diversity. The rather simplistic distinction between private and public issues originally provided by Crick seems now to be in need of further elaboration and Crick acknowledged as much in his foreword to Kiwan's book. However, there are still dilemmas about the nature of this perhaps more particular inclusive approach. The dangers of a knee-jerk response to the murders of people in London in 2005 are apparent if, unless we are very careful, diversity will be seen as a problem. Ajegbo's report (2007) emerged from a group established by the government to look at diversity and citizenship in the wake of those atrocities in London, and ultimately to a new citizenship strand of 'living together in the U.K.' We need to be wary of allocating responsibility to schools for all society's ills and we should see the challenges of making too simplistic a conflation between citizenship and Britishness (Sears, Davies & Reid 2008). Finally, we also should be careful to consider diversity with appropriate range. There is some very valuable work being completed in citizenship education about gender by Arnot (2008) and others but little is heard of this matter from policy makers working on citizenship education.

The Local, National and Global

The Crick Report made clear that there was a need for a 'change in the political culture of *this country*' (1998, p. 7; italics added). To further emphasise this point the Lord Chancellor in the same report declared that:

> We should not, must not, dare not, be complacent about the health of *British* democracy. Unless we become a *nation* of engaged citizens our democracy is not secure. (1998, p. 8)

Research on teacher's perceptions of citizenship showed that it was felt principally to be about being respectful to our immediate neighbours (Davies, Gregory & Riley 1999). This limited and limiting approach should be of little surprise in any discussion about a *National* Curriculum subject. Even if the approach in curricular documents had been determinedly internationalist it would still, in this context, emphasise national perspectives. Citizenship education in its current form and despite the rhetoric of globalisation is very different from global education (Davies, Evans & Reid 2005). What lies at the root of this issue is the plasticity of the term *citizenship*. It may, as discussed earlier, provide focused access to the rights and responsibilities offered by a nation-state (in an exclusive or inclusive manner) as well as the benefits and challenges of a more expansive (or fragmented) cosmopolitanism. As such, currently, the national perspective of citizenship is curiously accepted and yet also rejected without a consequent acknowledgment of the multiple citizenships that are necessary to gain advantages.

Learning Citizenship

Teaching methods for citizenship education are still rather traditional although there is a wide range of activities in classrooms, in whole school contexts and in communities. The ethos or climate within these contexts are seen as important and at times, according to the largest evaluation currently being undertaken, are appropriate. But, this, of course, does not mean that success has been achieved. Of the many challenges that exist, three could be highlighted. Firstly, schools are obviously not democratic institutions: staff are not elected and decisions are taken by those who occupy key positions in a hierarchy. The need to find a way forward that is educational and thus consultative and not necessarily constitutional (Reid & Whittingham 1984) may not reflect immediately and explicitly on orientations regarding the power distribution within the school. Of course, this 'realist' position risks undermining the whole enterprise of citizenship education by postponing, perhaps indefinitely, democratic engagement. Secondly, teachers, despite ambitious claims to see education as just one in a series of integrated children's services, still operate within schools and classrooms. It may be possible for much more to be done in the realisation of learning through democratic involvement but the challenges of that are not insignificant. Finally, although new educational processes (e.g. in relation to assessment for as well as of learning, and the use of digital media to generate traditional and new forms of youth participation) are developing, there are still many questions that remain about what is intended and experienced. If these new forms of learning allow those who already enjoy high levels of resource (such as computers and the literacy skills needed to use them) to enjoy greater levels of engagement than others then a contradiction will continue between individual outcomes and egalitarian intention.

Ultimately, the challenge for citizenship education is to exist within a National Curriculum and a globalising world; to promote opportunities for individuals and groups; to celebrate diversity and tolerance; to allow for the achievement of a wide range of very high standards by methods that are equitable. These challenges are not insuperable. They are 'merely' the challenges faced by all teachers. The fact that citizenship education by its very nature throws these challenges into sharp relief should not lead us to give up on democracy or on school's capability to help people understand and engage.

REFERENCES

Ajegbo, Keith. (2007) *Citizenship and Diversity: Curriculum Review*. London, HMSO.

Arnot, Madeleine (2008) *Educating the Gendered Citizen*. London, Routledge.

Audigier, F. (2000) Audigier, Francois (1998) Basic concepts and core competences of education for democratic citizenship, DGIV/EDU/CIT (2000) 23 Strasbourg, Council of Europe. The quotation is from page 30 of that document.

Ball, Stephen (2007) *Education Plc: Understanding Private Sector Participation in Public Sector Education*. London, Routledge.

Biesta, Gert, Robert Lawy & Narice Kelly (2009) Understanding young people's citizenship learning in everyday life: The role of contexts, relationships and dispositions, *Education, Citizenship and Social Justice*, 4(1), pp. 5–24.

Brennan, Tom (1981) *Political Education in a Democracy*. Cambridge University Press.

Campbell, David E. (2008) Voice in the classroom: How an open classroom climate fosters political engagement among adolescents, *Political Behavior*, 30(4), pp. 437–454.

Crick, Bernard & Alex Porter (eds.) (1978) *Political Education and Political Literacy*. London, Longman.

Crick Report (1998) *Education for Citizenship and the Teaching of Democracy in Schools*. London, Qualifications and Curriculum Authority.

Curtis, Polly & Anthea Lipsett (2009) 100,000 families refused first choice of secondary school, *Guardian*, 3 March.

Davies, I., Gregory, I. and Riley, S.C. (1999) *Good Citizenship and Educational Provision*. Lewes, Falmer Press.

Davies, Ian, Mark Evans & Alan Reid (2005) Globalising citizenship education: A critique of global education and citizenship education, *British Journal of Educational Studies*, 53(1), pp. 66–89.

Dewey, John (1916/1966) *Democracy and Education*. London, Macmillan Free Press.

Ehman, Lee (1980) Change in high school students' political attitudes as a function of social studies classroom climate, *American Educational Research Journal*, 17, pp. 253–265.

Entwistle, Harold (1973) Towards an educational theory of political socialisation. Paper read at the Philosophy of Education Society Conference, New Orleans, 15 April.

Fullan, Michael (with Susan Stiegelbauer) (1991) *The New Meaning of Educational Change*. London, Cassell.

Giddens, Anthony (1998) *The Third Way: The Renewal of Social Democracy*. Cambridge, Polity.

Gollancz, Victor & David Somervell (1914) *Political Education at a Public School*. London, Collins.

Greenstein, Fred (1969) *Children and Politics*. London, Yale University Press.

Hahn, Carole (1998) *Becoming Political: Comparative Perspectives on Citizenship Education*. Albany, State University of New York Press.

Heater, Derek (1977) A burgeoning of interest: Political education in Britain, in Bernard Crick & Derek Heater (eds.) *Essays on Political Education*. Lewes, Falmer Press, pp. 51–81.

Hurd, Douglas (1988) Freedom will flourish where citizens accept responsibility, *The Independent*, 13 February.

Jefferys, Keith (2007) *Politics and the People*. London, Atlantic Books.

John, Peter D. & John Osborn (1992) The influence of school ethos on pupils' citizenship attitudes, *Educational Review*, 44(2) pp. 153–165.

Kakos, Michalis (2007) The interaction between students and teachers in citizenship education. Unpublished PhD thesis, University of York.

Kerr, David (2005) Citizenship education in England: Listening to young people: New insights from the Citizenship Education Longitudinal Study, *International Journal of Citizenship and Teacher Education*, 1(1), pp. 74–96.

———. (2007) Memorandum submitted by National Foundation for Educational Research (NFER), House of Commons Education and Skills Committee: Citizenship Education, Ev. 252–263, London, Stationery Office Limited.

Kiwan, Dina (2008) *Inclusive Citizenship*. London, Routledge.

Lister, Ian (1987) Political education in England 1974–84: A briefing paper presented to the Global Education Centre of the University of Minnesota, *Teaching Politics*, 16(2), pp. 3–25.

Malak-Minkiewicz, Barbara (2005) IEA and civic education studies: Pursuing a moving target. Paper presented at the conference Building Democracy in Europe through Citizenship Education, Frascati, Villa Tuscolana Hotel, November, http://www.invalsi.it/download/cidree/Malak.rtf (accessed 23 March 2009).

Marshall, Thomas H. (1963) Citizenship and social class, in *Sociology at the Crossroads and Other Essays*, http://www.lse.ac.uk/resources/LSEHistory/marshall.htm (accessed 23 March 2009).

Meikle, James (2006) Schools poor at teaching citizenship says Ofsted, *Guardian*, 28 September.

Ministry of Education (1949/1961) *Citizens Growing Up, Pamphlet No. 16*. London, HMSO.

National Curriculum (2009) *Citizenship Education*, http://curriculum.qca.org.uk/key-stages-3-and-4/subjects/citizenship/index.aspx (accessed 15 May 2009).

Oakshott, Michael (1956) Political education, in Peter Laslett (ed.) *Philosophy, Politics and Society*. Oxford, Basil Blackwell, pp. 194–214.

Osler, Audrey (2003) The Crick report and the future of multiethnic Britain, in Liam Gearon (ed.) *Teaching Citizenship in the Secondary School*. London, Routledge, pp. 42–53.

Reay, Diane, Gill Crozier, David James, Sumi Hollingworth, Katya Williams, Fiona Jamieson & Phoebe Beedell (2008) Re-invigorating democracy? White middle class identities and comprehensive schooling, *Sociological Review*, 56(2), pp. 238–255.

Reid, Alan & Bill Whittingham (1984) The constitutional classroom: A political education for democracy, *Teaching Politics*, 13(3), pp. 307–330.

Scruton, Roger (1985) *World Studies: Education as Indoctrination*. London, Institute for European Defence and Strategic Studies.

Sears, Alan, Ian Davies & Alan Reid (2008) Britishness. Unpublished paper presented at the conference Britishness: The View from Abroad, University of Huddersfield, 5–6 June.

Sears, Alan & Emory Hyslop-Margison (2007) Crisis as a vehicle for educational reform: The case of citizenship education, *Journal of Educational Thought*, 41(1), pp. 43–62.

Stradling, Robert (1977) *The Political Awareness of the School Leaver*. London, Hansard.

———. (1987) Political education and political socialisation in Britain: A ten year retrospective. Paper presented at the International Round Table Conference of the Research Committee on Political Education of the International Political Science Association, Ostkolleg der Bundeszentrale für Plitische Bildung, Cologne, 9–13 March.

Training and Development Agency for Schools (2009) *Types of Schools in England*, http://www.tda.gov.uk/teachers/overseas_trained_teachers/english_education_system/types_of_schools.aspx (accessed 23 March 2009).

Whitty, Geoff, Gabrielle Rowe & Peter Aggleton (1994) Subjects and themes in the secondary school curriculum, *Research Papers in Education*, 9(2), pp. 159–181.

Perceptions of the Past and
Education of Future Citizens in
Contemporary Russia

Nelli Piattoeva

INTRODUCTION

Since the disintegration of the USSR, Russia has experienced massive social, economical and geopolitical transformations. The advent of the Western principles of democracy and market economy integrated Russia into the world system—a revolutionary development for a country which over the previous seven decades had invested enormous financial and ideological resources into preserving a radically different political order and isolationism. The breakdown of the communist regime based on the idea of unity between ethnically and linguistically different but ideologically friendly nations discredited the political organisation of the Soviet state. This development paved the way for nationalism—the idea that the nation and the state should be congruent. It provided ethnic groups living on the territory of the former USSR with grounds to claim national sovereignty and led to the primacy of the national project on the political agendas of the newly independent states.

Russian Federation is one among the myriad of states established in the aftermath of the disintegration of the Soviet Union. However, Russia should be distinguished from all the other newcomers in that symbolically, politically and economically it holds an ambiguous position as the successor of the Soviet state. Since the collapse of the Union, Russia has had to deal with a number of complicated issues, including lack of a well-defined Russian identity and a new national idea that would resonate with people, as well as come to grips with the loss of territory, weakened military power and economic hardship. However, it is impossible to explore Russia's contemporary politics without viewing it in terms of the challenges imposed by globalisation. In other words, Russia has to deal with 'the turbulence of the immediate historical past' and also with the 'pressure exerted by the economic, political and cultural forces of Western globalization' (Hedetoft & Blum 2008, p. 21). For Russia, globalisation implies transformation from a 'hemispheric hegemon' to a 'middling power'. Thus, in addition to the 'domestic' consequences of globalisation, for example, economic vulnerability to and growing reliance on global markets, and social disenchantment and distrust between leaders and citizens, globalisation impinges on Russia's already wounded sovereignty and national security, thus making it even more susceptible to the global forces. Globalisation is a 'West'-driven project and Russian leaders find it hard to accept that Russia is not in the driving seat (Hedetoft & Blum 2008).

It goes without saying that as the political fundament of the state changes, education is both affected by the change and expected to contribute to the new political order by means of citizenship education. With this context in mind, this chapter explores citizenship education in Russia between the 1990s and 2000s. I argue that the constitution of citizenship education is shaped by the Soviet political legacy and its model of citizenship education, and the emerging citizen ideals linked to the internal and external political developments. By the latter I particularly mean the political elite's visions of the Russian state and nation, on the one hand, and the penetration of supranational discourses and global political trends on the other. It should be borne in mind that these factors have not yet led to the establishment of a coherent model of citizenship education. On the contrary, the domain of citizenship education is inconsistent and shows evidence of conflicting discourses of citizenship. I start with a short discussion of the two main philosophical traditions of citizenship and the role of education in the political processes of nation and state formation. This theoretical foreword will help to put the following sections on Russia into a wider historical and theoretical perspective.

CITIZENSHIP EDUCATION AND THE STATE

The early conceptions of citizenship first elaborated by Plato and Aristotle laid the foundation for the so-called civic-republican model with its emphasis on duty, civic virtue and participation. In Athens, citizens were expected to participate in governmental and judicial functions, whereas in Sparta, virtuous (male) citizens were educated in the spirit of selfless devotion and sacrifice to the state (Heater 1999, p. 45). Later in history, the ideas of stressing loyalty to and participation in the *polis* were crystallised in the writings of Rousseau on civic liberty and the centrality of civic duty to the preservation of the republic. He asserted that only in a republic may individuals attain true freedom. However, the republic could only exist through the support of its citizens. If citizens are not involved, they are subjecting their liberty to the arbitrary will of others. And, if they are unwilling to fight for it, the republic faces the threat of destruction by its external enemies (Heater 1999, pp. 53, 64).

Following the French Revolution, the civic-republican tradition of the community of citizens—the nation—had been defined in civic terms as rule by the people and their ultimate commitment to the public weal. The eighteenth century gave rise to the liberal model, which differed greatly from the civic-republican ideals. Rooted in the writings of John Locke on natural rights, the liberal tradition advocated citizens' rights to pursue self-interests and consequently abandoned the idea of citizens' duty vis-à-vis the state and fellow citizens central to the civic-republican model. Importantly, the liberal ideal required only a weak form of identification with the state (Heater 1999, pp. 5–7). Whereas the republican state was constituted *by* the people, the liberal state was conceptualised as separate *from* the people, fulfilling the function of a 'night watch' over citizens' private property. This radically different understanding of the state and the state–citizen bond necessitated a different concept of nationhood.

Nationalism gave rise to a nation-state model where borders of the political unit are equated with borders of the cultural unit. In this model, the ethnocultural nation is claimed to encompass all those living on the territory of the bounded state. Citizens are united by the myth of common cultural heritage, as opposed to a set of shared political principles and participation. The cultural definition of the nation aspires to veil existing social, cultural, political and economic heterogeneity of society. In reality, most modern states are much more heterogeneous than the ideal suggests. Despite that, the nation-state has become the only legitimate state model today and states search for ways to maintain national cohesion amidst ever increasing diversity of their constituent societies (Castles 2005).

What was the role of education in this development? As has been argued by Balibar (1991, p. 93), a social formation reproduces itself as a nation through a network of apparatuses and daily practices. Individuals are instituted as *homo nationalis* from cradle to grave, at the same time as they are instituted as *homo œconomicus, politicus, religiosus*. Hobsbawm's (1989, pp. 149–150) analysis of the formation of the nation-state asserted that nothing compared with the possibilities of the classroom to pursue the propaganda of a homogeneous nation, with teachers as patriotic agents of the state. The main purpose of state-controlled education was to become an integral part of the developing state apparatus and a vital means of promoting the new social order (Green 1990, p. 79). Education constitutes a powerful instrument in raising political loyalty and creating a cohesive national culture, as envisioned by the political elite. It is invested with the task of spreading the national language, forging a national identity, encouraging patriotic values, inculcating moral discipline and rooting citizenship in terms of justification of the state to the people and the duties of the people to the state (Green 1990, p. 80).

We could draw several general conclusions from the preceding text. First, since ancient times, citizenship has balanced between loyalty to the state (and later the nation) and compliance with its rules, on the one hand, and participation in and scrutiny of the governing bodies, on the other. Second, though debates on the role of education in citizen development date back to ancient Greece, only with the rise of state education systems has the link between the two been truly consolidated. With a gradual merger of citizenship and nationality, state schools were expected to foster integration in both the political and the national community. Finally, citizenship education in any society represents a fragile balance of rights and duties, obedience and criticism, participation and individualism, and, as the discussion on the Russian case will later demonstrate, this balance is sensitive to and reflects changes in the larger socio-political context. It is important to understand that rights, duties, participation and identity can be articulated in very different terms, largely depending on the political ideology they are rooted in. Thus, citizenship is a profoundly historical and embedded concept inseparable from the meaning of the polity itself.

THE SOVIET LEGACY

A few words need to be said about the main political principles of the Soviet state regarding citizenship and nationality. As mentioned earlier, contemporary Russia holds an ambiguous position as a successor of the Soviet regime. The Soviet legacy has inevitably left its mark on the institutions, political ideologies and citizenship identities of the new Russia. In the following, I discuss central attributes of the Soviet political thinking, which distinguish the USSR from the traditional European nation-state.

The Soviet Union was neither conceived nor organised as a nation-state. It displaced and institutionalised 'nation' and 'nationality' as sub-state rather than state-wide categories (Brubaker 1996, pp. 26–27). More so, nationhood was 'never predicated of the state-wide citizenry' (Brubaker 1996, p. 28). This thinking was manifested in the ethno-federal organisation of the USSR, which divided the country into a complex set of national territories with varying degrees of autonomy. Territorial-political nationhood was complemented by a cultural-personal variant—an elaborate system of ascribing nationality to each individual from birth. The nationality indicated in every citizen's passport was determined by descent, not residence. It was inherited from either parent by 'blood'. No doubt, there were attempts to counterbalance sub-state identities with loyalty to the Soviet state. After all, Russian remained the *lingua franca* of the Union and Russian history and culture were advanced by the communist authorities. However, the idea of the 'Soviet people' as means to construct a unified Soviet supranation adhering to a set of common political principles was superseded by the sub-state nationality as a central marker of distinct Soviet identities (Brubaker 1996; Simonsen 1999).

The position of the Russian republic (RSFSR)—the territorial predecessor of contemporary Russia—was somewhat different from the other national territories in that it was not defined as a homeland for the ethnic Russians. Instead, it was the centre of the Soviet Union and a base for its fundamental political and cultural institutions. The RSFSR did not have its own Russian Communist Party or the Academy of Science. And the history of the USSR was in fact the history of Russia; Russia did not have a separate history from that of the USSR (Kuzio 2001, p. 111). This peculiar arrangement explains why a survey conducted in the late 1970s and the early 1980s found that 80 percent of Georgians and Uzbeks considered their titular republic as their homeland, whereas 70 percent or more Russians, regardless of where they lived, named the Soviet Union as their homeland (Kolstø 2000). There was no single Soviet identity shared by all those residing on the territory of the USSR. Instead the Soviet Union gave rise to two forms of identification: one strongly linked to the sub-state nationhood, as in the case of non-Russians, and a supranational identity of Russians and Russophones.

The Soviet legacy left Russia with mutually contradicting notions of nationhood and nationality. On the one hand, ethno-federalism established a clear link between the nation and the polity—a sort of proto-nation-state akin to the Western state model. However, this principle was relegated to the level of sub-state territories and was never attributed to the entire Soviet state as such. Simultaneously, nationality as an innate characteristic and biological inheritance became the central marker of individual identity, while citizenship remained a hollow concept. Whatever rights people possessed were largely determined by their nationality. Emphasis on nationality meant that people were not considered as equals despite ethnic descent. On the contrary, nationality largely determined their chances in the political and social institutions.[1]

INTERPLAY BETWEEN HISTORICAL LEGACIES, POLITICAL CHANGES AND CITIZENSHIP EDUCATION

This section focuses on citizenship education in Russia from two perspectives. First, I study the meaning(s) of the Russian nation and national identity found in the policy documents since the end of the 1980s up to date. Second, I analyse the role of the citizen as it is expressed in the official education policy discourse. I focus on the rights and duties reserved for citizens, personal qualities each is expected to possess and expressions of political activity (participation). As discussed earlier, citizenship and national identity are two sides of the same coin. Thus the discussion on rights, duties and participation would remain incomplete if the question of citizen identity is left out. In order to interpret my findings, I contrast them to the political traditions of citizenship, Russia's historical legacy and recent developments in the society and politics at large. The analysis is based on the close reading of policy documents issued by the Russian federal state authorities, mostly by the Russian Ministry of Education. Thus my primary focus is on the macro-level, i.e. how citizenship education is articulated in the documents produced by the authorities, which means that the question of policy implementation remains a matter for separate inquiry.

Image of the Nation and National Identity

Since the Soviet Union, political authorities have striven to balance between ethnic diversity and state unity. In the Soviet Union the dilemma was temporarily solved by granting ethnic groups limited cultural rights and various degrees of political autonomies. The former extended to the realm of education. For instance, there was only one history text-book whose contents were strictly evaluated by the political centre before publishing. Once approved, it was translated into multiple languages and used uniformly throughout the country (Vaillant 1994, p. 142). Ethnic diversity was tolerated as long as it remained devoid of political agenda. After the collapse of the USSR, ethnic groups stood up to demand recognition. The secession of Soviet republics and the threat of further disintegration of the Russian republic itself required urgent action. Education became a battleground in the struggle to preserve unity and accommodate diversity.

Nationalisation became one of the primary objectives of education in the first years after the collapse of the Union. However, nation was understood in explicit sub-state terms (Janmaat & Piattoeva 2007; Piattoeva 2009). Prior to the dissolution of the Union there were suggestions among the highest political ranks that republics should be left to teach their own history (Vaillant 1994, pp. 145–146; 'School Social Studies Today: New Approaches', 1991). In radical contrast to previous decades, cultural rights of ethnic groups were extended to the study of history and traditions and, importantly, they were explicitly encouraged to develop identities distinct from the uniform state. Ironically, such a heavy emphasis on the sub-state nation was rooted in the Soviet political thinking, but now it included political forms. The tripartite organisation of the curriculum, sealed in the Law on Education (1992/2003), introduced the so-called national-regional and school components which made it possible to allocate some curricula time for the study of educational contents relevant to the local context. This legislative step marked an important decentralisation trend in education policies. Thus, educational transformations went parallel to the democratisation of society and a particularly strong political will to establish a federated state model.

In the mid-1990s conservative politicians started to blame the government for the total negligence of national consolidation. The political arena of these years was characterised by continuous power struggles between the centre and the regions, with the Chechen War (1994–1996) as the most extreme example of the political disputes (Tishkov 1997). At the same time, the many votes received by politicians whose primary election slogans referred to the restoration of the Soviet Union, patriotism and the inferior position of the ethnic Russians forced liberals in power to pay more attention to questions of national identity and the fragile balance between state unity and its culturally heterogeneous population (Tishkov 1997; Tolz 1998). Moreover, the economic hardship, which culminated in the financial crisis of the late 1990s and the crash of the rouble in 1998, further helped to undermine public confidence in democracy and the Westernising course. These events are generally associated with Russia's loss of prestige and its subordination and vulnerability to the hegemony of the 'West' (Hedetoft & Blum 2008). Such public perceptions establish conditions to support the return to a more conservative model of governance and a nationalistic agenda based on claims of Russia's uniqueness and a political path of its own.

Nevertheless, policy documents continued to insist on the development of national comprehensive schools as means to preserve and enhance cultures and languages of each people (*narod*) along with respect for culture, history and languages of the 'peoples' of Russia and 'universal cultural values' (National Security Council 1996, p. 6). The role reserved for the Russian language and culture remained purely integrating, as in the Soviet times, but very different from viewing the Russian language and culture as the cornerstones of the all-Russian nation (Janmaat & Piattoeva 2007; Piattoeva 2009). However, national schools or schools with an ethnocultural component, as they are now called, increasingly triggered suspicion. Whereas earlier, national schools were perceived as crucial to the preservation of unity, questions were raised as to their harmful effect on interethnic relations and state integrity. Cautious appeals for the all-Russian (state) values to dominate appeared as early as the mid-1990s (e.g. the Development Strategy of History and Social Science Education, MoE 1994). Some education documents of this period argued for more attention to citizen and patriotic education and the formation of a system of common national values (*obchenatsional'niie tsennosti*) (e.g. MoE 1998b). Delays in the preparation of the new curricula and text-books were blamed on the lack of agreement with respect to common national values (e.g. MoE 1994).

Concrete legislative steps in the direction of strengthening national cohesion in and through education were taken in the 2000s. The *Conception of National Education Policy* (MoE 2006) explained that the challenge lies in guaranteeing the unity of educational and cultural space, and protection and development of national cultures and regional cultural traditions. This document argues that regional educational objectives contradict the federal standard of education, regional programmes are prioritised over the federal curricula, the link to the Russian culture and language is weakened, and, importantly, national schools have been transformed into sites of ethnic mobilisation, giving rise to centrifugal processes. The document proposes to preserve the polyethnic character of the Russian society, satisfy the ethnocultural and linguistic needs of different cultural groups and unite the people of Russia into a *political nation*. However, measures listed in the document suggest that the primary aim is to reinforce the state's control over education. For instance, an expert council is expected to evaluate teaching materials in humanities as to their congruence with the goal of consolidating Russian society and raising citizens and patriots of Russia (MoE 2006).

The latest amendment to Article Seven of the Law on Education (1992/2008) technically abolished the tripartite education standard and replaced it with a single federal standard. It is feared that this radical change will eradicate schools catering to the cultural needs of non-Russians (Ponkin 2007). Following direct instructions of the former president, Vladimir Putin, the Academy of Science started the examination of all history text-books used in schools throughout Russia. As numerous researchers have pointed out, history text-books have returned to the traditional symbols of nation-building, patriotism and pride in the achievement of the Soviet past (Zajda 2007, pp. 295–296). However, the text-books have long been accused of prioritising stories about the Russian people, Russian statehood and Russian culture (Bogolubov et al. 1999, p. 540), thus indicating that there is no room for multiculturalism and histories of non-Russians in the official school history canon. Curiously, Article Six of Chapter Two of the Law on Education (1992/2008), which guarantees the right to receive basic education in one's mother tongue, has so far remained intact. Latest developments are thus comparable to the state of affairs during the Soviet period. The authorities see no threat in providing education in languages other than Russian on condition that the content of education is controlled. As long as people learn the history of Russia and develop loyalty to the Russian state, its symbols and institutions, education in the non-Russian languages may continue.

Citizen's Role

After the advent of *perestroika* in the mid-1980s, Soviet political leaders started a cautious process of the emancipation of political culture. It led to the critical examination of the Soviet past and the role of the Communist Party. In the educational sphere, questions were raised as to the role of the school in the one-sided ideological propaganda of the Party. All Soviet educational establishments were required to practise upbringing (*vospitanie*)—a particular type of political and moral socialisation based on collectivism, strict discipline, a conscientious attitude towards labour, Soviet patriotism, proletarian internationalism and opposition to all incompatible ideologies (religion, capitalism, imperialism and individualism) (Collias 1990; Halstead 1994). The democratisation of the Soviet society brought about the de-ideologisation of the education system in hope that it would foster the dissolution of the Soviet mentality (Webber 1999, pp. 33–35). As a result of the ideological shift, *upbringing* gained a negative connotation and became associated with vigorous political indoctrination (Kraevskii 2002, p. 82). Coincidentally, politicians, experts and teachers alike were wary of political propaganda in schools. The official view was that the primary task of the school was to preserve peace and stability and prevent any political movement or ideology from entering the school.

However, the political elite soon realised that the formation of a constitutional state and the development of democracy based on free elections require help from education (MoE 1996). The aim was to teach about citizens' rights articulated in the constitution and to ensure that the newly enfranchised voters:

> give preference to forces most likely to guarantee . . . a dignified life for people, legality and constitutional order characteristic of a democratic constitutional state. (MoE 1995, p. 2)

In other words, it was important to teach voters to consider the 'public good' ahead of personal interests. This argument reminds us of the role reserved for education in the historical period of the extension of franchise—to ensure social control, conformity and political compliance (cf. Green 1990). A particular type of citizenship education, often referred to as civic-legal (*grazhdansko-pravovoie*), mostly aimed at the development of constitutional culture expressed in terms of constitutional knowledge, skills of law-abiding behaviour and activeness in the performance of civic duties (MoE 1995).

Despite these claims, I propose that in the first years since the breakdown of the Soviet regime, citizen's role and the contents of citizenship education were constructed in opposition to the Soviet past and its far-reaching social control. In this respect, the reorientation of citizenship education could be perceived in terms of its contribution to the demolition of the Soviet mentality which stood in the way of successful economic and political transformation. The very concern with constitutional culture and citizen rights was portrayed as incompatible with the Soviet regime's preoccupation with patriotism and citizen duty, disregard for laws and ignorance of citizen rights expressed in the constitution. As one document argued, the law and constitutional culture were not among the central values of the Soviet system (MoE 1995, p. 1). The liberal tradition of citizenship seems to have left a profound mark on the articulation of citizenship education in the early 1990s, evident in the emphasis on rights (cf. Morozova 2000) and little concern over citizen's identification with the state. This conclusion raises the question of the extent of foreign influence on the articulation of citizenship education.

Certain discourses found in the documents replicate the supranational discourse on citizenship. They penetrate national borders through organisational (e.g. UN, Council of Europe, OECD, Civitas International) and academic links. For instance, references to human rights were common in the documents issued in the 1990s on the topics of citizenship (*grazhdanskoie*) and civic-legal (*grazhdansko-pravovoie*) education. Ministerial circulars called for more and better teaching of human rights in schools. Education in human rights was closely linked to the promotion of 'common human values'—an ambiguous category employed to replace the highly politicised Soviet moral basis. Moreover, education in human rights was perceived as a pressing obligation of the new Russian state, which quickly signed a number of international declarations thus affirming its commitment to respect and promote key international principles (Antonov 1996, p. 50). For instance, Russia's entry into the Council of Europe facilitated education in human rights, following the Recommendation of the Committee of Ministers on Teaching about Human Rights (MoE 1998a). Globalisation manifests itself in the development of global political norms which limit national sovereignty, as they legitimate intervention and interference on the basis of incompliance with the global moral architecture, e.g. human rights, democratic principles, etc. (e.g. Hedetoft & Blum 2008). Thus Russia's embracement of global citizenship education discourses represents signs of its incorporation into the supranational educational governance and the need to sustain global legitimacy by adhering to the established global moral code, whether in practice or rhetoric.

Since the end of the 1990s, ideas stressing individual rights and citizen responsibilities in a young democracy have been superseded by the discourse of patriotism. The ideas of state patriotism were articulated in two extensive programmes of patriotic education for the years 2001–2005 and 2006–2010 (Russian Government 2001, 2005). Patriotic upbringing is widely perceived as the principal responsibility of the state. The programme adopted in the summer of 2005 declares that patriotism should develop into the core spiritual component of Russia (Russian Government 2005, p. 4). It is defined as love for the 'Motherland', loyalty to the 'Fatherland', a determination to serve its interests, as well as a readiness to protect the 'Fatherland' up to the point of self-sacrifice (MoE 2003, p. 2). Patriotism starts with love for one's 'small Motherland', i.e. a sub-state territory, and matures into a state patriotic consciousness and love for one's 'Fatherland' (MoE 2003, p. 3). Moreover, patriotism is premised on the priority of social and state affairs over individual interests and constitutes the highest purpose of life and actions of individuals, social groups and segments of society (MoE 2003, p. 3).

The preceding quotation illustrates that the discourse of patriotism shares ideas with the civic-republican citizenship model in terms of its emphasis on loyalty, duty and the significance of patriotism for personal fulfillment and identity. However, a crucial difference between the classical ideas and the Russian contemporary discourse lies in the perception of the state. Whereas in the civic-republican tradition people constitute the nation and the state through participation and consideration of the public good, the Russian state is constituted as a power apparatus independent from the citizenry while claiming their ultimate loyalty. Whereas in the civic-republican terms freedom could only be guaranteed through political involvement—to avoid the arbitrary will of others—in the contemporary Russian discourse freedom comes from the act of unquestioned loyalty itself.

The primacy of loyalty unfolds in the distinct military character of state patriotism. The militarisation of patriotic education turns 'citizen' into a 'soldier' with loyalty, duty and self-sacrifice to the state as the central citizen virtues (Piattoeva 2009). Thus it comes as no surprise that in July 2005 the amended version of the Law on Education returned lessons in national defence and military duties to schools and institutions of vocational training (Law on Education 1992/2008; Vinogradov & Litovkin 2005). Such a gendered perception of patriotism attributes an exceptional status to the male citizens, who can fulfill their duty to the state as devoted soldiers.

The victory of the Soviet army in the Great Patriotic War (Russian term for the Second World War, 1941–1945) is evoked to strengthen national cohesion. More so, the glorious past is carefully protected from critical interpretations. For instance, a Russian encyclopedia of the Great Patriotic War was published to counterbalance a Russian history book sponsored by the Soros Foundation, as it paid little attention to the war period.[2] There is a tendency to create and defend a national narrative—an ultimate historical 'truth'—which is evident in the growing control over history teaching and text-books described earlier. Similar to the Soviet period, the Great Patriotic War is employed as a symbol of Russia's powerful status vis-à-vis the international community and unity of different ethnic groups in fighting for the common good in the name of the state.[3]

CONCLUSION

Russia's challenges in the realm of citizenship education stem from the complex political developments set off by the disintegration of the Soviet Union, the collapse of the bipolar world order and the ideological borderlines which insulated Russia from the influence of the 'West'. As the analysis concentrated on the level of education policies, with the empirical data drawn from the official documents and legislation, there is no way of knowing how policies are received on the grass roots level. However, this general policy framework constrains, both institutionally and discursively, the local modifications of citizenship education. It is also important to bear in mind that the general recentralisation of domestic politics and control over education aim at bringing policy and implementation into closer congruence.

The analysis incorporated three sets of explanatory lenses in order to understand citizenship discourses found in the documents. First, I referred to the two main philosophical traditions of citizenship, the liberal and the civic-republican. This framework helps to situate Russian citizenship education projects within a broader philosophical framework and enables further comparison between Russia and other countries. Both liberal and civic-republican ideals have clearly left their mark on the conceptualisation of citizenship education, with the former prominent in the beginning of the 1990s and the latter gaining in strength in the 2000s. However, the political-philosophical traditions were modified to fit the specific Russian context. The embeddedness of both citizenship and citizenship education made the other two sets of interpretative lenses indispensable, i.e. the Soviet legacy and the contemporary socio-political scenery.

The analysis of the historical context concentrated on the perceptions of nationhood and citizenship in Soviet period. The conceptual heritage left by the Soviet regime helps to explain why nationhood is still often understood in ethnic terms and as a sub-state category. The educational changes initiated by the state authorities in the 2000s are framed in the language of state integrity and common national values. Therefore they attest to the government's growing desire to dissociate from the Soviet vocabulary and create a unified *state-nation* in line with the Western political principles. Nation-building is inevitably accompanied by *nation destroying* (Connor 1972)—a potential outcome of the ongoing re-evaluation of education materials and the recentralisation of the curricula. However, owing to the Soviet legacy, i.e. the institutionalisation of nationhood as a central political principle and a marker of individual identity, the state policies are likely to face resistance.

The fall of the iron curtain paved the way for Russia's incorporation into the global polity. The emerging transnational alliances enable the discourses of human rights, universal values and democracy to traverse geographical and mental borders. The Russian government needs to make use of the supranational vocabulary in order to maintain its international legitimacy. However, the impacts of globalisation manifested in Russia's acceptance of global moral principles do not easily fit with the simultaneous need to reconstruct national identity, state cohesion and trust in political institutions. As a result, the domain of citizenship education is inhabited by antithetical discourses. Especially the rise of state patriotism defined in terms of unquestioned loyalty to the state seems to have little in common with human rights, democratic constitution and participation. In the two antithetical discourses, the notions of rights, duties, participation and identity are given different, almost opposite, meanings. However, it is equally important to acknowledge that the liberal conception of citizenship education, with its emphasis on fair play by the constitutional rules, represents a thin notion of citizenship and does not encourage much critical thinking.

In a multinational and multiconfessional Russia, 'nation' remains highly contested, thus it is more viable, politically, to articulate patriotism as a state-oriented identity. Russian patriotic education draws heavily on the Soviet tradition of political upbringing. It leads to the militarisation of citizenship both in terms of highlighting the role of military service as a fundamental citizen responsibility and reducing citizenship to the mere exercise of loyalty and self-sacrifice. The Soviet past constitutes one of the central reference points for the political decision making in general and education policies in particular. The USSR is either depicted in negative terms as a faulty mentality to be dismantled, or it is regarded as a source of pride and past glory to be restored. The argumentation employed in the latest education documents attests to the growing popularity of the latter vision. In this respect, the elite's perception of the past dictates the education of tomorrow's citizens.

NOTES

1. For instance, people's nationality entry in the passport either opened the way to prestigious higher education institutions through affirmative action programmes or denied opportunities to members of unwanted ethnicities, such as the Jews. The same was true of employment prospects and political careers (Brubaker 1996, p. 31).
2. Interview with a senior official responsible for patriotic education in the Federal Ministry of Education (May 2005).
3. On the use of the war in the Soviet period, see Collias (1990).

REFERENCES

Antonov, V. (1996) Circular on the new teaching material about the Universal Declaration of Human Rights for the elementary school, *Vestnik Obrazovania*, 9, pp. 50–55 (in Russian).

Balibar, Etienne (1991) The nation form: History and ideology, in Etienne Balibar & Immanuel Wallerstein (eds.) *Race, Nation, Class. Ambiguous Identities.* London, Verso, pp. 86–106.

Bogolubov, Leonid, Galina Klokova, Galina Kovalyova & David Poltorak (1999) The challenge of civic education in the new Russia, in Judith Torney-Purta, John Schwille & Jo-Ann Amadeo (eds.) *Civic Education across Countries, Twenty-Four National Case Studies from the IEA Civic Education Project.* Amsterdam, IEA, pp. 523–543.

Brubaker, Roger (1996) *Nationalism Reframed. Nationhood and the National Question in the New Europe.* Cambridge, Cambridge University Press.

Castles, Stephen (2005) Hierarchical citizenship in a world of unequal nation-states, *PS Political Science and Politics*, 38(4), pp. 689–692.

Collias, Karen A (1990) Making Soviet citizens: Patriotic and internationalist education in the formation of a Soviet state identity, in H.R. Huttenbach (ed.) *Soviet Nationality Policies. Ruling Ethnic Groups in the USSR.* London and New York, Mansell, pp. 73–93.

Connor, Walker (1972) Nation-building or nation-destroying? *World Politics*, (24)3, pp. 319–355.

Green, Andy (1990) *Education and State Formation.* New York, St. Martin's Press.

Halstead, Mark J. (1994) Moral and spiritual education in Russia, *Cambridge Journal of Education*, 24(3), pp. 423–439.

Heater, Derek (1999) *What is Citizenship?* Malden, MA, Polity Press.

Hedetoft, Ulf & Douglas W. Blum (2008) Introduction: Russia and globalisation—a historical and conceptual framework, in Douglas W. Blum (ed.) *Russia* and Globalisation. *Identity, Security and Society in an Era of Change.* Baltimore, The Johns Hopkins University Press, pp. 1–34.

Hobsbawm, Eric J. (1987) *The Age of Empire 1875–1914.* New York, Vintage Books.

Janmaat, Jan G. & Nelli Piattoeva (2007) Citizenship education in Ukraine and Russia: Reconciling nation-building and active citizenship, *Comparative Education* 43(4), pp. 527–552.

Kolstø, Pål (2000) *Political Construction Sites. Nation-Building in Russia and the Post-Soviet States.* Boulder, CO, Westview Press.

Kraevskii, Volodar V. (2002) Upbringing or education? *Russian Education and Society,* 44(8), pp. 81–94.

Kuzio, Taras (2001) Historiography and national identity among the Eastern Slavs, towards a new framework, *National Identities,* 3(2), pp. 109–132.

Law on Education (1992/2003) http://www.ed.gov.ru/min/pravo/272,prin (accessed 4 June 2004).

———. (1992/2008) http://www.mon.gov.ru/dok/fz/obr/3986/ (accessed 9 January 2009).

Ministry of Education (1994) The development strategy of historical and social science education in comprehensive schools: The collegium's decision, 28 December, 24(1) (in Russian), http://center.fio.ru/method/getblob.asp?id=10000131 (accessed 9 January 2009).

———. (1995) On improving the constitutional culture and education in voting rights and the electoral process (in Russian), http://teacher.fio.ru/getblob. asp?id=10000151 (accessed 9 January 2009).

———. (1996) On civic-legal education of students in comprehensive schools of the Russian Federation (in Russian), http://teacher.fio.ru/getblob.asp?id=10000186 (accessed 9 January 2009).

———. (1998a) On the study of human rights in the comprehensive schools of the Russian Federation in the academic year 1998/99, *Vestnik Obrazovania,* 8, pp. 73–75 (in Russian).

———. (1998b) On teaching courses in history and social studies in the comprehensive education institutions of the Russian Federation in the academic year 1998/99, *Vestnik Obrazovania,* 9, pp. 69–71 (in Russian).

———. (2003) *The Concept of Patriotic Upbringing of the Citizens of the Russian Federation* (in Russian), http://www.ed.gov.ru/junior/rub/patriot/ (accessed 13 October 2008).

———. (2006) *Conception of the National Education Policy of the Russian Federation, Approved by Ministerial Decree no. 201 on August 3, 2006* (in Russian), http://www.edu.ru/db-mon/mo/Data/d_06/prm201–1.htm (accessed 9 February 2009).

Morozova, Svetlana A. (2000) Citizenship education in democratic Russia, in G.A. Bordovskii et al. (eds.) (2000) *Citizenship Education: Materials of the International Project* (in Russian). St. Petersburg, Herzen State Pedagogical University, pp. 27–36.

National Security Council (1996) *The Conception of State National Policy of the Russian Federation, Approved by a Presidential Decree no. 909 on June 15, 1996* (in Russian), http://www.scrf.gov.ru/documents/27.html (accessed 26 January 2009).

Piattoeva, Nelli (2009) Citizenship and nationality in changing Europe. A comparative study of the aims of citizenship education in Russian and Finnish national education policy texts, *Journal of Curriculum Studies,* Vol. 41, Issue 6, pp. 723–744.

Ponkin, Ivor (2007) Do not liquidate the tripartite standard: It will not improve the situation in education, *Uchitel'skaia Gazeta,* 47 (in Russian), http://www.ug.ru/ issues07/?action=topic&toid=2117 (accessed 24 January 2009).

Russian Government (2001) *State Programme Patriotic Up-Bringing of the Citizens of the Russian Federation for 2001–2005* (in Russian), http://www.redstar.ru/2001/02/02_02/document.html (accessed 13 October 2008).

———. (2005) *State Programme Patriotic Upbringing of the Citizens of the Russian Federation for 2006–2010* (in Russian), http://www.ed.gov.ru/ntp/fp/patr/ (accessed 13 October 2008).

School social studies today: New approaches (1991), *Vestnik Obrazovania*, 1, pp. 78–83 (in Russian).

Simonsen, Sven G. (1999) Inheriting the Soviet policy toolbox: Russia's dilemma over ascriptive nationality, *Europe-Asia Studies* 51(6), pp. 1069–1087.

Tishkov, Valery (1997) *Ethnicity, Nationalism and Conflict in and after the Soviet Union: The Mind Aflame*. Oslo, International Peace Research Institute.

Tolz, Vera (1998) Conflicting 'homeland myths' and nation-state building in post-communist Russia, *Slavic Review*, 57(2), pp. 267–294.

Vaillant, Janet G. (1994) Reform in history and social studies education in Russian secondary schools, in Anthony Jones (ed.) *Education and Society in the New Russia*. Armonk, NY, M.E. Sharpe, pp. 141–168.

Vinogradov, M. & D. Litovkin (2005) Duma returned compulsory military training to schools, *Izvestia*, 8 July (in Russian), www.izvestia.ru (accessed 16 September 2008).

Webber, Stephen (1999) *School, Reform and Society in the New Russia*. Chippenham, Anthony Rowe.

Zajda, Joseph (2007) The new history school textbooks in the Russian Federation: 1992–2004, *Compare*, 37(3), pp. 291–306.

10 'Common-Sense Citizenship', 'Citizenship Tourism' and Citizenship Education in an Era of Globalisation

The Case of Ireland During the Celtic Tiger Era

Audrey Bryan

INTRODUCTION

This chapter examines state-crafted strategies for 'managing diversity' in Ireland during the so-called 'Celtic Tiger' era (Blommaert & Verschueren 1998, p. 11), which lasted from the mid-1990s until the global economic downturn of 2008. It focuses on two seemingly disparate dimensions of diversity management which came to dominate the legislative and educational domains during this period, namely, the state's efforts to curtail the automatic right to citizenship to certain children born in Ireland, as well as statutory attempts to manage the negative side-effects of unaccepted diversity through educational initiatives designed to 'celebrate' and 'respect' diversity and alleviate racism.

In keeping with the volume's focus on how different nation-states are impacted by, and respond to, globalisation, the chapter is primarily concerned with the movement or 'global flow' of people, or what Arjun Appadurai (1996) calls 'ethnoscapes'. So intense was migration to Ireland in the late 1990s and early 2000s that according to the 2006 census, 15 percent of those normally resident in Ireland had been born outside the state, and 10 percent were of foreign nationality (Central Statistics Office 2007).

These global flows of people are directly and indirectly linked to broader networks and flows of trade, finance, investment and culture that were also major features of the Celtic Tiger economy, which I outline in more detail in the following. The Irish state restructured itself in response to globalisation during the Celtic Tiger era, away from a welfare state model towards a competition state which prioritised the needs of global capital over those of its own citizens (Kirby & Murphy 2007). I suggest that this resulted in new forms of inequality and insecurity that can be linked to the intensification of racist sentiment against exogenous and indigenous 'Others' within the Irish national space (Garner 2004; Loyal 2003).

The idea of the Celtic Tiger economy, akin to the 'tiger' economies of South-East Asia, first emerged in the mid-1990s, as evidence of Ireland's nascent economic boom began to accumulate (Coulter 2003). In a relatively short space of time, the Irish economy experienced unprecedented growth, largely as a consequence of changes in the operation of global capitalism and the convenient base that the Republic offered to multinational corporations seeking to expand operations in Europe (e.g. Coulter 2003; Garner 2004). During this period, the demographic profile of Irish society became rapidly and significantly more ethnically and racially diverse. The trend of immigration that accompanied the birth of the so-called 'Celtic Tiger' economy resulted in a newfound emphasis on issues related to national identity, citizenship, cultural diversity and 'integration' in an Irish context, as well as a marked intensification of racism in Irish society. Against a backdrop of increased immigration and rising levels of hostility against minorities, the education system—and intercultural education in particular—has come to be viewed as 'one of the key responses to the changing shape of Irish society and to the existence of racism and discriminatory attitudes in Ireland' (National Council for Curriculum and Assessment [NCCA] 2005, p. 17). Intercultural education in this context has been defined as a 'synthesis of the learning from multicultural and anti-racist education approaches . . . used internationally in the 1960s to the 1990s' (NCCA 2005, p. 3).

Drawing upon recent political-economic, legislative and educational developments, this chapter examines some of the complex and contradictory ways in which the borders of Irish citizenship, and relatedly, understandings of Irishness, have shifted over the last decade, reflecting a tension between a narrowly conceived sense of ethnic citizenship, on the one hand, and the reality of increasing social diversity on the other (Loyal 2003). In the political and legislative domain, I focus on the Citizenship Referendum of 2004 as an illustration of the ways in which restrictive and ethnically nationalist understandings of Irishness were reinforced during the Celtic Tiger era. I then examine recent educational interventions designed to 'help alleviate racism,' to 'normalise' and celebrate diversity and to reconfigure Irish national identity around a civic, rather than an ethnic ideal. At the heart of the analysis is the question of how to understand and interpret the paradoxical coexistence of political-economic arrangements and legislative developments that were implicated in the intensification of racism alongside a host of other state-sanctioned social policies and programmes aimed at promoting inclusiveness and contesting racism within Irish society. Offering a critique of the civic nationalist potential of citizenship and intercultural education initiatives implemented during the Celtic Tiger era, I examine the seemingly contradictory coexistence of state-led anti-racist initiatives and interventions grounded in civic nationalism alongside state-led racist initiatives which construct Irishness along narrowly prescribed, ethnic nationalist lines. Subjecting some of the 'impressive rhetoric' of citizenship and intercultural education to critical scrutiny (Gleeson 2009, p. 89), I argue that the inclusive and anti-racist aims and civic nationalist ideologies of these interrelated curricular interventions are often not realised in practice, but rather function as a means of enabling the state to attempt to maintain legitimacy within a context of state-led racist policies and political-economic arrangements and escalating racism.

The chapter is organised as follows: I begin by providing an overview of the rapid social and demographic transformation that Irish society underwent in the late 1990s and first decade of the twenty-first century. I then explain the intensification of racism that occurred during the largest economic boom ever witnessed by the state (Garner 2007a). Following this, I examine political, legislative and educational policy responses to the increased racial and ethnic diversification of Irish society that occurred during the Celtic Tiger era. Firstly, I outline political discourses about the entitlement to Irish citizenship mobilised around the time of the citizenship referendum in June of 2004, which resulted in a constitutional amendment attaching residence qualifications to the hitherto automatic right to citizenship available through *ius soli* (or birthright citizenship). More specifically, I examine the construction of a moral panic about 'citizenship tourism' and appeals to 'common-sense citizenship' that were mobilised during the campaign, resulting in a change in the law that had previously enabled children born in Ireland to so-called 'non-national' parents to access Irish citizenship by virtue of their having been born on Irish soil (Garner 2007a). Shifting the focus more directly to the education system, I next examine educational responses to the increased ethnic diversification of Irish society, including the purported role of citizenship education in promoting intercultural and anti-racist education. Examining citizenship in these different domains, I seek to highlight, as well as explain, apparent contradictions between the ethnic nationalist construction of Irishness as discursively and materially produced through citizenship legislation enacted during the Celtic tiger era, and the ideology of civic nationalism transmitted in recent state-sanctioned educational policy documents.

THE BIRTH OF THE CELTIC TIGER AND NEW CONFIGURATIONS OF RACISM IN IRISH SOCIETY

The idea that Irish society is multicultural is commonly understood as a recent development in Ireland's demographic history, despite the historical presence of a host of culturally diverse groups in Ireland. The perception of Irish cultural homogeneity has been linked to the political project of Irish nationalism that emerged following Ireland's independence from

Britain in the 1920s. This project, which was based upon racialised and exclusionary foundations, constructed Irishness as a homogenous entity that was essentially white, Catholic, nationalistic and rural (e.g. Connolly 2006; Loyal 2003; McVeigh & Lentin 2002). The next section examines the implications of this presumption of cultural homogeneity for 'Others' within the Irish national space, whose presence became a major focus of public and political attention during the Celtic Tiger era.

In the 1980s, Ireland experienced a severe economic recession, characterised by high unemployment rates, substantial public debt and mass emigration. It lagged so far behind most other EU member states on all indices of economic performance that it bore many of the hallmarks of a 'Third World' country (Coulter 2003). Yet, less than a decade later, many politicians and social commentators were celebrating an economic boom that earned the Irish economy the label the 'Celtic Tiger'. Fiscal and other incentives (including very low taxation on profits) made Ireland an investment paradise for multinational firms seeking to gain access to the European Union market, especially those involved in the information technology and pharmaceuticals industries, resulting in a major increase in foreign direct investment and a dramatic decrease in unemployment. Certain indigenous industries, especially in the information technology sector, also experienced significant growth during this period (O'Riain 2000).

By the end of the 1990s, economic experts were warning that a labour shortage could pose a serious problem to continued economic growth. In an effort to foster greater economic growth and meet demands for labour, the government reached out to so-called non-Irish nationals and returning Irish emigrants alike. Simultaneously, social unrest and poverty in various parts of the world were forcing a small yet significant number of refugees and asylum seekers, primarily from Africa and Asia as well as various parts of the former Soviet Union and Romania, to seek refuge in Ireland.

As the population of Ireland became more ethnically diverse in the late 1990s and first decade of the twenty-first century, evidence of growing anti-immigrant sentiment became apparent, exemplified by sensationalist media reports which depicted immigrants, refugees and asylum seekers in a predominantly negative and stereotypical light (Devereux & Breen 2004).

Collectively, media coverage presented immigrants (and asylum seekers in particular) as a threat to the integrity of the Irish national space and its scarce resources, and the coverage was implicated in fuelling public hostility towards those 'non-Irish-looking' individuals who were perceived to be undeserving or illegitimate (Garner, 2007c). Eurobarometer polls designed to measure levels of racism and xenophobia in European member states, carried out in Ireland in 1997 and 2000, provide evidence of rising levels of hostility towards minority groups during this period. Whereas in 1997, 16 percent of Irish respondents agreed that the presence of people from minority groups offered grounds for insecurity, three years later, that percentage had increased to 42 percent (Thalhammer et al. 2001). Moreover, the proportion agreeing that it is a good thing for society to be made up of people from different 'races', religions and cultures fell from 76 percent in 1997 to 61 percent in 2000 (Thalhammer et al. 2001).

Increasing hostility towards migrants and indigenous minorities has been linked to a set of political-economic arrangements which provided the structural basis for the intensification of racism in Celtic Tiger Ireland. Garner (2004), for example, outlines a series of ideological and economic processes that gave rise to new configurations of racism that emerged during the boom period (p. 228). He alludes to trends such as accelerated income and wealth polarisation, regional wealth discrepancies and an overall perceived drop in the quality of life, as explanatory factors against which the emergence of new racist ideas and practices must be read. Other facets of the Celtic Tiger paradox included new modes of employment and increasingly flexible labour market practices (in the form of badly paid, poorly protected, part-time and temporary employment contracts), competitive pressures, an out-of-control property market and soaring cost of living more generally (Loyal 2003). This constellation of factors, combined with the Irish economy's vulnerability to the increasingly rapid changes that characterise the global economy and its reliance on multinational capital, as well as a decline in the proportion of national income devoted to state spending, resulted in heightened material inequalities and psychological vulnerabilities (Loyal 2003; Garner 2004). Similarly, in their examination of how the Irish state restructured itself in response to globalisation, Kirby and Murphy (2007) outline Ireland's gravitation towards a 'competition state' during the Celtic Tiger era, characterised by a 'particularly ungenerous approach towards social provision' which prioritised efficiency and enterprise over security, entitlements and other social considerations, resulting in new forms of inequality and uncertainty (p. 20). From this vantage-point, racism can be understood as a response to socio-economic conditions which heighten material vulnerabilities and anxieties—anxieties that are projected onto vulnerable groups like Travellers, asylum seekers and economic migrants who are deemed privileged recipients of scarce national resources, such as welfare payments, jobs or land (Garner 2004; Hage 2003; Rizvi 1991).

The following section examines how the Irish government was implicated in generating and exploiting these anxieties to ensure that a referendum altering the hitherto unfettered entitlement to citizenship available through *ius soli* would be passed. It examines how the parameters of citizenship shifted during the Celtic Tiger era to reflect a defensive approach to immigration and a narrow and restrictive definition of what it means to be Irish, based on ethnic nationalist ideology which maintains that belonging to the nation is determined by blood ties, common origin and specific cultural traditions that are not chosen, but rather obtained through the contingencies of birth and inheritance (Montgomery 2005a, 2005b).

HEADLINES AND BLOODLINES: THE REFRAMING OF CITIZENSHIP DURING THE CELTIC TIGER ERA

Under the Citizenship Acts of 1956 and 1986, children born in the Irish Republic acquired Irish nationality through *ius soli*, meaning that Irish citizenship was the birthright of any individual born on Irish soil, including immigrants and asylum seekers. A one grandparent route to citizenship also applied, enabling those who were not born in Ireland, but who had at least one grandparent who had been born in Ireland to apply for citizenship, even though the applicant themselves may never have lived in or entered the Irish state. The 'Good Friday' or 'Belfast' Agreement, which was signed in 1998, led to a series of constitutional changes both north and south of the border, one of which was the Citizenship Act of 2001 which granted Irish nationality directly to those in the north who had up until then only been able to claim Irish nationality through a grandparent born before 1922.

The phrase 'Irish Born Children' (IBC) entered political discourse in the 1990s. A 1989 Supreme Court ruling (*Fajujonu v. Minister for Justice*) determined that Irish children whose parents were non-Irish nationals have a 'constitutional right to the company, care, and parentage of their parents within Ireland' (Annual Review of Population Law 1989). In the late 1990s and early 2000s, immigration lawyers and department of justice officials advised applicants to avail of the IBC route to residency, because of the lengthy time (up to two and a half years) it was taking to process asylum applications at the time.

In 2003, the Fajujonu ruling was successfully challenged by the newly appointed justice minister, Michael McDowell, by a 5–2 decision in the Supreme Court, thereby removing automatic access to residence rights though the IBC route, and creating a situation whereby parents applying for residence through this route would now have to have their case dealt with on a case-by-case basis (Garner 2007c). Symbolically, the normalisation of the term *IBC* meant the emergence of racialised distinctions within Irish mainstream politics between Irish children born in the state whose *parents* were not Irish nationals and those whose parents were (Garner 2007b). This administrative distinction between Irish children versus IBC implicitly emphasised the prioritisation of bloodlines over residency, and paved the way for the enactment of citizenship legislation based on 'policies of blood-line derived exclusivity', wherein Irish citizenship had to be earned by those IBCs who lacked Irish bloodlines (Garner 2007a, p. 447).

Intent on closing what he deemed to be a 'loophole' which allowed people to access Irish residence too easily, Minister McDowell announced that a referendum would be held in June of 2004 on the issue of amending the 2001 Citizenship Act. McDowell proposed the introduction of a three-year residence qualification for non-Irish national parents, before their IBC would be entitled to citizenship. Meanwhile, the right to Irish citizenship for those with at least one grandparent born in Ireland would remain, thereby privileging membership of the nation through bloodlines over membership through birthplace (Garner 2007b).

'COMMON-SENSE CITIZENSHIP' AND 'CITIZENSHIP TOURISM'

Despite a broad coalition of non-governmental and other groups vocally opposed to the referendum, the minister's constitutional amendment received almost 80 percent of electoral support. Garner (2007a) identifies four overlapping arguments that were advanced by government officials as to why the Citizenship Act should be amended to reflect a 'common-sense' approach to citizenship in an Irish context. These included (a) the argument that the concept of birthright citizenship (*ius soli*) did not comply with European Union norms, (b) that birth on Irish territory was, in and of itself, not sufficient to allow citizenship and that existing law enabled those without 'social' or 'cultural' links with Ireland to access membership of the nation, (c) the identification of so-called 'citizenship tourism' as a threat to the immigration system, and the Irish nation more broadly and (d) the IBC 'loophole' was threatening the integrity of Ireland's immigration system by enabling people to apply for asylum and then not have to follow through the application in order to gain residence. In support of the claim of citizenship tourism, attention was drawn to the apparent phenomenon of so-called 'non-national' women arriving in Ireland in the latter stages of pregnancy to give birth in order to claim citizenship rights. McDowell and his supporters implied that the Irish immigration system was being exploited by heavily pregnant 'citizenship' or 'maternity tourists' attempting to take advantage of *ius soli*. In support of his claim, McDowell argued that sixty thousand foreign women had given birth in Irish maternity hospitals in the previous year, and that hospital managers had expressed concerns about the strain that an influx of foreign pregnant women was placing on hospital resources.

The political discourse surrounding the citizenship referendum is a clear illustration of a discursive strategy of *deracialisation* employed by politicians who seek to implement policy decisions which discriminate against racialised groups by couching their arguments in deracialised language and stressing non-racist criteria, such as overcrowding, or an additional strain on scarce resources, as their justification (Troyna 1993). Indeed, the results of the referendum convey the extent to which the discursive demonisation of foreign women had powerful material effects. The ideological deployment of a discourse of 'common-sense citizenship' was used to deflect direct accusations of racism while simultaneously promoting ideas predicated on popular racist assumptions about the need to defend the national territory and to protect Irish cultural heritage and limited national resources from 'undeserving', 'illegitimate' and unassimilable 'Others' (Crowley, Gilmartin & Kitchin 2006; Garner 2007b; Rizvi 1993).

Elucidating the implications of the Irish Nationality and Citizenship Act 2004, Garner suggests that the constitutional amendment '. . . restores primacy (not exclusivity) to the jus sanguinis route to Irishness and, in practice, excludes people from particular parts of the world' (Garner 2007b, p. 126). Both discursively and materially, the referendum helped to solidify restrictive and exclusionary understandings of Irish citizenship and belonging, based on a common cultural heritage that relies on a presumption of homogeneity, and a concomitant denial of cultural diversity as a historical feature of Irish society (Crowley, Gilmartin & Kitchin 2006).

Somewhat paradoxically, the legislative and political developments alluded to earlier, which resulted in an intensification of racism during the Celtic Tiger era, coexisted alongside a host of other state-sanctioned initiatives aimed at promoting inclusiveness and at contesting racism within Irish society (Fanning 2002). These included various pieces of anti-discrimination legislation, and the establishment of government bodies charged with addressing racism in Irish society (for a fuller elucidation of these initiatives, see Bryan 2008; Crowley, Gilmartin & Kitchin 2006; Fanning 2002). Many of these bodies and programmes identified the education system—and citizenship education in particular—as having an important role in fostering interculturalism, inclusiveness and anti-racism in society. Contrary to the ethnic nationalist ideology underlying arguments advanced during the 'common-sense citizenship' campaign, intercultural educational initiatives enacted during the Celtic Tiger era were theoretically premised upon the notion of civic nationalism.

How then might we theorise the paradoxical co-existence of political-economic developments and political campaigns that were implicated in the intensification of racism and the promotion of narrowly restrictive, ethnically nationalist understandings of what it means to be Irish alongside a host of other state-sanctioned social and educational policies and initiatives aimed at promoting inclusiveness along civic nationalist lines and at contesting racism within Irish society? Intercultural interventions which are enacted within a broader context of racist political discourses and political-economic arrangements that promote economic disparities and uncertainties and fuel anxieties can be seen as acts of compensatory legitimation (Weiler 1984), or what Steven Klees (2008), referring to movements like Education for All and the Millennium Development Goals in the arena of international development, more recently has coined the 'good cop, bad cop' scenario. Rising levels of public hostility, fuelled by negative political commentary about migrants and asylum seekers, and policies which promote anxiety and economic insecurity call into question the legitimacy of the social order (this is the bad cop). To compensate for this, the state must introduce initiatives, like intercultural education, aimed at ameliorating racism and thus restoring legitimacy (this is the good cop). Yet, as I argue in more detail elsewhere, in actuality, these interventions were weak versions of anti-racism which failed to tackle the root causes of racism, or to promote truly inclusive understandings of Irishness (Bryan 2008; Bryan forthcoming a, b). Intercultural education, therefore, had the effect of placating its proponents with the idea that something was being done about the problem of racism in Irish society, thereby eliminating the need for any real interrogation of its structural dimensions and the political-economic arrangements and political discourses that were ultimately responsible for its intensification (Solomon et al. 2005). The next section provides a more detailed overview of citizenship education in an Irish context, including a critique of state-sanctioned approaches to intercultural and anti-racist education in school that were developed and implemented during the last decade.

CITIZENSHIP EDUCATION IN HISTORICAL CONTEXT

This section provides a brief overview of how civics and citizenship education have been constructed historically in an Irish context, before examining some of the ways in which citizenship and intercultural education were conceived during the Celtic Tiger era. Citizenship education had been a contentious issue since the foundation of the Irish State in the early 1920s (Hyland 1993). The Catholic Church was against civics as a separate subject on the school curriculum as it feared it would encroach on a range of areas traditionally the domain of religious education, such areas as moral education and personal development. In 1967, civics was introduced as a compulsory programme in secondary schools, albeit as a marginal, non-examination subject. The syllabus was 'bland' and uncontroversial, focusing primarily on education for national citizenship and the accumulation of facts about specific topics, state institutions and public organisations (Clarke 2002; Hyland 1993). It was highly nationalistic in its orientation, describing the ideal citizen as passive and compliant, yet prepared to defend the national territory if necessary (Department of Education 1967). In practice, civics was 'quietly ignored' in schools, and as early as the early 1970s, it was 'a dying subject' (Gleeson 2009; NCCA 1997, p. 1). It wasn't until the early 1990s, with the publication of a discussion paper on Civic Social and Political Education (CSPE) at the secondary level that citizenship education re-emerged on the educational and political agenda. This led to the establishment of CSPE as a mandatory examination subject at junior certificate (lower secondary) level in the late 1990s.

CIVIC, SOCIAL AND POLITICAL EDUCATION AND INTERCULTURAL EDUCATION IN THE CELTIC TIGER ERA

Civic, Social and Political Education seeks to promote 'active exploration and study of citizenship at all levels (personal, local, national, global) in the context of contemporary social and political issues' (Department of Education and Science 2006, p. 7). The curriculum is framed around seven key organising concepts including: 'democracy,' 'citizenship,' 'interdependence', 'human dignity,' 'stewardship,' 'rights and responsibilities' and 'development'. From the point of view of the present chapter, one of the most important aims of CSPE is to 'encourage pupils to apply positive attitudes, imagination and empathy in learning about, and encountering, other people and cultures' (Department of Education and Science 2006, p. 7). The aims of CSPE are closely aligned with another 'adjectival education' initiative which was developed during the first decade of the twenty-first century, namely, intercultural education, which evolved as the Irish population continued to diversify and evidence of increased hostility towards minorities became more apparent. Intercultural education is defined as 'a synthesis of the learning from multicultural education approaches and anti-racist education approaches which were commonly used internationally in the 1960s to the 1990s' (NCCA 2006, p. i), and is viewed as a key mechanism through which racism and racial inequality can be ameliorated in Ireland (NCCA 2006, p. i).

In 2005 and 2006, the NCCA produced intercultural guidelines for primary and post-primary schools. These guidelines promote intercultural education as a means of underscoring 'the normality of diversity in all parts of human life' (NCCA 2006, p. i). According to the guidelines, intercultural education 'helps to prevent racism' (NCCA 2006, p. 16), enables students to develop 'positive emotional responses to diversity and an empathy with those discriminated against' (p. 16), and enables them to 'recognise and challenge prejudice and discrimination' where they exist (NCCA 2005, p. 30). As such, intercultural education is deemed 'one of the key responses to the changing shape of Irish society and to the existence of racism and discriminatory attitudes in Ireland' (NCCA 2005, p. 17). Finally, intercultural education also seeks to reconfigure Irish national identity around a *civic,* rather than an *ethnic* ideal, such that multiple 'cultures', 'ethnicities' and 'religious traditions' can be embraced (Tormey & O'Shea 2003). The goal of cultivating civic nationalism is based in part on the criticism that the 'traditional view of Irishness—one that does not recognise the cultural and ethnic diversity which has long existed in Ireland—has made many Irish people from minority groups feel excluded' (NCCA 2005, p. 13). The capacity of citizenship education to promote intercultural values and understanding is also emphasised in these guidelines.

While the development of subjects like CSPE and intercultural education more specifically are promoted as progressive measures geared towards fostering more inclusive (civic as opposed to ethnically nationalist) versions of Irish identity and the normalisation and celebration of diversity, I maintain that this goal is compromised and complicated for a host of reasons, not least of which because the intercultural educational dimensions of the curriculum are essentially an 'add-and-stir' approach that seeks to accommodate change without altering the existing curriculum to any significant extent (Bryan 2008). Drawing on a corpus of recently published policy documents, and curriculum materials currently being used in Irish secondary schools, I examined the ways in which instructional materials (including citizenship and intercultural curricular content) problematically, if unwittingly, abnormalise diversity in Irish society and actually reinscribe narrow and restrictive, ethnically nationalist versions of Irishness reminiscent of the post-independence era of the 1920s (Bryan 2008). For example, a section on 'Refugees and Asylum Seekers in Ireland' in one recently produced CSPE text-book describes how:

> Over the last decade Ireland has become a *multicultural* society. This means there are people living and working in Ireland from many other cultures and countries. (Murphy & Ryan 2006, p. 2.19; emphasis in original)

While the text is helpful as a means of countering the 'general misconception that Ireland is being "flooded" with asylum seekers' by providing statistics on 'the actual numbers of asylum seekers who have travelled to Ireland in recent years' (Murphy & Ryan 2006, p. 2.19), it also presumes cultural homogeneity as the norm in Irish society by stating that Ireland only became multicultural 'over the last decade'. This representation has the effect of abnormalising—as opposed to normalising—diversity by proclaiming cultural diversity a new and aberrant phenomenon, and therefore implying that it is something which is at once unusual and alien to the Irish nation (Bryan 2009a).

Other CSPE curriculum resources which are designed specifically to teach about cultural diversity ironically, albeit unwittingly, reinscribe exclusionary understandings of what it means to be Irish. For example, an activity in *Changing Perspectives: Cultural Values, Diversity, and Equality in Ireland and the Wider World* presents different versions of an exercise about stereotyping, namely a 'version for a class with Irish students only' and a 'version for a culturally diverse class' (Gannon 2002, p. 13). The goal of convincing teachers and students that cultural diversity is truly integral to, and normal within, Irish society is questionable if 'Irish students' and 'students from differing cultural backgrounds' are considered mutually exclusive to the point that two separate versions of the activity are warranted (p. 13). While the exercise states that it seeks to provide 'a more complete picture of who people really are,' the implication is that 'culturally diverse' students are not 'really' Irish—in fact, that they cannot be Irish—and equally, that 'Irish students' are culturally homogenous. As such, the exercise contradicts its own core message that 'diversity . . . exists in all cultures/nationalities' (p. 13) and that it is a normal and integral feature of society (Bloomaert & Verschueren 1998). These examples are indicative of a dichotomy between the 'impressive rhetoric' of Citizenship education in an Irish context on the one hand and a very different reality on the other (Gleeson 2009, p. 89), wherein the actual knowledge about interculturalism as it is constructed in the formal curriculum is at odds with many of the key messages that interculturalism as an ideology seeks to underscore (Bryan 2008).

(IN)CONCLUSION? CITIZENSHIP AND CITIZENSHIP EDUCATION IN THE POST–CELTIC TIGER ERA

The foregoing analysis has focused on the seemingly paradoxical coexistence of state-led anti-racist initiatives and interventions grounded in civic nationalism which were promoted during the Celtic Tiger era alongside state-led racist initiatives (as illustrated by the common-sense citizenship campaign) which construct Irishness along narrowly prescribed, ethnic nationalist lines. Yet examining some of these apparently anti-racist and inclusive interventions in more detail, we see that they are often weak versions of interculturalism and anti-racism which ironically reinscribe restrictive understandings of Irishness based in the presumption of cultural homogeneity, and do little to alter existing patterns of racialised domination and oppression. From this vantage-point, the implementation of intercultural education in schools fulfills a political function of providing an educational palliative to minorities while pre-empting resistance, thereby muting consideration of alternative policy responses that would yield genuine egalitarian outcomes and effects for racialised minorities in Ireland (Bryan 2008).

This chapter has focused on the subject of civics and its role in contesting and reproducing racism in the educational domain. Equally important is the very structure of the Irish education system itself, which actively promotes segregation along, *inter alia*, gender, class and religious lines. Although a more thorough analysis of educational structures and practices implicated in producing racism is beyond the scope of this chapter, from the point of view of inclusion and diversity, it is notable that the majority of schools in Ireland are denominationally controlled and that most of these are under Roman Catholic management (Lodge & Lynch 2004). Furthermore, denominational schools enjoy exemptions from equality legislation in order to protect their ethos, which allows them to actively discriminate against certain students by giving preference in enrolment to students of the denomination of the school (Devine 2005; Nowlan 2008). The fact that denominational schools are legally permitted to refuse to admit a student who does not belong to the denomination of the school is hardly conducive to the rhetoric or spirit of respecting and celebrating diversity which is so fundamental to Irish interculturalism and anti-racism.

The foregoing critique is not meant to imply that schooling, or citizenship education, should not, or cannot, play a role in teaching about cultural diversity and against racism. In fact, I would argue that if we are to better understand and overcome racism in society, there needs to be sustained attention to the role that schooling could play in contesting racism. Moreover, the seemingly paradoxical nature of government policy over the last decade or so, as well as the contradictions between the professed rhetoric and the reality of citizenship education as it is enacted in curriculum resources opens up spaces for counter-hegemonic, genuinely egalitarian, anti-racist struggle.

It remains to be seen whether a new proposed elective subject in citizenship education at upper-secondary level, provisionally titled Politics and Society (NCCA 2009), will help to overcome the contradiction between the professed rhetoric about inclusion and diversity in Irish society and the realities of its institutions (Benon, Garvin, Lynch, & Roche 1985; Gleeson, 2009). As the boom years of the Celtic Tiger give way to a new post–Celtic Tiger era characterised by skyrocketing levels of unemployment, substantial salary cuts, increasing public debt and forced migration due to a lack of employment opportunities, levels of racism against indigenous and exogenous 'Others' who are deemed to be privileged recipients of ever more scarce national resources are likely to rise once more. The need for alternative radical pedagogical anti-racist strategies in tandem with broader political-economic reforms that promote greater levels of equity, not greater levels of economic disparity and insecurity, are all the more timely if we are to avoid further projection of hostility and anxiety onto vulnerable groups like asylum seekers and refugees.

ACKNOWLEDGMENTS

I would like to thank Melíosa Bracken, Andy Storey and the editors of this volume for their helpful comments on an earlier version of this chapter.

REFERENCES

Annual Review of Population Law (1989) *Fajujonu v. Minister for Justice*, 8 December, 16, p. 168.

Appadurai, Arjun (1996) Disjuncture and difference in the global cultural economy, in Arjun Appadurai (ed.) *Modernity at Large: Cultural Dimensions of Globalization*. Minneapolis, University of Minnesota Press, pp. 32–43.

Benson, Ciarán, Garvin, Tom, Lynch, Kathleen & Billy Roche (1985). Ideology, Interests and Irish Education. *The Crane Bag*, 9, 2, Irish Ideologies (1985), 12–24.

Blommaert, Jan & Jef Verschueren (1998) *Debating Diversity: Analyzing the Discourse of Tolerance*. London and New York, Routledge.

Bryan, Audrey (2008) The co-articulation of national identity and interculturalism in the Irish curriculum: educating for democratic citizenship? *London Review of Education*, 6(1), pp. 47–58.

———. (2009) The intersectionality of discourses on nationalism and interculturalism in the Republic of Ireland: Teaching against racism? *Race, Ethnicity and Education*, 12(3), 297–317.

Bryan, Audrey (2009b) 'Migration Nation': Intercultural education and anti-racism as symbolic violence in Celtic Tiger Ireland. In F. Vavrus & L. Bartlett, Lesley (Eds.), *Critical Approaches to comparative education: Vertical case studies from Africa, Europe, the Middle East and the Americas.* New York. Palgrave. Macmillan.

Central Statistics Office (2007) *Census 2006: Principal Demographic Results.* Dublin, Stationary Office.

Clarke, Marie (2002) Citizenship education and assessment, in D. Scott (ed.) *Curriculum and Citizenship Education: International Perspectives on Curriculum.* Westport, CT, Greenwood Publishing Group, pp. 111–130.

Connolly, Paul (2006) 'It goes without saying (well, sometimes)': Racism, whiteness and identity in Northern Ireland, in Julian Agyeman & Sarah Neal (eds.) The New Countryside? Ethnicity, Nation and Exclusion in Contemporary Rural Britain. Bristol, Policy Press, pp. 21–45.

Coulter, Colin (2003) The end of Irish history? Introduction, in Colin Coulter & Steve Coleman (eds.) *The End of Irish History? Critical Approaches to the Celtic Tiger.* Manchester, Manchester University Press, pp. 1–33.

Crowley, Una, Mary Gilmartin & Rob Kitchin (2006) *'Vote Yes for Common Sense Citizenship': Immigration and the Paradoxes at the Heart of Ireland's 'Céad Míle Fáilte', NIRSA Working Paper 30.* Maynooth, National Institute for Regional and Spatial Analysis.

Department of Education (1967) *Rules and Programmes for Secondary Schools.* Dublin, Stationary Office.

Department of Education and Science (2006) *Civic, Social and Political Education Syllabus.* Dublin, Stationary Office.

Devereux, Eoin & Michael Breen (2004) No racists here: Public opinion and media treatment of asylum seekers and refugees, in Neil Collins & Terry Cradden (eds.) *Political Issues in Ireland Today.* Manchester, Manchester University Press, pp. 168–187.

Devine, Dympna (2005) Welcome to the Celtic Tiger? Teacher responses to immigration and increasing ethnic diversity in Irish schools, *International Studies in Sociology of Education,* 15(1), pp. 49–70.

Fanning, Bryan (2002) *Racism and Social Change in the Republic of Ireland.* Manchester, Manchester University Press.

Gannon, Mary (2002) *Changing Perspectives: Cultural Values, Diversity and Equality in Ireland and the Wider World,* City of Dublin Vocational Educational Committee Curriculum Development Unit.

Garner, Steve (2004) *Racism in the Irish Experience.* London, Pluto.

———. (2007a) Babies, bodies and entitlement: Gendered aspects of access to citizenship in the Republic of Ireland, *Parliamentary Affairs,* 60(3), pp. 437–451.

———. (2007b) Ireland and immigration: Explaining the absence of the far right, *Patterns of Prejudice,* 41(2), pp. 109–130.

———. (2007c) *Whiteness: An Introduction.* New York, Routledge.

Gleeson, Jim (2009) The influence of school and policy contexts on the implementation of CSPE, in Gerry Jeffers & Una O'Connor (eds.) *Education for Citizenship and Diversity in Irish Contexts.* Dublin, IPA, pp. 74–95.

Hage, Ghassan (2003) *Against Paranoid Nationalism: Searching for Hope in a Shrinking Society.* Annandale, New South Wales, Pluto Press.

Hyland, Áine (1993) Address to the first meeting of the teachers involved in the pilot scheme for the introduction of civic, social and political education at junior cycle level. Unpublished paper presented to DES NCCA in-service course participants. Dublin Castle.

Kirby, Peadar & Mary Murphy (2007) Ireland as a 'competition state', *IPEG Papers in Global Political Economy,* 28, pp. 1–24.

Klees, Stephen (2008) Reflections on theory, method, and practice in comparative and international education, *Comparative Education Review*, 52(3), pp. 301–328.

Lodge, Anne & Kathleen Lynch (eds.) (2004) *Diversity at School*. Dublin, IPA/ Equality Authority.

Loyal, Steve (2003) Welcome to the Celtic Tiger: Racism, immigration and the state, in Colin Coulter & Steve Coleman (eds.) *The End of Irish History: Critical Reflections on the Celtic Tiger*. Manchester, Manchester University Press, pp. 74–94.

McVeigh, Robbie & Ronit Lentin (2002) Situated racisms: A theoretical introduction, in Robbie Lentin & Ronit McVeigh (eds.) *Racism and Anti-racism in Ireland*. Belfast, Beyond the Pale, pp. 1–48.

Montgomery, Ken (2005a) Banal race-thinking: Ties of blood, Canadian history textbooks and ethnic nationalism, *Paedagogica Historica*, 41(3), pp. 313–336.

———. (2005b) *'A Better Place to Live': National Mythologies, Canadian History Textbooks, and the Reproduction of White Supremacy*. Ottawa, University of Ottawa.

Murphy, Deirdre & Jim Ryan (2006) *One World: Studies in Civic Social Political Education for Junior Certificate*. Dublin, EDCO.

National Council for Curriculum and Assessment (1997) *The Development and Work of the CSE Pilot Project 1993–1996*. Dublin, NCCA.

———. (2005) *Intercultural Education in the Primary School, Guidelines for Schools*. Dublin, NCCA.

———. (2006) *Intercultural Education in the Primary School. Guidelines for Schools*. Dublin, NCCA.

———. (2009) *Politics and Society: Draft Syllabus for Consultation*, http://ncca-consultation.com/ncca/index2.php?option=com_flippingbook&view=boo k&id=3&Itemid=72 (accessed June 1st, 2009).

Nowlan, Emer (2008) Underneath the bandaid: Supporting bilingual students in Irish schools, *Irish Educational Studies*, 27(3), pp. 253–266.

O'Riain, Seán (2000) The flexible developmental state: globalization, information technology and the 'Celtic Tiger', *Politics and Society*, 28(2), pp. 157–193.

Rizvi, Fazal (1991) The idea of ethnicity and the politics of multicultural education, in David Dawkins (ed.) *Power and Politics in Education*. London, Falmer Press, pp. 161–196.

———. (1993) *Critical Introduction: Researching Racism and Education*. Buckingham, PA, Open University Press.

Solomon, Patrick, John Portelli, Beverly-Jean Daniel & Arlene Campbell (2005) The discourse of denial: How white teacher candidates construct race, racism and 'white privilege', *Race Ethnicity and Education*, 8(2), pp. 147–169.

Thalhammer, Eva, Vlasta Zucha, Edith Enzenhofer, Brigitte Salfinger & Gunther Ogris (2001) *Attitudes towards Minority Groups in the European Union. A Special Analysis of the Eurobarometer 2000 Survey on Behalf of the European Monitoring Centre on Racism and Xenophobia*. Vienna, SORA.

Tormey, Roland & Majell O'Shea (2003, June 17) Rethinking Ireland through the national curriculum. Paper presented at the *UNESCO Conference on Intercultural Education, Jyväskylä, Finland, 15–18 June*.

Troyna, Barry (1993) *Racism and Education: Research Perspectives*. Buckingham, PA, Open University Press.

Weiler, Hans (1984) The political economy of education and development, *Prospects*, 19(4), pp. 468–477.

11 A Paradigm Shift in the Political Culture and in Educating for Citizenship?

The Case of the United States of America

Thomas J. Scott and John J. Cogan

INTRODUCTION

The election of Barack Obama as the forty-fourth president of the United States of America on 4 November 2008 signaled a paradigm shift in American politics and potentially in the way youth and young adults are formally educated into their roles as 'citizens'. First, the Obama campaign was planned and carried out in a 'grass roots' manner grounded in the belief that the only way to energise and recapture the electorate into political life in the country was to convince regular voters that they did have the power to make change and to hold their elected officials accountable for what they promised to do once in office. Young voters were targeted specifically in this strategy.

Second, the campaign used state-of-the-art twenty-first-century technology to build this grass roots base in all fifty states, thus jettisoning the 'red-states/blue-states' strategy of the past three decades of campaigning in the United States, i.e. red states being Republican strongholds; blue states being primarily Democratic. Obama again and again noted that while we may hold differing beliefs, values and political views, all of us are citizens of the United States of America and need to work together to address the many critical issues facing the nation. Obama's use of various technologies to build a base of support through such media as the Internet, cell phones, MySpace and Facebook revolutionised the campaign, not only in terms of the broad and diverse populations it brought to the campaign, but also by raising hundreds of millions of dollars in campaign contributions from individuals in small amounts.

Third, the campaign focused specifically upon segments of the voting populace that had been largely ignored in the past, people of colour and young voters. These groups had been disenfranchised for a very long time and were, at first, skeptical of the campaign overtures. But candidate Obama's continuing appeal to these groups, as well as to many others, ultimately captured the largest body of young and diverse voters in a half century. The use of technologies that the young voter understood and used daily was a key to bringing them on board. Candidate Obama was in regular contact with his supporters through these technologies. It has built an enormous and diverse base for the Democratic Party.

Fourth, the Obama campaign, from day one, began a major voter registration initiative in all fifty states, as well as a massive 'get out the vote' programme in the last days of the campaign and on Election Day. Young people were a key factor in both the voter registration and voter drives and in doing so energised not only themselves but those with whom they interacted.

The spin-off effect of these strategies was that when students returned to high school and college in September, they began to demand different foci in their civics, government and related courses. No longer satisfied to just read text-books, take quizzes and tests and complete contrived assignments, they demanded that their teachers engage in 'active' pedagogies that interfaced with the congressional and presidential campaigns taking place throughout the nation. Many teachers responded positively to this; others did not. But if President Obama can keep these youth and young adults involved in the governance of the nation then the clamour from high school and college students for more 'active' citizenship education could grow exponentially. The Obama administration continues to use the technologies to link with the public in many ways, including putting legislation on Web sites for all to see, providing a way to track the actual spending of government programmes in order to increase transparency with electronic conduits to give feedback to the president on how he's doing and suggestions for improvement and critiques when they feel he's strayed off-message. At the time of writing we are only in the first year of the Obama presidency and the scene has moved from campaigning for the office of president to the business of governing the nation. Only time will tell if the bold moves of the campaign can be translated into the day-to-day business of governance. But at this point, it is clear from interviews that youth and young adults are as involved as ever in this presidency. This could have a monumental impact on the teaching of civics, government and political courses in the nation's schools and colleges in the future. But first let's set the scene for the argument which will be articulated in this chapter.

BACKGROUND AND CONTEXT

All of this comes at a time when the structure of the American public education system is undergoing fundamental changes. There has been a steady movement from the first administration of Ronald Reagan to centralise educational policy, curriculum standards, assessment of student progress and pedagogical practice. The United States throughout its history has not had a centralised Ministry of Education responsible for administering educational policy, curriculum, graduation standards or teacher licensure. Instead, individual states are given the constitutional power to create and administer systems of public education. The result for most of the nation's history has been a highly decentralised system characterised by disparate policy approaches that often conform to local educational needs and political realities. But beginning with Reagan, policies were introduced to gradually change this historic and constitutional structure to bring more centrality and cohesion to the system. Each succeeding U.S. president following Reagan has continued this movement. Most recently, George W. Bush promulgated the No Child Left Behind (NCLB) legislation that basically tied federal funds for educational programmes to the performance of all students in the nation's schools through a programme of 'high-stakes' testing. NCLB will be discussed in detail later in this chapter but suffice to say that it has had a major impact upon education and schooling in the United States in this decade.

These changes are set against the historical backdrop of the existence of nearly fifteen thousand independent and locally controlled school districts that are responsible for implementing educational policy. More than ninety thousand public schools attempt to align national, state and district curriculum mandates with each school's curriculum, where a teaching corps that has an established tradition of autonomy and pedagogical isolation then delivers the curriculum in their classrooms.

All of this presents interesting challenges for achieving agreement about the meaning of the concept of citizenship. In a pluralistic nation like the United States, citizenship has a multiplicity of meanings that are closely dependent upon class identity, the historical experience of cultural groups, gender differences and racial identities. Establishing an acceptable definition of what it means to be a 'citizen' in a milieu of fluid and often conflicting identity politics is problematic. Complicating definitional issues is the question of how citizenship is measured. Should it be measured solely by birth, the recognition of specific rights or by civic agency? For example, do we measure active citizenship through voting, working in a soup kitchen, dutifully paying taxes or a combination of all of these?

In this chapter we examine the history of citizenship education in the nation's schools, describe the impact of NCLB upon citizenship education in schools and finally discuss three areas related to globalisation that have been neglected by NCLB and will have significant impact upon citizenship education in the future: population diversity, the use of information technologies and creating a globally literate citizenry. But before getting to this we need to place educating for citizenship in the context of the nation's schooling history.

HISTORY OF CIVIC EDUCATION CURRICULUM IN THE UNITED STATES

Modern civic education in the United States dates back to the year 1916. Before this date, the social subjects in the curriculum were history and geography, and civics was taught mainly through the history curriculum. The 'Civics Study Group', formed under the Commission on the Reorganization of Secondary Education (National Education Association 1916), proposed two major changes that would have a long-term impact on the teaching of civics and government in U.S. schools.

First, the commission proposed the development of a new course at the ninth-grade level to be called Community Civics. This was to be a foundational course since many students left school for the workplace after grade nine. Second, at grade twelve, the final year of high school for those who went on to complete secondary education, a Problems of Democracy course was developed to build upon the foundational concepts and principles of the grade nine 'civics' course but focusing more specifically upon the problems, issues and conditions which students would face in their daily lives upon leaving formal schooling. This course was designed to help school-leavers develop the skills necessary to examine civic problems and issues and fulfill their roles and responsibilities as citizens living in a democratic society. The goal here was to develop participatory citizenship, yet in practice very little participation has ever been achieved in most U.S. civics or government courses (Justice 2008; Niemi & Niemi 2007). Instead, this twelfth-grade course is for the most part a content knowledge course that overviews the structure, organisation, function and symbols of American government. There have been attempts over the years to modify these offerings, but in the main these have been the two courses designed to educate for citizenship in the secondary school curriculum over the last century.

However, the 1990s saw a new era in civic education curriculum development. The publication in 1991 of a new framework for civic education called CIVITAS (Center for Civic Education 1991), followed in 1994 by the *National Standards for Civics and Government* (Center for Civic Education 1994), signaled major changes to the 1916 recommendations. The CIVITAS document was the theoretical framework in the development of the *National Standards for Civics and Government* (1994). This document, along with *Expectations of Excellence* (National Council for the Social Studies 1994), which were curriculum standards for the social studies in general in the United States, renewed the debate about the role of civics and government in the curriculum, and in particular how to develop knowledge, skills and behaviours for citizenship. The major change was that the *National Standards in Civics and Government* focused on the entire K–12 curriculum, a departure from the previous two course offerings in the past at grades nine and twelve.

The *National Standards in Civics and Government* (Center for Civic Education 1994) came the closest to anything the nation has ever had in terms of 'citizenship education policy'. As noted earlier, the historically decentralised system of schooling in the United States has only recently begun to focus more upon what might be termed a 'national' curriculum.

This has evolved through the development of national 'curriculum standards' documents in the various subject areas, including civics and government. A survey by Pederson and Cogan (2000; see also Galston 2004; Ross 2004; Westheimer & Kahne 2004) of the fifty states revealed no real unified policy on civics education. Rather an eclectic approach prevails with most states having simply adopted the *National Standards in Civics and Government* document and/or the *Expectations of Excellence* standards of the NCSS and made them their *de facto* policy. However, nothing has reshaped U.S. schooling in general and its role in educating for citizenship more than the NCLB legislation of the recent G.W. Bush administration. Some have cynically renamed the bill No Child Left Untested. Let us now examine this legislation in more detail and consider its impact on citizenship education.

NO CHILD LEFT BEHIND AND CITIZENSHIP EDUCATION

Eight years of political leadership characterised by a unilateral perception of America's role in the world, an extremist neo-liberal economic agenda and a domestic culture of fear reflected by the ephemeral war on terror has created significant challenges for citizenship education and the development of an engaged citizenry in the United States. For example, after the terrorist attacks of 9/11, rather than attempting to rally the American people around a patriotic vision of shared sacrifice and collective preparedness for the war on terror, the Bush administration encouraged citizens to go shopping and 'Get Down to Disney World in Florida', thus appealing to a debased value of materialism and self-serving consumption (see Bacevich 2008). From this response to the most severe terrorist attack in U.S. history, it was clear what was truly of value in Bush's America: the market as sacrosanct.

George Bush's educational policy viewed citizenship in myopic, econometric terms. NCLB (2001), the euphemism for the Bush version of the Elementary and Secondary Education Act which became law in 2002, was a reactionary and, in many respects, rhetorical public policy response to the problems of poverty and socio-economic inequities in American society. As a misguided attempt to address the economic realities of globalisation which many neo-conservatives saw as threatening to American economic hegemony, NCLB had no foundation in educational theory, philosophy or pedagogy: it was a policy driven solely by ideology.

In his 2004 bid for re-election George W. Bush characterised NCLB as an essential reform to promote job growth and economic security (Bush 2004). By associating NCLB with economic outcomes, Bush clearly abandoned the Jeffersonian philosophy of public schools as a vehicle of citizenship and a means of developing an engaged citizenry responsible for carrying out the civic dispositions necessary for the expansion and strengthening of democratic practice. As one critic of NCLB stressed, 'In the endless parade of education "reform", a focus on technical skills has replaced the pursuit of ideas, democratic ideals, and civic courage (Gibboney 2008, p. 24).

With NCLB's overemphasis on standardised testing, its focus on mathematics and reading instruction at the expense of subjects not 'worthy' of being tested, such as social studies and the arts, and its policy driven exclusively by quantitative data, the public school system became disconnected from its civic responsibility. A narrowing of the curriculum, pedagogy focused on test preparation of arcane facts and figures and a lack of emphasis on critical thinking, discussion and problem-solving became the hallmark of educational reform during the Bush presidency. Twelfth-grade results on NAEP civics tests from 1998 to 2006 saw no statistical improvement (see Lutkus & Weiss 2007), raising concern that civic instruction and curriculum development at the secondary level were not sufficient to meet the citizenship needs of new graduates. These outcomes fell short of creating the requisite skill set necessary for students to adapt to the intellectual demands of citizenship in a global age. Calls to re-energise civic instruction in schools came from such organisations as the Center for Information and Research on Civic Learning and Engagement (CIRCLE) and The Center for Civic Education. A concerted effort to expand civic-oriented curriculum offerings and teacher training has emerged with a particular focus on establishing support for civic education in public policy channels and state legislatures. Although some reformers hope civic education will be integrated throughout the school curriculum, social studies classes remain the primary arena in which civic education occurs in most schools.

In retrospect, NCLB was negligent of the realities of twenty-first-century America. Beyond testing students to death and stressing rhetorical concern for the academic needs of minority students, NCLB made no attempt to instill within students the necessary skills, aptitudes and behaviours that would equip them for the transformational nature of contemporary globalisation. In particular, NCLB neglected three aspects of globalisation that will have a significant impact on citizenship education in the future: the increasing diversity of the public school population; the role of technology in creating informed, participatory citizens; and the necessity of creating a globally literate citizenry who possess the capacity to visualise the integrated nature of issues that are local and global simultaneously. The following overview of each of these aspects not only provides a critique of the current state of citizenship education in the United States but a glimpse of the direction we feel citizenship education must take to remain a viable means of developing citizens for a future dictated by social, political and economic transformation. We will now turn to the issue of diversity in schools in the United States and its interface with citizenship education.

MULTICULTURALISM AND CITIZENSHIP
EDUCATION IN THE UNITED STATES

Currently, the United States is experiencing dynamic growth in racial and cultural diversity. According to a study of population projections conducted by the Pew Hispanic Center from 2005 to 2050, 82 percent of the population increase will be due to immigrants coming to the United States and their U.S.-born descendents. By 2050, one in five Americans will be an immigrant (Passel & Cohn 2008). The United States Department of Homeland Security (DHS) (2008) estimates over thirty million people living in the United States were foreign born, nearly 11.8 million of whom were considered 'unauthorised immigrants' as of 1 January 2007. DHS claims since the year 2000, the numbers of 'unauthorised' immigrants increased by more than three million people. Of this number 14 percent (nearly 1.7 million) were under the age of eighteen years. The top ten countries of origin for these immigrants were from the developing world: Mexico, Philippines, China, India, Brazil and several countries in Central America. Census data show the District of Columbia and the states of Texas, Hawaii, New Mexico and California are considered "majority-minority" states while the states of Maryland, Mississippi, Georgia, New York and Arizona have minority populations of nearly 40 percent (United States Census Bureau 2005).

Two crucial questions emerge from these projections. Are America's public schools adequately prepared for this transformation of American society? What specific curricular and pedagogical adaptations will be necessary to provide this diverse student population with the skills required for citizenship in a global age? For over two centuries the intersection of democracy and citizenship in the United States has traditionally been its public school system. In American classrooms, students of multifarious races, religions, linguistic backgrounds and class identities shared the same public space in which they were presented with a common set of values, norms and cultural constructs considered essential to a singular American identity. Assimilation of the 'Other' into the American ideal of *E Pluribus Unum*[1] was the prevailing method to deal with diversity in American schools. Traditionally, American schools perpetuated a singular purpose: to subdue multiculturalism and promote a unitary conception of citizenship; one that focused on the 'exceptionalism' of American values, political beliefs and cultural superiority (see Tyack 2003).

Currently, many public schools in the United States have not adequately adjusted to this new multicultural dynamic. Banks (2008) attributes this to the 'complicated, contextual, and overlapping identities of immigrant students' (p. 134; see also Bosniak 2006–2007). This is an especially acute problem for students whose parents are unauthorised (i.e. they entered the United States illegally, not necessarily by choice), since they exist in a netherworld; their connection to school is often ephemeral, their citizenship status uncertain and the official school bureaucracy is often unable or unwilling to meet these students' needs. More often than not, unauthorised students simply wither on the vine, caught in a bureaucratic trap in which they are offered a free public education but are not really able to utilise it as a mechanism toward legal status.

In some instances public schools have found themselves complicit in denying educational services to the children of unauthorised workers, despite the 1982 U.S. Supreme Court ruling *Plyler v. Doe*, which struck down the decision of a Texas school district to deny public education services to the children of unauthorised immigrants (see Stover 2008; Sneed 2007; Zehr 2007). Crackdowns on unauthorised workers by U.S. Immigration and Customs Enforcement agents have forced schools with large immigrant student populations to engage in delicate negotiations with law enforcement personnel on the one hand while trying to protect immigrant students' rights and family stability on the other (Stover 2008; Zehr 2008; Joel 2007). Research by Fine and colleagues (2007) found high-stakes tests are more likely to be required for high school graduation in states with the greatest immigration rates. The authors state:

> Once the collateral consequences are considered—pushout, dropout, constricted curricula and pedagogies, limited enrollments for overage students, schools not reaching Adequate Yearly Progress (AYP)—it is clear that high stakes testing policies are increasingly becoming a tool of border control, producing alienated bodies likely to drop out as if that were a natural condition of immigration; narrowing access to the gated communities of higher education, as if that were accountability. (2007, p. 79)

Traditional social and cultural networks are usually unavailable to many immigrant groups, forcing them to maintain transnational networks that provide attachment to communities that are geographically outside the one in which they reside (Spiro 2008). Developing a sense of political association and the singular identity of an American may become an abstraction for many immigrant populations whether they reside legally or illegally in the United States.

In addition to the struggle over nationality, many immigrants, including those who are unauthorised, 'move between multiple meanings of citizenship' (Sassen 2005, p. 85). For example, Sassen stresses that immigrant students often attend school regularly, obey the law, adhere to school policies or hold jobs. In essence, they meet many of the expectations of citizenship without the legal association to the state. As Putnam (2007) notes, 'adapting over time to immigration and diversity requires the reconstruction of social identities, not merely of the immigrants themselves but also of the newly more diverse society as a whole' (p. 159).

To fill the void between expectation, legality and social acceptance, public schools must make a concerted effort to provide the skills and dispositions these students need to eventually transition from an unauthorised, illegal status to the formal status of citizen. For example, Banks and colleagues (2005) provide a means of overcoming the issues of competing identities and multiple forms of citizenship by suggesting that schools develop curriculum that examines citizenship both within the nation-state and between nation-states. The study of immigration and its impact on citizenship and the formation of cultural identity in the United States should be a critical dimension of the civic education curriculum for all students. Unfortunately, the study of diversity in the United States is often neglected in the curriculum or trivialised in many text-books. If we are to adequately prepare students for life in a multicultural society and if a new 'social identity' is to become a reality in the United States, the increasing diversity of the nation must become an important part of the citizenship education curriculum. However, the use of technology by the young will also play a significant and growing role in educating for citizenship.

THE AUDACITY OF ENGAGEMENT: THE ROLE OF TECHNOLOGY AND CITIZENSHIP EDUCATION

The election of Barack Obama as president heralds a significant departure from the policies of the preceding eight years of the Bush administration. In the 2008 election Obama mobilised the dynamics of America's multicultural society and transcended the traditional constraints of class, gender, race, age and party affiliation (Scott 2008) in his victory over Republican Senator John McCain. Young voters played an important role in this mobilisation.

Pew Research Center (2008a) suggest that the 2008 election was characterised by an 'age gap—the divergence between the candidate preferences of the youngest and oldest voters was the widest in decades, perhaps ever' (para. 5). According to the Center's post-election analysis of voters under the age of thirty, 66 percent voted for Obama. Further, 28 percent of young voters in key battleground states attended a campaign event, more than any other age-group (Pew Research Center 2008b). The youth voter turnout was estimated to be between 52 percent and 53 percent with an estimated twenty-three million young Americans under the age of thirty voting, an increase of over three million more young voters than in 2004 (CIRCLE 2008). After decades of marginalisation, young voters have come to realise the value and power of political activism. They represent the 'new wave' of an American electorate that is increasingly diverse, technologically astute and politically active. According to the Pew Research Center (2008a), not only are these young voters more secular than older voters, they tend to support increased government involvement in daily life, oppose the war in Iraq, possess more liberal views on social norms and trend toward political liberalism. It is clear the 2008 election represented a push-back by most young voters against eight years of neo-conservatism and the politics of privilege associated with Bush policies.

The Obama campaign utilised technology in novel ways to organise his supporters. As Danielle Allen (2008) has observed, the campaign 'used its website to disseminate tools for grass-roots organising and made its campaign infrastructure infinitely expandable as groups replicated over and over, learning from and copying one another' (p. A15). To a large extent, Obama operationalised the decades-old vision of the Internet as a space for enhancing democracy. He capitalised on young voters' attraction to social networking sites and their passion for using technology as a source of information as well as communication. In a survey undertaken by the Pew Research Center, 42 percent of those aged eighteen to twenty-nine say they learned about the 2008 campaign through the Internet. Two-thirds of eighteen- to twenty-nine-year-olds claimed they used social networking sites, 27 percent of whom used these sites to acquire information about the candidates and their campaigns (Pew Research Center for the People and the Press 2008). As Cornfield (2008) notes:

> It appears to be the internet's capacity to enhance small group activity and social movement coordination, and the reciprocal flows of emotional power back from small groups and social movements into online dialogues, archives, and databases, that provides a crucial dynamic for the civic surge. (p. 72)

The future Obama presidency is predicated on the continued active engagement of the American citizenry. In a forum on service learning held at Columbia University on 11 September 2008, Obama stated:

> Part of what we're going to do is create transparency and account-ability in how government works so that you can be an active citizen holding your public servants and elected officials accountable. That's one other aspect of citizenship; paying attention to what's taking place. (ServiceNation 2008)

An Obama presidency could revolutionise the interaction between citizens and government. Obama has pledged to maximise the utility of technology as a mechanism to enhance citizen engagement by establishing links between citizens and governmental agencies. In the process, tremendous expectations are placed on citizens to exercise civic agency through deliberation, debate and assessment of public policy. Some of the innovations he proposes include:

- Make government data available online in universal formats to allow citizens to 'comment on the data, derive value and take action' in their communities.

- Establish pilot programmes to open up government decision making and involve the public in the work of government agencies by tapping the expertise of the American citizenry.
- Require executive branch appointees and rule-making agencies to conduct significant business in public, so citizens can watch a live Internet feed of their proceedings. These feeds will also be archived.
- Use Web tools to allow citizens to track online federal grants, contracts, earmarks and lobbyist contacts with government officials.
- Give the American public the opportunity to review and comment on the White House Web site for five days prior to the signing of any non-emergency legislation.
- Employ technologies such as wikis, blogs and social networking tools to modernise cross-agency and public communication and information sharing to improve government decision making (Obama 2008, p. 4).

A critical question emerges from Obama's ambitious vision of an engaged citizenry committed to good governance: is the content of citizenship education as it is commonly taught in most American public schools capable of meeting this challenge? Participatory citizenship of the sort envisioned by Obama requires a type of citizenship education characterised by dynamic pedagogy in which students *do politics* rather than *study about politics* in a text-book. However, as Justice (2008) has noted, much citizenship education in the United States is traditional in scope and characterised by passivity. Thus a potential dichotomy emerges from the type of citizen Obama envisions and the type of citizen that commonly graduates from America's public schools. For Obama's vision of participatory democracy to be realised, a significant transformation must occur in the curriculum and pedagogy of citizenship education. Moreover, the Obama presidency must make a concerted effort to eliminate the gap in civic knowledge and engagement that exists between upper- and middle-class white students and minority students, immigrants and low-income white students (see Levine 2009; McConnell 2008). This population composite now reflects the enormous changes and challenges occurring globally.

THE LITERATE CITIZEN IN AN AGE OF GLOBALISATION

Globalisation has created a new approach related to the content of citizenship education; students in the twenty-first century must engage in comparative, expansive and temporal inquiry if they are to become engaged citizens. First, students must increasingly become aware of how globalisation is affecting their daily lives. Zakaria (2008) has observed that the twenty-first century will be characterised by a multipolar world, one in which the United States will be viewed as a nation among equals rather than an economic and political hegemon. From a curricular standpoint, citizenship education must focus on the reality that future international issues will entail increasing amounts of multinational co-operation and negotiation. Banks (2008) advocates 'transformative citizenship education' which attempts to recognise and validate the cultural identity of students on the one hand, while clarifying and reflecting on how these identities are interrelated on a local, national and international level on the other. Likewise, Cogan and Derricott (1998, 2000) and Cogan, Grossman and Liu (2000) have called for a *multidimensional* citizenship education that merges personal belief, political agency and the recognition that the community-based problems faced by students in the twenty-first century are intricately related to global events (see also Merryfield 2008; Scott 2004).

To adapt to the complexity of a globalised world, the curriculum must fuse the local and the global; students must become cognizant that the domestic policy they shape as citizens has an impact on citizens in other parts of the world. Thus the curriculum of citizenship education can no longer be based solely on national imperatives—it must now be presented from a comparative basis, focusing on how political and economic decisions made in the United States are perceived in countries throughout the world. Teachers must focus on analysing the historical antecedents of issues, examine them in contemporary terms and help students make deductions regarding future implications the issues might have on their local communities as well as the larger international community. Only through the relationship of past, present and future can students find relevance in complex issues and enhance the possibility they will acquire the civic agency necessary to address those issues that may prove threatening to their collective security.

Obama's campaign pledge of promoting transparency in government provides teachers with an exciting opportunity to practise and refine the civic skills of deliberation, argument and advocacy, enhancing the political efficacy of their students. As Hess states (2008), in addition to expecting students to stay informed, participate in civic life and understand the operation of government, they must also 'participate effectively in *political* life by staying informed *about events and issues that animate political decisions in their communities, understand the procedures and processes used to create and enforce political decisions, and influence those decisions*' (p. 374; emphasis added).

Obama's technology initiatives play an important role in expanding traditional skills associated with citizenship. A curriculum infused with interactive government Web sites like the Office of Public Engagement (www. whitehouse.gov/ope), social networking sites like YouTube, Facebook or PBwiki and government transparency sites like GovTrack.us, OpenCongress.org, Recovery.gov and OpenSecrets.org will keep students politically informed while promoting engagement in real-time political decision making. This is a potentially revolutionary development in citizenship education whereby classrooms would become important centres of democratic discourse and decision making as students, and other citizens, acquire the capacity to influence public policy.

Blogs, wikis, YouTube, threaded discussion sites and widgets provide fast, continuous and in-depth possibilities for political analysis, debate and informed decision making all within the realm of the classroom. One significant obstacle to this possibility has been lack of access to high-speed Internet capacity. Obama's pledge to expand broadband could play an important role in making access more equitable, eradicating the digital divide which has marginalised many minority communities and pockets of chronic poverty in the United States (see Horrigan 2009; Hesseldahl 2008).

Henry Giroux stresses that education:

> should be concerned with teaching students not only how to think, but how to come to grips with a sense of their own individual and social responsibility and to be responsible for their actions as part of a broader attempt to be engaged citizens, who can participate in Democratic public life. (Polychroniou 2008, pp. 2–3)

Despite the tremendous political and economic challenges facing the United States, there is a sense of optimism that after decades of political apathy and alienation, especially on the part of America's youth, the United States has reached a watershed moment as far as the country's democratic potential.

CONCLUSION

In summary, the potential for a significant paradigm shift in the political culture of the United States, and in due course a major change in the way youth and young adults are educated for their roles as citizens, is real. Given the interface of the election of Barack Obama as president coupled with demographic shifts in the nation as outlined in this chapter and increased use of information technologies especially by young citizens and voters, increasing levels of globalisation will require the development of citizens who are global in their perspectives and knowledge base. We are currently at the intersection of these major forces that will force educational policy makers and educational practitioners to rethink how we educate for citizenship in schools and higher education institutions. Knowledge from textbooks and tests about that knowledge will not be enough to meet the many challenges facing the nation and the world. Nothing less than an 'active' citizenship that gets youth and young adults engaged in the political life of their communities, their nations and their world will be acceptable. Many educators and teachers will be reluctant to move from traditional pedagogies that are largely passive to these more active and progressive strategies.

But they will no longer have a choice. Because just as the American populace demanded change in the political and economic direction of the nation on 4 November 2008 with the election of Barack Obama to the presidency, the people who elected him, including millions of young voters, many voting for the first time, will demand that the form and substance of their education for citizenship must also change.

ACKNOWLEDGMENTS

Some of the material presented in this chapter has been published previously in Thomas Scott and John Cogan (2004) Democracy at the crossroads: Political tensions concerning educating for citizenship in the United States, in David Grossman, Wing-On Lee and Kerry Kennedy (eds.) *Citizenship Curriculum in Asia and the Pacific*, Hong Kong, CERC. Permission to use this material has been granted by the Comparative Education Research Center at the University of Hong Kong.

NOTES

1. From the Latin 'out of many, one', which became the motto of the United States in the late eighteenth century and is commonly used to describe the U.S. national identity.

REFERENCES

Allen, Danielle (2008) Citizenship 2.0, *Washington Post*, 25 November, p. A15.
Bacevich, Andrew (2008) He told us to go shopping. Now the bill is due, *Washington Post*, 5 October, p. B03.
Banks, James (2008) Diversity, group identity, and citizenship education in a global age, *Educational Researcher*, 37(3), pp. 129–139.
Banks, James A., Cherry A.M. Banks, Carlos E. Cortes, Carole L. Hahn, Merry M. Merryfield, Kogila A. Moodley, Stephen Murphy-Shigematsu, Audrey Osler, Caryn Park & Walter C. Parker (2005) *Democracy and Diversity: Principles and Concepts for Educating Citizens in a Global Age*. Seattle, Center for Multicultural Education, University of Washington.
Bosniak, Linda (2006–2007) Varieties of citizenship, *Fordham Law Review*, 75, pp. 2449–2453.
Bush, George W. (2004) The essential work of democracy, *Phi Delta Kappan*, 86(2), pp. 114–121.
Center for Civic Education (1991) *CIVITAS: A Framework for Civic Education*. Calabasas, CA, Center for Civic Education.
———. (1994) *National Standards for Civics and Government*. Calabasas, CA, Center for Civic Education.
CIRCLE (2008) *Young Voters in the 2008 Presidential Election: Fact Sheet*. Medford, MA, The Center for Information and Research on Civic Learning and Engagement.

Cogan, John J. & Ray Derricott (1998) *Citizenship for the 21st Century: An International Perspective on Education.* London, Falmer.

———. (2000) *Citizenship for the 21st Century: An International Perspective on Education.* London, Falmer.

Cogan, John, David Grossman & Mei-hui Liu (2000) Citizenship: The democratic imagination in a global/local context, *Social Education*, 64(1), pp. 48–52.

Cornfield, Michael (2008) Come and play: Citizenship and the internet, *The Hedgehog Review*, 10(3), pp. 66–79.

Department of Homeland Security (2008) *Estimates of the Unauthorized Immigrant Population Residing in the US, January 2007.* Office of Immigration Statistics, http://www.dhs/gov/xlibrary/assets/statistics/Publications/ois_ill_pe_2007.pdf (accessed 13 December 2008).

Fine, Michelle, Reva Jaffe-Walter, Pedro Pedraza, Valerie Futch & Brett Stoudt (2007) Swimming: On oxygen, resistance, and possibility for immigrant youth under siege, *Anthropology and Education Quarterly*, 38(1), pp. 76–96.

Galston, William (2004) Civic education and political participation, *PS: Political Science and Politics*, 37(2),http://eee.apsanet.org (accessed 29 September 2004).

Gibboney, Richard (2008) Why an undemocratic capitalism has brought public education to its knees: A manifesto, *Phi Delta Kappan*, 90(1), pp. 21–31.

Hess, Diana (2008) Democratic education to reduce the divide, *Social Education*, 72(7), pp. 373–376.

Hesseldahl, Arik (2008) Bringing broadband to the urban poor, *BusinessWeek Online*, 31 December, p. 7, http://www.businessweek.com/technology/content/dec2008/tc20081230_015542.htm (accessed 15 May 2009).

Horrigan, John (2009) *Stimulating Broadband: If Obama Builds It, Will They Log On? Pew Internet and American Life Project*, http://www.pewinternet.org/Reports/2009/Stimulating-Broadband-If-Obama-builds-it-will-They-log-on.aspx (accessed 15 May 2009).

Joel, Stephen (2007) My obligations during an immigration crackdown, *School Administrator*, 64(10), pp. 14–15.

Justice, Benjamin (2008) Looking back to see ahead: Some thoughts on the history of civic education in the United States, in Beth Rubin & James M. Giarelli (eds.) *Civic Education for Diverse Citizens in Global Times: Rethinking Theory and Practice.* New York, Lawrence Erlbaum Associates, pp. 239–261.

Levine, Peter (2009) The civic opportunity gap, *Educational Leadership*, 66(8), pp. 20–25.

Lutkus, Anthony & Andrew Weiss (2007) *The Nation's Report Card: Civics 2006 (NCES 2007–476), U.S. Department of Education, National Center for Education Statistics.* Washington, DC, U.S. Government Printing Office, http://nces.ed.gov/nationsreportcard/pubs/main2006/2007476.asp (accessed 18 May 2009).

McConnell, T. (2008) Not by votes alone: The vital imperative of restoring the civic mission of schools, *Social Education*, 72(6), pp. 312–313.

Merryfield, Merry (2008) Scaffolding social studies for global awareness, *Social Education*, 72(7), pp. 363–366.

National Council for the Social Studies (1994) *Expectations of Excellence.* Washington, DC, Author.

National Education Association (1916) *The Reorganization of the Secondary School Curriculum.* Washington, DC, Commission on the Reorganization of Secondary Education.

Niemi, Nancy & Richard Niemi (2007. Partisanship, participation, and political trust as taught (or not) in high school history and government classes, *Theory and Research in Social Education*, 35(1), pp. 32–61.

Obama, Barack (2008) Connecting and empowering all Americans through technology and innovation, http://www.barackobama.com/pdf/issues/technology/Fact_Sheet_Innovation_and_Technology.pdf (accessed 13 December 2008).

Passel, J. & D. Cohn (2008) *US Population Projections 2005–2050*. Washington, DC, Pew Research Center, Social & Demographic Trends, Pew Hispanic Center.

Pederson, Patricia & John J. Cogan (2000) Developing democratic values: The case of the USA, *Asia Pacific Journal of Education*, 20(1), pp. 93–105.

Pew Research Center (2008a) *Post Election Perspectives*. Pew Research Center Publications, http://pewresearch.org/pubs/1039/post-election-perspectives (accessed 25 November 2008).

———. (2008b) *Young Voters in the 2008 Election*. Pew Research Center Publications, http://pewresearch.org/pubs/1031/young-voters-in-the-2008-election (accessed 25 November 2008).

Pew Research Center for the People and the Press (2008) *Internet's Broader Role in Campaign 2008. Social Networking and Online Videos Take Off*, http://people-press.org/report/384/internets-broader-role-in-campaign-2008 (accessed 6 February 2009).

Polychroniou, Chronis (2008) Henry Giroux: Rethinking the promise of critical education under an Obama regime, *Truthout*, (interview), http://www.truthout.org/article/henry-giroux-rethinking-promise-critical-education (accessed 5 December 2008).

Putnam, Robert (2007) E Pluribus Unum: Diversity and community in the twenty-first century (the John Skytte Lecture), *Scandinavian Political Studies*, 30(2), pp. 137–174.

Ross, E. Wayne (2004) Negotiating the politics of citizenship education, *PS: Political Science and Politics*, 37(2), http://www.apsanet.org (accessed 29 September 2004).

Sassen, Saskia (2005) The repositioning of citizenship and alienage: Emergent subjects and spaces for politics, *Globalizations*, 2(1), pp. 79–94.

Scott, Thomas (2004) Pedagogy for global citizenship: Resisting standardization and high stakes testing in an age of globalization, *Pacific-Asian Education*, 16(1), pp. 17–29.

———. (2008) The 2008 election in the United States: A new direction for education? *Cahiers Pedagogiques*, htto://www.cahiers-pedagogiques.com/article.php3?id_article=4020 (accessed 2 November 2008).

ServiceNation (2008) *Transcript: ServiceNation Presidential Forum at Columbia University, September 11, 2008*, http://www.clipsandcomment.com/2008/09/11/transcript-servicenation-presidential-forum-at-columbia-university (accessed 3 December 2008).

Sneed, Maree (2007) Questioning immigration status when students enroll, *School Administrator*, 64(10), p. 12.

Spiro, Peter (2008) *Beyond Citizenship: American Identity after Globalization*. New York, Oxford University Press.

Stover, Del (2008) Caught in the middle, *American School Board Journal*, September, pp. 24–27.

Tyack, David (2003) *Seeking Common Ground*. Cambridge, MA, Harvard University Press.

United States Census Bureau (2005) Texas becomes nation's newest 'majority-minority' state, Census Bureau announces, U.S. Census Bureau News, CB05–118, http://www.census.gov/Press-Release/www/releases/archives/population/005514.html (accessed 13 December 2008).

Westheimer, J. & J. Kahne (2004) What kind of citizen? The politics of educating for democracy, *American Educational Research Journal*, 41(2), pp. 237–269.

Zakaria, Fareed (2008) *The Post-American World*. New York, W.W. Norton.
Zehr, Mary Ann (2007) Amid immigration debate, settled ground, *Education Week*, 26(39), 6 June, pp. 1–13.
———. (2008) Iowa school district left coping with immigration raid's impact, *Education Week*, 21 May, p. 7.

12 The State and the Citizen in Mexican Civic Education

An Evolving Story

Bradley A.U. Levinson

INTRODUCTION

In this chapter, I sketch the history of the relationship between modern state formation, the inculcation of citizenship subjectivities and the development of the curricular space called civic education in Mexico. I place most emphasis on contemporary developments at the secondary level since 1993. In developing this account, I am concerned with illuminating the complicated and uneven relationship between civil society, the state and the forms that civic education takes. While it may appear easy from policy documents to identify the prevailing historical trends in Mexican citizenship education—from 'socialist' solidarity to national (albeit authoritarian) unity to neo-liberal entrepreneurialism—the reality on the ground is in fact more complicated. The picture that emerges is of a loosely coupled, internally complex state, partially responsive to civil society concerns and globally circulating discourses, and an even more loosely coupled relationship between centralised educational bureaucracy and local educational practice. Rather than engage in much explicit theorisation, I try to let the unfolding narrative relate the key theoretical points about how the state may try to use civic education to form citizens, and how such efforts may succeed or fail on the ground.

AFTER THE REVOLUTION: THE VICISSITUDES OF THE STATE AND CIVIC EDUCATION IN MEXICO

The 1917 Mexican Constitution, forged during the years of the revolution against the dictatorship of Porfirio Diaz, is an updated version of the original Liberal Constitution of 1857. It remains the law in Mexico. Although the constitution provides for a progressive federal republic, with a separation of executive, judicial and legislative powers, a bicameral congress and considerable state and municipal autonomy, the reality in post-revolutionary Mexico has been distinct. Deeply rooted in the habits of colonial and dictatorial rule, Mexico quickly turned into what many have called a presidentialist regime. The concentration of power in the president's office led to a subordinate judiciary and a rubber-stamp legislature. By 1929, the president had formed the political party that eventually came to be known as the Institutional Revolutionary Party (*Partido Revolucionario Institucional* or PRI). Drawing together different sectors of society (skilled labour, the peasantry, business groups, etc.), the PRI developed a disciplined corporatist machine that helped identify the party with the state and perpetuate single-party rule. Importantly, the national teachers' union (SNTE) effectively came to serve as one of the bastions of PRI support. Although a nominally democratic nation, for over seventy years the PRI ruled Mexico with an iron hand, using a combination of carrot and stick, and sometimes outright electoral fraud, to keep itself in power. In addition to holding a constant majority in the Congress and controlling all major ministry appointments, the PRI controlled most mayoralties and virtually all state governorships.

It was not until the late 1970s that significant electoral reforms began to open the possibility for meaningful opposition politics in Mexico. Several important mayoralties and governorships fell to opposition parties during the 1980s, and in 1988 the PRI resorted to massive electoral fraud in order to reclaim the presidency from the renegade candidate Cuauhtémoc Cárdenas. The PRI attempted to recover legitimacy throughout the 1990s by agreeing to further electoral reforms and conducting more transparent business, yet certain democratic gains were irreversible. Economic crisis deepened, and so too did the presence of new democratic actors in civil society determined to force the peaceful resolution of social problems, through civil disobedience if necessary. Chief amongst these non-governmental organisations were those devoted to human rights, women's rights, indigenous peoples, economic justice and the environment.

Throughout these changes, the national ministry of public education, called the *Secretaría de Educación Pública*, or simply SEP, has played an important role. An ideological child of the revolution, the SEP was created in 1921 to advance the integrative and developmentalist agenda of the nascent state. Modeled on the French system, and highly centralised in Mexico City, the huge bureaucracy of the SEP now controls most of the formal educational enterprise in Mexico. Through the operation of most teacher education programmes, the hiring of all teachers and the production of common text-books for all of basic education, the SEP has historically been a key instrument of state formation and the creation of national identity (Joseph & Nugent 1994; Ornelas 1995). Important modernisation reforms since 1993 have arguably curtailed the power of the SEP. For instance, administrative decentralisation has put the states in charge of budgeting and teacher hiring; and since the declaration of 'middle basic education', or *secundaria* (grades seven to nine, roughly ages twelve to fifteen), as part of the cycle of compulsory schooling, text-books for this level are now produced outside the SEP. Still, matters of curriculum and educational planning remain highly concentrated in the SEP.

The practice of civic education in Mexico has a history that is roughly co-terminous with the SEP itself. Before the revolution and the creation of the SEP, Mexican liberals from the time of Benito Juárez forward had implemented modest civic education curriculum in public primary schools, but these only served a very small portion of the population. It was not until the period after the revolution that civics (*civismo*) became prominent. Primary school included very basic lessons in government, but above all, civics appears to have been taught experientially through nationalist civic ceremonies, which attempted to inculcate a strong sense of national pride and identity and allegiance to the state (see, for example, Vaughan 1997). This was to be expected. Strong regional loyalties and sentiments had animated much of the revolutionary fervour, and throughout the 1920s and into the 1930s the anti-clerical state continued to wage a war against Christian rebels in different parts of the republic. This 'hot' war was thus accompanied by a colder war of civic education for the hearts and minds of children.

From early on, the SEP decided to focus much of its attention on the kind of civic education that would be imparted through the *secundaria*. In 1928 a separate Office of Secondary Education was created, and at this time the *secundaria* became explicitly conceived as an institution serving the 'adolescent' life stage (Levinson 1999; Meneses Morales 1986). Moisés Sáenz, considered by most the founder of the *secundaria*, had studied at Columbia University with John Dewey. The Mexican *secundaria* proposed by Sáenz emphasised the importance of curtailing selfish individualism and creating a sense of social solidarity. The goal of the *secundaria* was to balance the desire for a curriculum more specialised than the *primaria*—a curriculum that would offer students the chance to explore their vocational options—with the themes of integration and national unity. Such origins reveal an implicit emphasis on what we might call the 'co-operative citizen'.

The presidency of Lázaro Cárdenas (1934–1940), the great populist reformer, oversaw a significant growth in secondary enrollments. Now with an avowedly socialist educational programme, children of workers were strongly encouraged to continue their schooling as the *secundaria* turned more 'technical' and the curriculum included more hours devoted to practical, productive activities. Yet the teaching of history and civics was also given renewed emphasis, and in 1932 the curriculum added a course in 'civic culture' to the other required academic courses for each of the three years. This course focused on political, economic and legal 'problems' in Mexico. By 1937, the course in civic culture had been changed to 'Socialist Information and Practice' and students increasingly learned about class conflict and imperialism as a way of understanding Mexican history. They participated in student government and mutual aid societies to practise co-operative social work, and made frequent trips to shops and factories in order to gain a fuller appreciation of working-class life (Meneses Morales 1988, pp. 115–119).

The short-lived socialist experiment ended abruptly in 1940, when presidential power changed to the more conservative Ávila Camacho. Under Ávila Camacho's first education secretary, Véjar Vázquez, the school became the 'school of love' and then the 'school of unity'. As the *secundaria* continued to expand, then, official educational discourse reinstated the signal importance of 'national unity' and reconciliation above class struggle.

As the Mexican state entered a period of more comfortable alliance with national and transnational capital, the official discourse of this period constructed the interests of the nation, of subordinated classes and of capital as convergent; each party could win in the formula for national development, modernisation and the stabilisation of a 'revolutionary' regime. This formula provided the basic continuity in policy and practice around the *secundaria* more or less until 1992. Indeed, in the period from 1950 to 1970, there was a 1,000 percent increase in *secundaria* enrollments, mainly due to the growing participation of female students, who came to form half the student body in most *secundaria*s by the late 1970s.

From 1992 to 1993, a series of educational 'modernisation' measures included an important amendment to the Constitutional Article Number 3, which made *secundaria* attendance compulsory, thereby raising the stakes of civic education at that level. The new law also stipulated teaching the values of critical reflection, democratic participation and human rights. From 1993 to 1999, civic education was granted just three hours per week in both the first and second years of *secundaria*. A new subject, Educational Orientation (*Orientación Educativa*), was added to the third year, along with a three-hour elective course determined according to local needs and interests. Many social workers, psychologists and 'vocational counsellors' whose work had been restricted to vocational aptitude tests or discussions about sexual development made their first regular appearance in classrooms at this time.

THE CREATION OF THE NEW FCE PROGRAMME OF 1999

The next serious reform of Mexican civic education began in the mid-1990s. During the last PRI presidential administration (1994–2000), the secretary of education initiated an ambitious new civic education programme for all three years of middle basic education (*secundaria*). The programme eventually came to be known as 'Civic and Ethical Formation' (*Formación Cívica y Etica*, or FCE).[1] The policy process for the reform of civic education in Mexico received a strong impulse, according to many, from then president Ernesto Zedillo (1994–2000), who had actually served as secretary of education during the prior presidential administration, from 1988 to 1994. Zedillo had been the primary architect of the modernisation reforms of 1992 and 1993, which made participatory and 'relevant' education a cornerstone of national development. Zedillo's presidency highlighted the goals of achieving educational 'equity, quality and relevance' (*pertinencia*).

Clearly Zedillo addressed social concerns that had been brewing for over a decade. In previous research, I have identified at least three powerful societal discourses that formed and expanded throughout the 1980s and 1990s. Each of these discourses expressed certain understandings of democracy, and each would impact the eventual formation of a new programme for citizenship education. Such discourses emerged out of rather different social sectors and movements, but each articulated a set of existential concerns that cut across broad sectors of Mexican society. Each also highlighted a different set of 'values' that needed to be recovered or constructed.

One discourse, which I call 'lost values' (*valores perdidos*), drew attention to the signs of what many observers call 'social disintegration', such as increased violence, corruption, divorce and disregard for adult authority. The assumption made by this discourse was that traditional values of respect, honesty and obedience had once effectively ordered society, but had fallen into disuse. There was a strong sense of proper social hierarchy having become challenged and turned upside down. Most powerfully articulated through conservative Catholic organisations such as the national 'Parents' Union' (UNPF), but also evident amongst older public school-teachers who lamented the waning of national pride and school discipline, the discourse on lost values resonated with a much broader public. The often explicit solution proposed by this discourse was the recovery of 'lost' values—typically through religious education or other kinds of catechistic instruction, and the reassertion of paternal control.

Another discourse, which I call the active and 'critical citizen' (*el ciudadano crítico*), highlighted the importance of creating deeper democratic habits and a political culture that would support a democratic transition over the longer term. Most strongly articulated by a generation of left-leaning Mexican intellectuals and leaders who had come of age in the political opposition to the PRI-dominated state, the discourse of the 'critical citizen' called for a new participatory sensibility amongst citizens, most of whom were seen as having grown complacent, fatalistic or too accustomed to state largesse. The discourse of the critical citizen implicitly valued equality over hierarchy—and prioritised gender equity. Although originating among the well educated, this discourse resonated across broad sectors of society that had been irrevocably changed by experiences of immigration and/or consumption of popular media.

The third discourse, which I call 'accountability' (*rendición de cuentas*), called for greater transparency in public management and more valid and neutral forms of evaluation in assessing educational 'quality'. One of the important assumptions of this discourse was that the goals of transparency and quality called for both institutional and personal transformations. On the one hand, new kinds of institutional arrangements, such as the creation of a quasi-independent National Institute for Educational Evaluation (INEE) or the implementation of a merit-based assessment of teacher performance, would leverage higher quality and greater public account-ability. On the other hand, the discourse called for the cultivation of a new subjectivity which placed responsibility for public outcomes—such as student learning—on individuals as well as institutions. In this sense, the new democratic citizen had to learn to become more responsible—that is, accountable—for his/her actions.

THE NEW CIVIC EDUCATION AND THE
INFLUENCE OF SOCIETAL DISCOURSES

An analysis of two key documents—the *Annotated Program of Studies*, and the *Teachers' Guide* (SEP 2000, 2001)—provides the major organis-ing themes and principles of the course in FCE. Throughout the text, the authors emphasise a communicative pedagogical stance and a new role for the teacher as facilitator of knowledge construction rather than provider of information. Such a new role is intimately linked to the urgent need for stu-dents to take control of their learning and to begin practising democratic virtues:

> [The program] seeks to strengthen the student's capacity for critical analysis, for group work and participation in both individual and col-lective decision-making processes based on the values of a democratic life. (SEP 2000, p. 14)
> The students will learn equally from their classmates and their teachers, manifesting in this way the importance of a dialogical and horizontal educational process. (SEP 2000, pp. 21–22)

The documents criticise the heavy emphasis on information in the previ-ous curriculum, for instance:

> in [the old civics] the contents were dominated by detailed description of our public institutions and the recital of human rights, to the detri-ment of a more systematic development of abilities and attitudes that might lead to greater civic participation. Even though important con-cepts and information were presented, because they showed no clear relation to their lives such concepts could not be easily experienced by the students as a priority in their education. In the new subject (FCE), we seek to make the connections between civics and students' lives more apparent. (SEP 2001, p. 3)

Correspondingly, the new plan established a number of 'pedagogical and didactic guidelines' for teachers. Such guidelines include clear directions to 'relate themes to students' lives' and to 'foment ... attitudes of respect and acceptance that encourage freedom of expression for all, taking special care to promote gender equity' (SEP 2001, p. 3). Clearly, these new guidelines create a significant break with the older, teacher-centred approach to civics instruction. Responding to the call for a more 'relevant' education, they also share key postulates with the discourse of the critical citizen.

The three years of *secundaria* study were organised around three main themes running throughout the FCE program. The first theme, focused on ethics, consists of 'reflection about human nature and human values'. Before long, the course centres on the perennial issue of gender relations and has students discussing what it means to 'be a woman and be a man' (SEP 2000, p. 39). The second theme considers both 'problems and possibilities for adolescents and youth'. A major section of the first year, called Youth and Goals (*juventud y proyectos*), opens an explicit reflection about the promises of adolescence. Students are encouraged to project their aspirations into the future, to imagine their possibilities. The language appears borrowed from humanistic psychology: 'personal realisation', 'life cycle and life goals' and 'human potential'. The first year ends with forty hours of instructional time spent exploring how to 'live in society'. Concepts include interdependence, communication, emotional connection (*afectividad*), enjoyment (*gozo*), solidarity and reciprocity, as well as the 'spirit of service, creativity, and work' (SEP 2000, p. 50).

In the second year under the rubric of democracy, students learn about the 'values of living together' (*valores de la convivencia*), as well as the more specific 'civic values and citizenship formation'. What are considered the key values of democracy are imparted to students: liberty, equality, equity, justice, respect, tolerance, solidarity and responsibility (SEP 2000, p. 55). After exploring the 'values of living together' in the immediate *secundaria* context, teachers and students make the leap to the nation, exploring concepts such as 'nationalism, love of country, and national pride' as well as 'unity and cultural pluralism'. Students are asked to examine the 'possibility of participating in, and influencing, matters of national interest' (SEP 2000, p. 85). Finally, the second year ends with a further opening out to the study of 'humanity' and the 'relationship to the environment' (SEP 2000, p. 89).

The third and final year centres on traditional civics concepts of 'social organisation, democracy, citizenship participation, and forms of government in Mexico', in other words, the constitution, the political structure (elections, parties, etc.), the governance structure (federal, state and municipal agencies) and the separation of powers (executive, legislative and judicial).

The 1999 FCE programme ends with an ambitious final project meant to foster 'responsibility, collective decision-making, and participation'. Through this project, students should learn how to arrive at decisions through consensus; how to conduct an empirical investigation and divide the work fairly amongst themselves; and how to present the results of an investigation to authorities and peers in order to effect positive change (SEP 2000, pp. 103–104).

Clearly, the Mexican FCE programme places primary emphasis on the enactment and embodiment of democratic values in everyday classroom practice. Not surprisingly given Mexico's history, the values and dispositions of democracy include a strong emphasis on group work, solidarity and the collective good. This is one of the key aspects of Mexican education for democratic citizenship that would seem to distinguish it from those strictly liberal models sponsored by the countries of the North, which tend to place higher emphasis on deliberation and the rights of possessive individualism. Mexico's strong history of collective traditions and identities may have served authoritarianism well, but a democratic education must now balance the forces of collectivism with a focus on individual rights and conscience. Yet in the articulation of this balance, the FCE still highlights the importance of collective life and responsibilities. Individual conscience is no longer prescribed, but nonetheless must be developed intersubjectively. The student-citizen is the subject of a political imaginary in which personal reflexivity, respectful dialogue and collective responsibility are paramount. Moreover, an analysis of the major themes and goals of the FCE programme shows the authors attempting to address the concerns about values expressed in each of the societal discourses identified earlier, yet still anchored most strongly in what I call the discourse of the 'critical citizen'. Thus, as the FCE bears the imprint of its authors' and sponsors' personal and ideological trajectories; of international experiences and familiarity with international materials; and of the intention to be as inclusive as possible of societal concerns.

ANOTHER VISION OF CITIZENSHIP: EDUCATION FOR A CULTURE OF LAWFULNESS

The year 2000 was a watershed year in Mexican political history in terms of democratic promise. In July, the long-standing single-party rule was effectively ended in Mexico with the election of the opposition candidate, Vicente Fox, and with the achievement of an opposition majority in the bicameral Congress. Fox's party, *Partido de Acción Nacional* (PAN), made inroads into all major ministries and significant new appointments within the SEP.

After 2000, it was the subsecretary for basic education, Lorenzo Gómez-Morín Fuentes, who really drove the development of further civic education reform. Hoping to expand the impact of civic education and 'articulate' its components across different educational levels, Gómez-Morín initiated a comprehensive set of reforms aimed at building an integral process of 'citizenship formation' (*formación ciudadana*). As part of this campaign, Gómez-Morín commissioned the development of curricula in FCE for the fifth and sixth grades of primary school, as well as the first year or two of high school, or *educación media superior*. In 2001, he sponsored an unprecedented agreement for collaborative work between the Ministry of Education, the Ministry of the Interior (*Gobernación*) and the Federal Electoral Institute (IFE). These three agencies all have some aspect of citizenship education included among their various responsibilities, yet never before had they worked together in any systematic way. Finally, at the *secundaria* level, Gómez-Morín brought to the SEP a pet programme for citizenship education that he had piloted in his home state of Baja California. This programme, originally called Culture of Lawfulness (CL), was adapted to the Mexican context, where it has come to be called Citizenship Formation, Towards a Culture of Lawfulness (*Formación Ciudadana, Hacia una Cultura de la Legalidad*). The FCE programme, meanwhile, in operation for less than two years, was allowed to continue as it was.

The original version of education for the CL is a project of the Washington DC–based National Strategy Information Center (NSIC), a conservative think tank created in the 1980s by Roy Godson, a professor of government at Georgetown University. With a background in intelligence work, Godson is a specialist in transnational security, organised crime and anti-corruption programmes. He developed the CL framework primarily through his collaborative work in Sicily, Italy, where he played a major role in combating the Mafia and helping create what has come to be called the 'Sicilian Renaissance'. Later, he refined his ideas about the programme through further anti-crime work in Hong Kong.

In a 'Guide to Developing a Culture of Lawfulness', Godson (2000) lays out some of the key principles and assumptions that guide his work. The concept of culture is central. According to Godson, regulatory and law enforcement approaches to crime prevention alone will not work. Rather:

> what is needed is a complementary strategy that amounts to a fundamental shift in values. The regulatory approach needs to be accompanied by society or culture sympathetic to the rule of law. (Godson 2000, p. 3)

The discourses on citizenship and democracy are quite muted in Godson's work, while the relation between the 'rule of law' and democracy is left largely implicit. Nevertheless, Godson's programme has been tied to efforts at creating greater democratic 'governability' in many 'transition' regimes. In the case of Mexico, Godson's programme has been appropriated as part of a broader effort to 'form citizens' for an emerging democratic society. In the political imaginary of the Gómez-Morín administration, a good citizen is one who knows the law, obeys it and helps others to obey it as well.

In Godson's scheme to create a culture of lawfulness, school-based education is crucial. He calls schools the 'most important, widespread, and strategic civic education organizations' and he specifically mentions the 'early secondary' years as the best time to 'reach children before they become involved in serious criminality and come to take it for granted that they live in a culture of corruption' (Godson 2000, p. 5). Out of this focus on education, Godson and his staff helped create specific curriculum materials for school instruction (Schneider 1999). In an effort to battle drug-related crime and corruption in the large border cities of Tijuana and Mexicali in the late 1990s, he was invited by then secretary of education Lorenzo Gómez-Morín to pilot the programme in Baja, California. Collaborating with local curriculum specialists, a thirty-six-lesson course, organised into three separate units, was designed for students in their third year (ninth grade) of *secundaria*: Values, Self-Esteem and a Culture of Lawfulness; Organised Crime and Corruption; and Furthering the Rule of Law, Resistance Techniques and What Students Can Do.

Among the more prominent curriculum materials were a Spanish translation of William Golding's classic novel *Lord of the Flies*, which tells the story of how several shipwrecked boys succumb to their 'savage' instincts and follow the most ruthless leader, and the 1990 movie *Goodfellas*, which portrays the cruelty of Mafia activity. Each of these materials appears to serve as the basis for dialogue and reflection about how to avoid the temptations of illegal power. Curiously, the school programme appears to combine a more dialogical pedagogy, like the FCE, with heavy-handed moralising. On the one hand, students are encouraged to critically discern corruption and other instances of the abuse of public power. On the other hand, students are also taught clear rights and wrongs as stipulated by existing law, and they are encouraged to assume an obedient stance vis-à-vis the law. The course is much more prescriptive than the FCE, and much more academic as well. Demonstrating thorough knowledge of laws and constitutional principles is deemed absolutely prerequisite to the formation of proper attitudes and behaviour.

Judging the programme a rousing success,[2] Subsecretary Gómez-Morín arrived on the national scene in 2001 eager to expand it to other states. In Baja California, in the same year, the programme expanded to cover approximately twenty thousand students. Meanwhile, other states were learning of the innovation in Baja, and soon the programme was being piloted in *secundarias* in four other Mexican states (mostly border states or states with histories of strong drug trafficking), as well as two of the 'delegations' within the federal district of Mexico City. By 2004, some 522 schools, 869 teachers and 88,000 students were involved with the programme, and it was projected to expand on a pilot basis to yet five more states.[3] However, by 2007 the implementation of the new educational reform ECL had never been fully incorporated into national curriculum or policy. Rather, in the spirit of decentralisation, many Mexican states opted to develop ECL (Education in the Culture of Lawfulness) as one of a small number of options that *secundarias* could choose to implement for a third-year state-specific elective course.

Clearly, the pedagogical premises and conceptions of democracy of the FCE and the ECL differ in significant ways. Among the core meanings of

ECL is the postulate that to be a 'good citizen' is to fight crime, and hence one must know and appreciate the law, thereby contributing to a 'culture of lawfulness'. To be a good citizen is also to obey the state rather than one's possible clientelistic obligations outside the law. In contrast to the FCE, where the model of the 'critical citizen' is prominent, ECL is more fundamentally rooted in societal discourses on 'lost values' and 'accountability'. On the one hand, the programme suggests a golden age when citizens firmly valued the law, before the corrosive influence of extralegal actors, such as drug traffickers (*narcotraficantes*). Now such values have been eroded, if not lost. ECL proposes to recover these values through a blend of moralising, cautionary tale and exhortation. On the other hand, the programme is anchored in a strong respect for formal procedural law, and the kind of transparency or accountability that ideally accompanies such law. In a country like Mexico, struggling with a legacy of violent corruption and the public cynicism that such corruption engenders, such a focus resonates strongly throughout civil society.

THE 2006 REFORM AND BEYOND: IMPLEMENTATION CHALLENGES AND THE CONUNDRUM OF THE STATE

In 1993 a strongly democratic conception of citizenship first appeared in Mexican education, with the reinstatement of civic education as a separate subject in the context of a 'critical' and 'participatory' education reform. Although 1993 marked the heyday of neo-liberal political economic reforms in Mexico (especially the sale of state enterprises and the shrinking of the public sector), educational policy did not wholly reflect neo-liberal priorities and rationalities. If anything, this trend toward heterogeneity was strengthened in 1999 with the launching of the new FCE programme, which only dimly reflected neo-liberal themes of competition, accountability, entrepreneurialism and individual responsibility. Meanwhile, the ECL programme with its more conservative, neo-liberal version of democratic citizenship education, has still never achieved national status, and it probably never will.

It is clear, then, that at the level of federal civic education policy there may be coexisting and even contradictory initiatives and programmes within the same state ministry. Such variation may reflect the different routes by which global and societal discourses and concerns have been distilled through the policy formation process, as well as the different contexts and commitments out of which policy makers emerge. Prior to 1993, there is little evidence that civic education was open to multiple interpretations through the policy process. An analysis of policy documents, curriculum and text-books generally yields a picture of ideological and organisational consistency. After 1993, and especially after 1999, the picture appears more complex. This may be due to the growing complexity of the SEP itself, as well as a certain democratisation of the policy process, in which the state appears more responsive to civil society concerns and less prone to mere orchestration from above.

Critical scholarship on Latin American education has tended to lament the so-called 'neo-liberal state', seeing it as buckling under to global monetary prerogatives and abandoning goals of social justice for goals of economic efficiency and growth (e.g. Ball, Fischman & Gvirtz 2003). Yet the state is never in any case unitary or monolithic. It rarely exercises ideological discipline or coherence across its different branches and ministries. It may seem quite solid in its self-presentation, and quite unitary in its policy pronouncements, but in fact, a closer examination reveals all kinds of fissures and contradictions. Just by looking closely at the SEP as one small corner of the Mexican state, we can already see such contradictions.

What about the challenge of translating policy and curriculum into pedagogical practice on the ground? Here, too, there is much to say about the contradictions and loosely coupled relations between a federal bureaucracy and the states, regions and schools charged with implementing policy. I will close by briefly discussing some of these challenges and the ways they question the intentionality of the state. If teachers may be described as 'agents of the state', their manner of implementing civic education still largely betrays the intended new democratic citizen imagined by state policy.

Recent field studies in Mexico have revealed the challenges and contradictions of implementation (e.g. Araujo et al. 2005; Elizondo et al. 2007; Juarez Hernandez 2006; Landeros Aguirre 2006; Levinson 2004). Most of these studies were conducted in the early 2000s, after the 1999 FCE was implemented. The single most common finding is that teachers have largely failed to adopt new pedagogical styles and methods. They may be discussing aspects of democracy, but not modeling it.

When I posed the question, 'What is the greatest challenge posed to the successful implementation of the new FCE program?' the almost unanimous response of policy makers, administrators and teachers alike was some version of 'teacher training'. Teachers themselves, when discussing their experiences with FCE, often call for more training and better in-service 'courses', which currently are only sporadically offered and of poor quality. With few exceptions, they recognise that their own training does not adequately prepare them to teach the course. They even note that the new programmes explicitly call for teachers to 'change', to adopt a new 'stance' in relation to their students, but that the guidance and resources needed to effect such a change are rarely forthcoming (Levinson 2004). And few incentives exist to encourage reticent teachers to examine and change their old teaching habits.

Part of this problem is clearly structural. The national teachers' union in Mexico is powerful and corrupt, and at the level of the *secundaria* hiring often occurs through favoritism, seniority and a system of gradual accumulation of 'hours'. Once they acquire some hours, and begin accumulating more over the years, it is virtually impossible for teachers to lose them. Thus, when FCE was created as a new subject in 1999, it was staffed mostly with psychologists and social workers who'd been teaching the 1993 subject *Orientación Educativa*, and who'd thereby gained an initial foothold in the regular school classroom or with old 'civic education' teachers. Even though new FCE teachers are now being produced in the normal schools, there are few positions available to them until the current generation of teachers retires. Moreover, the corps of in-service teacher trainers is mostly drawn from the regional set of *jefes de enseñanza*, who are also in their positions due to seniority in the union hierarchy (*escalafón*). Most *jefes de enseñanza* come into their positions as a kind of pre-retirement perk after having served as school principals or state-wide administrators. Many years may have passed since they taught in a classroom, and there is little accountability for their job performance.

This same system of hourly hiring also accounts for the structural obstacles in creating a truly collegial, joint process of curriculum planning and teaching. Teachers come and go throughout the schoolday, often juggling several jobs, both in and out of schools. They are rarely paid for 'planning hours' beyond their actual student contact hours in classrooms. Teachers of FCE tend to have the most fractured, mobile schedules of all. Thus, the goal of teacher collaboration (*trabajo colegiado*) in planning and teaching is dead on arrival. Such collaboration is one of the main goals of the 2006 reform, with the 'transversal' themes of environment, gender and values supposedly at the heart of joint planning.[4] Little of this is practically realised.

Finally, there are also rather more cultural factors that militate against effective implementation of democratic citizenship education. Because Mexican educational policy making has always been subject to the vicissitudes of the six-year presidential administrations known as *sexenios*, continuity has often been difficult to achieve. Teachers that have been in schools for a number of years will note the grand rhetoric that accompanies the inauguration of a new *sexenio*; they observe the arrival and departure of educational reforms, and they see that very little changes in the end. Mixed with this sense of inertia is often a more active critique of the duplicity of the state. Many teachers have developed a profound suspicion of educational authorities, seeing them as willfully complicit with an agenda of obfuscation, projecting polished surfaces that have little substance behind them. They see training programmes as mere exercises in 'simulation', conducted to fulfill bureaucratic imperatives but lacking substance or seriousness. Ultimately, this is a problem of trust that will take years to address.

These are just a few of the challenges faced by the state in implementing effective civic education reform. The ironies are abundant. The Mexican state has decentralised important aspects of educational decision making and hiring, but continues to centralise the curriculum process in the national ministry. And even though the curriculum process is still centralised, there is little ideological coherence between, say, current state economic policy and the core principles of the citizenship education curriculum. Finally, the imposing power of the state, historically, accounts for a good deal of the dysfunctional structures, attitudes and relationships that complicate reform. Yet paradoxically, a strong state will still be necessary to break the anti-democratic power of the national teachers' union, facilitate civil society co-operation and stakeholder buy-in and build professional capacity in local states and regions. The story of Mexican civic education for democracy continues to evolve.

ACKNOWLEDGMENTS

Some of the material presented in this chapter has been published previously in Bradley Levinson (2005) Programs for democratic citizenship education in Mexico's Ministry of Education: Local appropriations of global cultural flows, *Indiana Journal of Global Legal Studies*, 12(l), pp. 251–284. Permission to use this material has been granted by the Indiana University Press.

NOTES

1. In the Mexican lexicon, *educación* has always had a broader meaning than mere *instrucción*, and *formación* indicates a fuller approach than *educación*. While instruction, and even education, can refer to the transmission and acquisition of facts and knowledge through mental processes, formation points to habit and affect, with the intention of shaping forms of perception and conduct in everyday life. The Mexican *secundaria* has always presumed to be *formativo* and *integral* (holistic), thus the new FCE programme does not so much propose a new focus as recover and reinforce one of the *secundaria*'s perennial goals.
2. Using a survey instrument and focus groups, the NSIC itself has conducted an evaluation of the project in Baja California, and has claimed significant improvement in 'knowledge and attitudes' related to crime prevention (Godson & Kenney 2001). To my knowledge, no independent evaluation has been conducted.
3. The national education plan for 2001–2006 specifically mentions the goal of implementing the ECL programme in 50 percent of all Mexican *secundarias*—most of them urban—by the end of the administrative period.
4. In 2006, a newly modified version of FCE was unfolded as part of an ambitious reform of the entire *secundaria* curriculum. In its thematic content and pedagogical orientation, this version of FCE did not differ substantially from that of 1999. The same eight weekly hours were now distributed differently across the three years of *secundaria*, and changes were made mainly in thematic sequencing and pedagogical guidelines. Like the remainder of the new curriculum, learning outcomes were now phrased in terms of desirable 'competencies'. In many ways, the constructivist orientation and democratic ethos of the 1999 FCE were harbingers of the broader 2006 reform altogether. After 2006, all teachers were increasingly trained (and exhorted) to use more dialogical, participatory, engaged methods, and to centre instruction less on subject-matter

content and more on students' experiences and prior knowledge. One sign of the centrality of the FCE programme to broader school reform was the prominence of so-called 'transversal' themes which had previously been 'located' exclusively within FCE but which now were supposed to cut across virtually all school subjects and activities. Specifically, these transversal themes included environmental education, values education and education about sex and gender equity. By a process of interdisciplinary integration, it was hoped that students would gain a 'critical education' through which they would come to recognise the 'commitments and responsibilities that are incumbent upon them and the society in which they live' (SEP 2006, p. 20).

REFERENCES

Araujo-Olivera, Stella, Maria Teresa, Yurén Camarena, Marcos J. Estrada Ruíz & Miriam de la Cruz Reyes (2005) Respeto, democracia y política, negación del consenso: El caso de la formación cívica y ética en las escuelas de Morelos, *Revista Mexicana de Investigación Educativa*, 10(24), pp. 15–42.

Ball, Stephen, Gustavo Fischman & Silvina Gvirtz (2003) *Crisis and Hope: The Educational Hopscotch of Latin America*. New York, Routledge Falmer.

Elizondo, Huerta, Aurora, Anders Stig Christiansen & Dalia Ruiz Avila (2007) Democracia y ética en la escuela secundaria: Estudio de caso, *Revista Mexicana de Investigación Educativa*, 12(32), pp. 243–260.

Godson, Roy (2000) Guide to developing a culture of lawfulness. Paper presented at the Symposium on the Role of Civil Society in Countering Organized Crime: Global Implications of the Palermo, Sicily Renaissance, Palermo, Italy, 14 December.

Godson, Roy & Dennis J. Kenney (2001) Fostering a culture of lawfulness on the Mexico–US border: Evaluation of a pilot school-based program, in John Bailey & Jorge Chabat (eds.) *Transnational Crime and Public Security: Challenges to Mexico and the United States*. San Diego, Center for US-Mexican Studies, University of California/San Diego, pp. 410–440.

Joseph, Gilbert & Daniel Nugent (1994) *Everyday Forms of State Formation: Revolution and the Negotiation of Rule in Modern Mexico*. Durham, NC, Duke University Press.

Juarez Hernandez, Ana Francisca (2006) *Estrategias de Enseñanza en Formación Cívica y Ética en secundaria*. Mexico City, Departamento de Investigaciones Educativas.

Landeros Aguirre, Leticia Gabriela (2006) *Trayectorias y concepciones educativas en profesores de la asignatura Formación Cívica y Ética para la educación secundaria*. Mexico City, Departamento de Investigaciones Educativas.

Levinson, Bradley (1999) 'Una etapa siempre difícil': Concepts of adolescence and secondary education in Mexico, *Comparative Education Review*, 43(2), pp. 129–161.

———. (2004) Hopes and challenges for the new civic education in Mexico: Toward a democratic citizen without adjectives, *International Journal of Educational Development*, 24(3), pp. 269–282.

Meneses Morales, Ernesto (1986) *Tendencias Educativas Oficiales en México, 1911–1934*. Mexico, Centro de Estudios Educativos, Mexico City.

———. (1988) *Tendencias Educativas Oficiales en México, 1934–1964*. Mexico, Centro de Estudios Educativos. Mexico City.

Ornelas, Carlos (1995) *El sistema Educativo Mexicano*. Mexico City, Secretaría de Educación Pública/CIDE.

Schneider, Jane (1999) Educating against the Mafia: A report from Sicily, *Civnet's Journal for Civil Society*, 3 (accessed on 26 March 2008).

Secretaría de Educación Pública (2000) *Formación Cívica y Ética: Programas de estudio comentados.* Mexico City, Secretaría de Educación Pública.

———. (2001) *Formación Cívica y Ética, Educación Secundaria: Libro para el maestro.* Mexico City, Secretaría de Educación Pública.

———. (2006) *Plan de Estudios 2006: Educación Secundaria.* Mexico City, Secretaría de Educación Pública.

Vaughan, Mary Kay (1997) *Cultural Politics in Revolution: Teachers, Peasants, and Schools in Mexico, 1930–1940.* Tucson, University of Arizona Press.

13 Possibilities and Problems
Citizenship Education in a Multinational State: The Case of Canada

Alan Sears

INTRODUCTION

In 1838 John George Lambton, first Earl of Durham, was sent by the new Queen Victoria to British North America to try and sort out the mess created the year before by rebellions in the colonies of both Upper and Lower Canada (what are today the provinces of Ontario and Québec). In his influential report, Lord Durham (1839) wrote:

> I expected to find a contest between a government and a people: I found two nations warring in the bosom of a single state: I found a struggle, not of principles, but of races; and I perceived that it would be idle to attempt any amelioration of laws or institutions until we could first succeed in terminating the deadly animosity that now separates the inhabitants of Lower Canada into the hostile divisions of French and English.

Durham's proposed solutions to this clash of nations included the recommendation that the two colonies be united in the hope that French Canadians would eventually be assimilated into the dominant English majority.

While Durham's key ideas were initially adopted, their long-term failure, at least in terms of the hoped for assimilation and the creation thereby of a single Canadian nation, is well illustrated by a motion passed by the Canadian House of Commons in November of 2006 which states, 'That this House recognize that the Québécois[1] form a nation within a united Canada' (CBC News 2006). This gave parliamentary and state recognition to the multinational nature of the Canadian state, something Québec nationalists, as well as Aboriginal leaders, political scientists and social theorists, had been advocating for some time (Taylor & Laforest 1993; Resnick 1994).

The central argument of this chapter is that the persistent, complex and structural nature of diversity, including multinationalism, in Canada has played a critical role in shaping historic and contemporary policies and practices related to citizenship and citizenship education in the country.

The chapter will explore how this basic characteristic of the Canadian nation-state has both opened possibilities and presented its own particular set of problems to developing coherent and effective policies in these areas particularly in the context of globalisation.

THE DEEP DIVERSITY OF THE CANADIAN STATE

Contemporary factors related to globalisation, including changing patterns of migration and citizenship, have created 'a growing awareness of the multiethnic nature of most contemporary nation-states and the need to account for this aspect of pluralism in public policy' (Johnson & Joshee 2007, p. 3). For Canada this is not a particularly new phenomenon. As Kymlicka (2007) points out, 'issues of accommodating diversity have been central to Canada's history' (p. 39). Jaenen (1981), for example, argues that certain conditions of Canada's historical development uniquely suited it for pluralism. He posits four factors: the English–French dualism, which has been 'a fundamental characteristic of Canadian society' (p. 81) since the Loyalist migration at the end of the eighteenth century; the more diverse British, rather than exclusively English, nature of early Anglophone Canada; the separation of church and state and relative religious liberty that has always existed in Canada; and the fact that control over education was made a provincial, rather than a federal, responsibility. One might add to this list the presence of a range of Aboriginal peoples in Canadian territory as well as the significant immigrant minorities present in the country.

Joshee and Winton (2007) contend this diversity was recognised early on in legal and constitutional structures. They point out, for example, that the Royal Proclamation of 1763 recognised Aboriginal rights to self-government and the Québec Act of 1774 provided for maintaining the French language and culture even though the territory of Québec had come under British control. The same ethos is reflected in the constitutional arrangements that established the Canadian state in 1867. 'The founding compact of Canada', they write, 'implicitly recognized the value of retaining a connection with one's ancestral culture' (p. 22). Those constitutional arrangements included a division of powers between the federal and provincial governments, largely established to protect 'la nation canadienne francaise' (Morton 1993, p. 51; see also Taylor & Laforest 1993) and prevent the kind of assimilation advocated by Lord Durham. Provincial powers include exclusive legislative jurisdiction in key areas important to maintaining a sense of ethnic and national distinctiveness including education, culture and language.

Constitutional reform over the years since 1867 has broadened the range of national minorities accorded constitutional recognition and protection and has also embedded multiculturalism as an interpretive frame for the constitution (Kymlicka & Norman 2000; Kymlicka 2003). For example,

Aboriginal rights, including treaty rights, are affirmed in the Constitution Act of 1982. The act also establishes English and French as the official languages of the province of New Brunswick, largely to protect the place of the Acadian people who have a definite understanding of themselves as a national group within Canada. Central to the act is the Canadian Charter of Rights and Freedoms with a clause that states, 'This Charter shall be interpreted in a manner consistent with the preservation and enhancement of the multicultural heritage of Canadians' (Department of Justice 1982).

As Kymlicka (2003) points out, over the past several decades the trend across virtually all Western democracies has been toward greater recognition and accommodation of diversity in several ways: increased autonomy for national minorities; a move away from polices of assimilation of immigrants toward integration; and greater recognition of the rights of indigenous peoples. Canadian policies have largely followed these trends and have not been particularly unique. However, 'Canada is distinctive,' he argues, 'in having to deal with all three forms of diversity at the same time' and 'in the extent to which it has not only legislated but also constitutionalized, practices of accommodation' (p. 374).

The centrality of diversity in Canadian history and contemporary circumstances has been a key factor in shaping policy in citizenship and citizenship education. In Kymlicka's words, 'Learning how to accommodate this internal diversity, while still maintaining a stable political order, has always been one of the main challenges facing Canada, and remains so today' (2003, p. 368). As will be explored below, in the context of citizenship education the Canadian state has responded in a range of ways over time, including attempting to eliminate diversity through the creation of an overriding, common national identity; the co-opting of diversity to form the core of that national identity; and the submerging of diversity into generic approaches to citizenship and citizenship education.

THE HISTORY OF CITIZENSHIP EDUCATION: SEARCHING FOR AN ELUSIVE NATIONAL IDENTITY

A key component of citizenship in any country is the people's identification with the nation, in other words, their sense of national identity. One result of the deep diversity present in Canada has been the search to discover, or create, some sense of shared national identity. An American observer writes, 'National identity is the quintessential Canadian issue'. He goes on to argue, 'Almost alone among modern developed countries Canada has continued to debate its self-conception to the present day' (Lipset 1990, p. 42). McLean (2007) documents early twentieth-century attempts by federal parliamentarians to create a national education system largely to address a perceived 'crisis of citizenship' (p. 7), including the lack of a sense of national identity. When the first Canadian Citizenship Act was proclaimed in 1947, a leading advocate of citizenship education wrote, 'Canada is legally a nation, but the Canadians are scarcely yet a people' (Kidd 1947). More recent writers have made the point that, while Canada exists as a state, it is not a nation in the sense of Canadians sharing a profound sense of 'group affinity and shared values' (Resnick 1994, p. 6; see also Taylor & Laforest 1993; Gwyn 1995; Sears 1996–1997). The fear of deep differences and lack of understanding among Canada's disparate peoples and regions has been a dominant theme in the literature in the fields of citizenship and citizenship education in Canada.

Curtis (1988) describes this process of 'public *construction*' (p. 111; emphasis in the original) in nineteenth-century Ontario. He argues that in establishing early public education the state was concerned with the overlapping functions of institution building and 'political characteriza- tion of the population' (p. 111). He documents the long and often contested process of centralising state control over schools, curriculum and teachers, contending that this was a deliberate effort to take control of education away from parents and local communities so the state could be more effec- tive in using education for political socialisation. According to Curtis, the elites who pushed for, and achieved, universal public schooling in Canada in the nineteenth century were concerned about 'the creation in the popu- lation of new habits, orientations, [and] desires' that were consistent with 'the bourgeois social order' including 'respect for legitimate authority and for standards of a "collective morality"' (p. 366). As Bruno-Joffré (2002) writes, 'The public school was conceived as an agency for national unity and social harmony' (p. 114).

The standards of collective morality to be inculcated in early English Canadian schools were essentially British in nature. In Canada's early years school history courses and other subjects focused on Britain and the Empire and patriotic ceremonies and symbols were not directed toward the new nation but toward the growing empire:

> English speaking children were raised with the historical myths of Brit- ish nationalism, as conveyed by adapted editions of the Irish National Reader and authors as diverse as MacCauly and G.A. Hently. What mere Canadian citizenship could compete with the claims of an empire that spanned the known universe? (Morton 1993, p. 55)

Bruno-Joffré (2002) argues that citizenship education in schools, at least until the end of the Second World War, was focused on supporting this orientation. During this period, she writes:

> the aim of public schools in English Canada was to create a homoge- neous nation built on a common English language, a common culture, a common identification with the British Empire and an acceptance of British institutions and practices. (p. 113)

While this approach to citizenship education did violence to the linguistic and cultural traditions of many, it was particularly devastating for Canada's Aboriginal peoples. Battiste and Semaganis (2002) describe something of this 'cognitive imperialism', arguing it was, and largely still is, an attempt to extinguish 'Aboriginal conceptions of society' (p. 93).

The focus on Britishness as a state constructed, unifying national identity began to wane during World War II for several reasons, including the decline of Britain and the British Empire as major forces in the world. Most importantly, however, it simply was not working. Although early public schooling was decidedly assimilationist, with the goal of 'Anglo conformity' around the ideal of the British Empire, it was largely unsuccessful in unifying the population. Non-British newcomers to Canada did not identify with the Empire and clung doggedly to their ethnic communities and loyalty to distant homelands (Granatstein 1993).

This first became a major concern for the federal government during the war when Canadians of non-British background demonstrated a distinct lack of interest in the war effort despite the government's best attempts to drum up support. A new department, the Nationalities Branch (which later became the Citizenship Branch), was created to focus on reaching out to ethnic groups and fostering a sense of belonging to the Canadian state (Sears 1996; Joshee 2004; Joshee & Winton 2007).

Following the war the Citizenship Branch, and the Department of the Secretary of State of which it was part, became a major force in shaping civic education across Canada. Although it was an arm of the federal government and therefore had no official role in public education, it used a variety of official and unofficial means to implement state policy in the area (Sears 1997). The creation of a unifying sense of national identity remained a central part of that policy. Over the years from the end of the war to the mid-1980s the federal state developed and implemented literally hundreds of programmes across a range of sectors to respond to perceived crises in national unity. These constructed and disseminated a series of national ideals it was hoped would be widely accepted by Canadians and form the basis for a lasting sense of national identity. These ideals roughly fit into the following time periods: Canada, the land of conquering pioneers, from the late forties through the fifties and into the early sixties; Canada, the bilingual/bicultural reality, from the early sixties to the mid-seventies; and Canada, the pluralist ideal, from the mid-seventies on (Sears 1996). None met the objective of uniting the country around a shared identity.

One of the central factors working against the acceptance of a broadly accepted set of national symbols and a concomitant sense of national identity in Canada has been the resistance from 'la nation canadienne francaise' particularly centred in Québec (Sears 1996–1997). Symbols and events that unify most countries are often sources of division across linguistic and cultural lines in Canada. Fulford (1993) illustrates this when he observes:

The key event in our past, the battle on the Plains of Abraham, was not a subject to be explored mythically, because there was no pan-Canadian way of calling it either a victory or a defeat; to this minute it remains a sensitive issue, perhaps the only eighteenth century battle anywhere, that cannot be discussed without anxiety. (p. 111)

Taylor sums it up succinctly, 'In Canada even history divides' (Taylor & Laforest 1993, p. 25).

School history, social studies and civics curricula have most often worked to perpetuate this division. A number of studies document the much different approaches to these subjects in Québec compared to the rest of Canada (Hodgetts 1968; Lévesque 2004). While school curricula, structures and patriotic ceremonies in English Canada sought to build a single, and largely Anglo, national identity, the same factors in Québec were concerned with 'la surviance'—the survival of the French language and culture in a North America dominated by an expansionist English majority. Social education focused on 'the canon of a Francophone nation struggling for political recognition and resisting outside domination' (Létourneau, forthcoming).

Recently Québec has instituted major reforms to high school history curricula, including far more overt emphasis on citizenship education. This has ignited a vociferous public debate in the province between those who wish to maintain the focus on a beleaguered but valiant French Canadian nation and those who support the shift of focus to students' 'acquisition of the skills and knowledge needed for understanding present day society' (Létourneau, forthcoming). Consistent with recent developments in the rest of Canada and across the democratic world, the new programme focuses on the creation of citizens as effective and engaged agents of social construction and change.

CONTEMPORARY ISSUES RELATED TO CITIZENSHIP AND CITIZENSHIP EDUCATION IN CANADA

The past fifteen to twenty years have seen the development of a widespread consensus across democratic countries in several key areas relating to citizenship education. This consensus has four attributes: a pervasive sense of crisis about disengagement from civic involvement particularly among young people (and, in recent years, with particular concerns about young immigrants); a commitment to citizenship education as a key means for addressing that disengagement; focusing citizenship education on a generally civic-republican conception of citizenship with an emphasis on civic responsibility and engagement; and proposing constructivist approaches to teaching and learning as models of best practice in civic education (Hughes & Sears 2008).

This consensus has led to the development of remarkably similar citizenship education programmes across the democratic world; in effect the globalisation of citizenship education. A key feature of these programmes is their generic nature; the way that national, ethnic and other forms of identity are submerged in a focus on democratic ideas and processes (Sears, Davies & Reid 2008). Citizens' backgrounds and senses of self and others do not matter as long as they engage in liberal democratic practice. Kiwan (2008) found this when she interviewed key policy makers and practitioners in civic education in Britain. She reports that they universally 'underplayed' (p. 50) identity-based conceptions of citizenship in favour of other models, including the participatory ones. When asked about this, Professor Bernard Crick, arguably the most influential single individual in the development of England's national curriculum in citizenship, said, 'We're not dealing with nationality, we're dealing with a skill, a knowledge, an attitude for citizenship' (Kiwan 2008, p. 46); an almost perfect description of a generic approach to citizenship and citizenship education.

As has already been pointed out, education is a provincial responsibility in Canada so there is a fair degree of variance in precise programmes and vehicles for citizenship education. In some provinces, Alberta being the clearest example, interdisciplinary social studies courses are the primary locations for dealing with citizenship while others, particularly Ontario and Québec, take a more disciplinary approach centred in history and geography courses.

Having said that, broadly speaking Canada shares in all aspects of the global consensus about citizenship education, including its generally generic nature. While pluralism and inclusion are central to the rhetoric of social studies and citizenship education policy and programmes across Canada, it has largely been an iconic rather than a deep pluralism. Since the 1970s the idea of education as a doorway for individuals and groups to feel included in the mainstream civic life of the country in Canada has extended to at least attempt to include the voices of Aboriginal peoples, women, diverse ethnic groups, disabled people, gays and lesbians. This has resulted in a widespread educational policy framework that promotes the 'pluralist ideal' (Sears, Clarke & Hughes 1999, p. 113). Central to the pluralist ideal is an activist conception of citizenship in which every citizen, or group of citizens, will have the knowledge, skills and dispositions needed to participate in the civic life of the country and feel welcome to do so. As Sears and Hughes put it, good citizens in this conception:

> are seen as people who are: knowledgeable about contemporary society and the issues it faces; disposed to work toward the common good; supportive of pluralism; and skilled at taking action to make their communities, nation, and the world a better place. (1996, p. 134)

It is important to note that what citizens are being included in, then, is not citizenship in the ethnic or sociological sense of belonging to a community but, rather, they are being included in the community of those who participate, who join in a process.

The subway and bus bombings in London in 2005 precipitated a rethinking of generic approaches to citizenship education in that country, including calls for the teaching of 'Britishness' in schools (Ajegbo, Kiwan & Sharma 2007). This concern for social harmony is not limited to England, however, and shows up in a number of contexts, including the call for 'Australian Values' to be taught in the schools of that country and the ubiquitous nature of social cohesion as a policy term across state agencies and programmes in Canada (Sears, Davies & Reid 2008; Joshee 2004). Almost universally, democratic jurisdictions are wrestling with the question of how civic education can build a strong sense of attachment to the common good without regressing to its assimilationist past. As Kiwan (2008) points out, there is 'a central tension in balancing unity and diversity, evident not only in discourses in England, but indeed internationally in a number of different nation-state contexts' (p. 42). This tension is evident in a wide range of state activities related to citizenship in Canada.

Beyond curricular polices and programmes related to citizenship education, Canada has also been part of recent global trends in governance more generally. Chan, Fisher and Rubenson (2007) write, 'As in the rest of the Anglo-Saxon world, neoliberalism has come to comprise the raison d'être of Canadian policies over the last two decades' (p. 235). Smith (2004) argues that the rhetoric and structural adjustments that accompanied this move in Canada led to a fundamental shift in the way the state sees citizens:

> No longer were Canadians expected to relate to their government as democratic citizens; rather they were perceived as consumers. As democratic citizens we have the right to participate, to shape the decisions that affect us. As customers we are judged to be self-interested, atomistic consumers of government services, the quality of which we judge by the information the government provides. (p. 306)

Similarly Joshee (2004) traces shifts in diversity policy over the years in Canada from the 'ideal of assimilation' (p. 138), through 'cultural diversity and citizenship' (p. 140) and 'focus on identity' (p. 141), to 'social justice and education' (p. 144) and, more recently, 'social cohesion' (p. 146). The latter, she argues elsewhere (Johnson & Joshee 2007), 'is rooted in a neoliberal approach that replicates existing inequalities based on race, class, and gender' (p. 11).

The structure of Canadian schooling has also been greatly impacted by neo-liberal reforms. 'In the last decade and a half, accountability has come to dominate the educational policy discourse in Canada and pervade the majority of government documents and policies' (Chan, Fisher & Rubenson 2007, p. 221). The thirty years following World War II witnessed an expansion in teacher autonomy and professionalism within many Western democracies, including Canada (Dale 1989; Hargreaves 2003). However, economic downturn and the election of neo-liberal governments in the late 1970s and early 1980s led to a taming of the profession. Within a neo-liberal framework, the role of teachers in administrating public education, establishing curricular objectives and instructional design was undermined by policy makers focused on instrumental objectives, standardised testing and evidence-based practice (Levin 2008).

While this sort of authoritarian atmosphere is not conducive to effective teaching for democratic citizenship, there is evidence that the inherent diversity of Canada and the Canadian state described earlier has provided some unique opportunities to resist some of the more negative impacts of globalisation and these provide the possibility of a more positive future for citizenship education. That same diversity has also created problems for the effective implementation of civic education policy and programmes in the country. I will now turn to a brief examination of some of those possibilities and problems.

POSSIBILITIES AND PROBLEMS FOR THE FUTURE OF CANADIAN CITIZENSHIP EDUCATION

One area where Canada's deep diversity has shaped public debate, policy and practice differently than in other jurisdictions, particularly the United States and Australia (see chapters in this volume), is multiculturalism broadly and attitudes toward immigrants in particular. There has certainly been some backlash toward the increasingly diverse nature of immigration to Canada and the state's policies in the area of multiculturalism. One best-selling book, for example, described trends and policies in these areas as 'mosaic madness' (Bibby 1990) and another lashed out at 'the cult of multiculturalism in Canada' (Bissoondath 1994). There has never been, however, widespread public hostility to diversity policy or a mainstream political party that has made opposition to either immigration or multiculturalism a major platform theme as the Howard government did in Australia (Reid & Gill, this volume). In fact, federal political parties generally go out of their way to woo immigrant communities through promises of enhanced programmes for those already in the country or easing barriers to future immigration, particularly in areas such as family reunification. For most politicians and policy makers in Canada multiculturalism is presented 'as the true and only basis of Canadian Identity' (Troper 2002, p. 159).

Joshee and Winton (2007) argue that Canada has developed a different set of national myths than the United States and part of that developing understanding is seeing the country as more internationalist in outlook and open to diversity internally. A number of scholars would concur with Hébert and Wilkinson (2002), who contend that Canada's unique history and mix of peoples has meant that 'Canadian citizenship exists today within multi-layered belongings and complex understandings' (p. 3; see also Taylor & Laforest 1993; Kymlicka & Norman 2000).

One of the places this state commitment to presenting diversity as a central and positive aspect of Canada is in public schooling. Moving away from the assimilationist policies of the past, policy and practice in education have changed significantly to the point where 'during the past thirty years, public schools have been the primary area where multiculturalism has been implemented as the new conception of identity formation' (Bruno-Jofré & Henley 2001, p. 51). Schools which were once mandated to eliminate diversity have become, officially at least, 'more concerned with the concept of inclusion—how to teach for tolerance, develop respect for diversity, and entrench anti-racism and equality programs in school curricula' (Shields & Ramsay 2004, p. 43; Hughes & Sears 2008).

One of the most overt manifestations of this focus on developing understanding and acceptance of diversity in citizenship education is the pervasive focus on perspective taking in the Alberta social studies curriculum. While the Alberta curriculum mandates teaching about a wide diversity of perspectives 'for historical and constitutional reasons' (Alberta Education 2005, p. 4), there is a particularly strong focus on Aboriginal and Francophone perspectives and experiences. Other Canadian jurisdictions also identify the development of understanding of and respect for multiple perspectives as central to social studies. While it is true that approaches to diversity in Canadian classrooms are often quite superficial, focusing more on building harmony and avoiding conflict than exploring difference in any deep or substantial way (Bickmore 2006), the fact that Canada has largely avoided the conservative reaction against immigration, diversity and multiculturalism opens space for more substantial work related to citizenship education in these areas.

Another area where Canada's diversity has mitigated the impact of neo-liberal/conservative reforms has been in the structure of educational governance. The diffuse nature of political control over education in Canada has meant that no single government has been able to impose its will on the education system as a whole. While the 1980s and 1990s saw a range of very conservative governments elected in provinces across the country, there were pockets of resistance. Several provinces, for example, resisted market-oriented moves to implement more choice in education through providing funding for charter or private schools. In fact, private schooling is a marginal presence in Canada relative to other jurisdictions and charter schools are only permitted in one province. During this period the province of Saskatchewan elected a social democratic government and was the most consistent jurisdiction in resisting trends toward centralisation, continuing policies of widespread consultation about educational matters and maintaining 'a policy of investing in teachers as curriculum developers' (Chan, Fisher & Rubenson 2007, p. 224).

While the substantial, symbolic and structural diversity of the Canadian state opens possibilities for resisting neo-liberal global trends, it also produces its own set of challenges to citizenship education. The most important of these is the lack of an overt and coherent federal presence in education. In commenting on a major Organization for Economic Co-operation and Development (OECD) report, Robertson (2006) points out, 'Among the OECD's member states, Canada stood alone; every other nation, including those which, like Canada, are structured as federations had devised a vehicle for articulating, debating, and adopting national policies and for coordinating education research' (p. 410). Hughes and Sears (2006, 2008) compare recent Canadian policy and practice in citizenship education with that in a range of democratic jurisdictions around the world. They identify a number of areas of capacity building that undergird substantial programmes and development in the field, including widespread public and professional debate about goals and objectives; pre- and in-service teacher education programmes; the development and dissemination of quality materials to support teaching; and programmes of research to monitor progress and feed information back to the system. They conclude, 'Other nations that face similar challenges to those we face in Canada have moved forward to build capacity to support quality teaching and learning related to democratic citizenship; Canada has not' (2006, p. 9).

The federal government is constitutionally excluded from legislating in the areas of public education but 'there is nothing in the Constitution Act that prevents the Canadian government from using its leadership role and spending powers to influence public schooling in Canada' (Ungerleider 2003, p. 277). It is the only level of government with the ability to generate a national conversation about citizenship and citizenship education and the resources to support substantial capacity building in the field. Until it takes up a more overt leadership role, Canada will continue to be a 'dabbler rather than a player' (Hughes & Sears 2006, p. 6) in the area of citizenship education.

CONCLUSION

Merryfield and Duty (2008) argue that globalisation presents both opportunities for new and effective forms of democratic citizenship and powerful potential limits on the practice of democracy. In terms of the former, Merryfield argues, 'Globalization has expanded the engagement and political efficacy of citizens in the twenty-first century' (p. 87). International organisations and movements provide citizens with new opportunities for engagement around issues of importance from the environment to international trade and monetary policy. On the other hand, she contends, the loss of national sovereignty to transnational corporations, the World Bank or international trade agreements has often resulted in significant weakening of individual choice and efficacy.

Just as globalisation presents both opportunities and barriers for democratic citizenship, I have argued through this chapter that the deep diversity of the Canadian state presents opportunities and problems for reimagining citizenship education for a global age. A central feature of globalisation is increasing mobility of peoples accompanied by a decreasing sense of attachment to particular nation-states (Merryfield & Duty 2008; Johnson & Joshee 2007). This calls for citizenship education that allows for multiple understandings of what it means to be a citizen and that will develop in children the ability to understand 'the points of view of people different from themselves' (Merryfield & Duty 2008, p. 87) both inside and outside of the state in which they live. The Canadian state has considerable experience incorporating ethnic and cultural differences as well as dealing with established national minorities that enjoy some measure of institutional and territorial autonomy. Canadian schools are moving positively in the direction of building the kind of understanding of other world-views called for by many advocates of global education. That is not to say that Canada has all the issues around identity and diversity figured out, but it is to say that our particular national context has laid a solid groundwork for moving forward in this area. As Kymlicka (2003) writes, 'identity politics in Canada is simply everyday democratic politics' (p. 384).

Canada's deep diversity also poses problems for developing the kinds of trans- or supranational understandings of citizenship that commonly exist today along with national understandings. As argued earlier, the Canadian state's internal struggles with multiple forms of diversity have often led to a national navel-gazing as it struggles to maintain social cohesion and foster some sense of national identity. There was a surge of interest in global education curricula in the late 1980s and early 1990s (Sears & Hughes 1996), but that has largely waned and Canadian social studies and citizenship programmes overwhelmingly focus on Canadian issues, themes and topics. Citizenship education in Canadian schools still focuses almost wholly on creating citizens to operate in the context of the nation-state.

Finally, the diffuse and fractured nature of educational governance in Canada has worked against the creation of clear and consistent policies in and support for citizenship education in the country. History and contemporary circumstances provide a considerable basis for Canada demonstrating leadership in cultivating innovative thinking about citizenship and citizenship education to address challenges raised by globalisation. As long as the federal government fails to take a lead role in fostering discussion and development of the field in Canada that potential will remain largely unrealised.

NOTE

1. Essentially, French Canadians in Québec.

REFERENCES

Ajegbo, Sir Keith, Dina Kiwan & Seema Sharma (2007) *Diversity and Citizenship Curriculum Review*. London, Department for Education and Skills.

Alberta Education (2005) *Social Studies K–12*, http://www.education.gov.ab.ca/k_12/curriculum/bySubject/social/sockto3.pdf (accessed 29 August 2005).

Battiste, Marie & Helen Semaganis (2002) First thoughts on First Nations citizenship issues in education, in Yvonne Hébert (ed.) *Citizenship in Transformation in Canada*. Toronto, University of Toronto Press, pp. 93–111.

Bibby, Reginald W. (1990) *Mosaic Madness: The Poverty and Potential of Life in Canada*. Toronto, Stoddart.

Bickmore, Kathy (2006) Democratic social cohesion (assimilation)? Representations of social conflict in Canadian public school curriculum, *Canadian Journal of Education*, 26(2), pp. 359–386.

Bissoondath, Neil (1994) *Selling Illusions: The Cult of Multiculturalism in Canada*. Toronto, Penguin.

Bruno-Jofré, Rosa (2002) Citizenship and schooling in Manitoba between the end of the First World War and the end of the Second World War, in Yvonne Hébert (ed.) *Citizenship in Transformation in Canada*. Toronto, University of Toronto Press, pp. 112–133.

Bruno-Jofré, Rosa & Dick Henley (2001) Public schooling in English Canada: Addressing difference in the context of globalization, in Rosa Bruno-Jofré & Natalia Aponiuk (eds.) *Educating Citizens for a Pluralistic Society*. Calgary, Canadian Ethnic Studies, pp. 49–70.

CBC News (2006) *House Passes Motion Recognizing Québécois as Nation*, http://www.cbc.ca/canada/story/2006/11/27/nation-vote.html (accessed 10 March 2009).

Chan, Adrienne S., Donald Fisher & Kjell Rubenson (2007) Conclusion, in Adrienne S. Chan, Donald Fisher & Kjell Rubenson (eds.) *The Evolution of Professionalism: Educational Policy in the Provinces and Territories of Canada*. Vancouver, University of British Columbia, Centre for Policy Studies in Higher Education and Training, pp. 219–241.

Curtis, Bruce (1988) *Building the Educational State: Canada West, 1836–1871*. London and Ontario, The Althouse Press.

Dale, Roger (1989) *The State and Educational Policy*. Toronto, OISE Press.

Department of Justice (1982) *Constitution Acts 1867–1982*, http://laws.justice.gc.ca/en/const/annex_e.html#1 (accessed 10 March 2009).

Durham, Lord (1839) *Lord Durham's Report on the Affairs of British North America*, http://faculty.marianopolis.edu/c.belanger/quebechistory/docs/durham/1.htm (accessed 10 March 2009).

Fulford, Robert (1993) A post-modern dominion: The changing nature of Canadian citizenship, in William Kaplan (ed.) *Belonging: The Meaning and Nature of Canadian Citizenship*. Montreal and Kingston, McGill-Queen's University Press, pp. 104–119.

Granatstein, Jack L. (1993) The 'hard' obligations of citizenship: The Second World War in Canada, in William Kaplan (ed.) *Belonging: The Meaning and Future of Canadian Citizenship*. Montreal and Kingston, McGill-Queen's University Press, pp. 36–49.

Gwyn, Richard J. (1995) *Nationalism without Walls: The Unbearable Lightness of Being Canadian*. Toronto, McClelland & Stewart.

Hargreaves, Andy (2003) *Teaching in the Knowledge Society: Education in the Age of Insecurity*. New York, Teachers College Press.

Hébert, Yvonne & Lori Wilkinson (2002) The citizenship debates: Conceptual, policy, experiential, and educational issues, in Yvonne Hébert (ed.) *Citizenship in Transformation in Canada*. Toronto, University of Toronto Press, pp. 3–36.

Hodgetts, A.B. (1968) *What Culture? What Heritage? A Study of Civic Education in Canada*. Toronto, OISE Press.

Hughes, Andrew S. & Alan Sears (2006) Citizenship education: Canada dabbles while the world plays on, *Education Canada*, 46(4), pp. 6–9.

———. (2008) The struggle for citizenship education in Canada: The centre cannot hold, in James Arthur, Ian Davies & Carole Hahn (eds.) *The SAGE Handbook of Education for Citizenship and Democracy*. London, Sage, pp. 124–138.

Jaenen, Cornelius J. (1981) Mutilated multiculturalism, in J.D. Wilson (ed.) *Canadian Education in the 1980s*. Calgary, Destelig, pp. 79–96.

Johnson, Lauri & Reva Joshee (2007) Introduction: Cross-border dialogue and multicultural policy webs, in Reva Joshee & Lauri Johnson (eds.) *Multicultural Education Policies in Canada and the United States*. Vancouver, UBC Press, pp. 3–13.

Joshee, Reva (2004) Citizenship and multicultural education in Canada: From assimilation to social cohesion, in James A. Banks (ed.) *Diversity and Citizenship Education: Global Perspectives*. San Francisco, Jossey-Bass, pp. 127–156.

Joshee, Reva & Susan Winton (2007) Past crossings: U.S. influences on the development of Canadian multicultural education policy, in Reva Joshee & Lauri Johnson (eds.) *Multicultural Education Policies in Canada and the United States*. Vancouver, UBC Press, pp. 17–27.

Kidd, J.R. (1947) A study to formulate a plan for the work of the Canadian Citizenship Council. Unpublished EdD thesis, Columbia, New York.

Kiwan, Dina (2008) Citizenship education in England at the crossroads? Four models of citizenship and their implications for ethnic and religious diversity, *Oxford Review of Education*, 34(1), pp. 39–58.

Kymlicka, Will (2003) Being Canadian, *Government and Opposition*, 38(3), pp. 357–385.

———. (2007) Ethnocultural diversity in a liberal state: Making sense of the Canadian model(s), in Keith Banting, Thomas J. Courchene & F. Leslie Seidle (eds.) *The Art of the State, Volume III: Belonging? Diversity, Recognition and Shared Citizenship in Canada*. Montreal, Institute for Research on Public Policy, pp. 39–86.

Kymlicka, Will & Wayne Norman (eds.) (2000) *Citizenship and Diverse Societies*. New York, Oxford University Press.

Létourneau, Jocelyn (Forthcoming) Teaching history, memory and identity: The debate on History education in Quebec, in Penney Clark (ed.) *History Teaching and Learning in Canada: A State of the Art Look*. Vancouver, UBC Press.

Lévesque, Stéphane (2004) History and social studies in Quebec: An historical perspective, in Alan Sears & Ian Wright (eds.) *Challenges and Prospects for Canadian Social Studies*. Vancouver, Pacific Educational Press, pp. 55–72.

Levin, Ben (2008) *How to Change 5000 Schools: A Practical and Positive Approach for Leading Change at Every Level*. Cambridge, MA, Harvard Education Press.

Lipset, Seymour Martin (1990) *Continental Divide: The Values and Institutions of the United States and Canada*. New York, Routledge.

McLean, Lorna (2007) Education, identity, and citizenship in early modern Canada, *Journal of Canadian Studies*, 41(1), pp. 5–30.

Merryfield, Merry M. & L. Duty (2008) Globalization, in James Arthur, Ian Davies & Carole Hahn (eds.) *The SAGE Handbook of Education for Citizenship and Democracy*. London, Sage, pp. 80–91.

Morton, Desmond (1993) Divided loyalties? Divided country? in William Kaplan (ed.) *Belonging: The Meaning and Future of Canadian Citizenship*. Montreal and Kingston, McGill-Queen's University Press, pp. 50–63.

Resnick, Phillip (1990) *The Masks of Proteus: Canadian Reflections on the State*. Kingston and Ontario, McGill-Queen's University Press.

Robertson, Heather-Jane (2006) An idea whose time keeps coming, *Phi Delta Kappan*, 87(5), pp. 410–412.

Sears, Alan (1996) Scarcely yet a people: State policy in citizenship education: 1947–1982. Unpublished PhD thesis, Vancouver, University of British Columbia.

———. (1996–1997) Something different to everyone: Conceptions of citizenship and citizenship education, *Canadian and International Education*, 25(2), pp. 53–67.

———. (1997) Instruments of policy: How the federal state influences citizenship education in Canada, *Canadian Ethnic Studies*, 29(2), pp. 1–21.

Sears, Alan, Gerry M. Clarke & Andrew S. Hughes (1999) Canadian citizenship education: The pluralist ideal and citizenship education for a post-modern state, in Judith Torney-Purta, John Schwille & Jo-Ann Amadeo (eds.) *Civic Education across Countries: Twenty-Four National Case Studies from the IEA Education Project*. Amsterdam, IEA, pp. 111–135.

Sears, Alan, Ian Davies & Alan Reid (2008) From Britishness to nothingness and back again. Paper presented at Britishness: The View from Abroad, University of Huddersfield, U.K., 5–6 June.

Sears, Alan & Andrew S. Hughes (1996) Citizenship education and current educational reform, *Canadian Journal of Education*, 21(2), pp. 123–142.

Shields, Patricia & Douglas Ramsay (2004) Social studies across English Canada, in Alan Sears & Ian Wright (eds.) *Challenges and Prospects for Canadian Social Studies*. Vancouver, Pacific Educational Press, pp. 38–54.

Smith, Peter J. (2004) The impact of globalization on citizenship: Decline or renaissance, in Pierre Boyer, Linda Cardinal & David John Headon (eds.) *From Subjects to Citizens: A Hundred Years of Citizenship in Australia and Canada*. Ottawa, University of Ottawa Press, pp. 301–328.

Taylor, Charles & Guy Laforest (1993) *Reconciling the Solitude: Essays on Canadian Federalism and Nationalism*. Montreal, McGill-Queen's University Press.

Troper, Harold (2002) The historical context for citizenship education in urban Canada, in Yvonne Hébert (ed.) *Citizenship in Transformation in Canada*. Toronto, University of Toronto Press, pp. 150–161.

Ungerleider, Charles (2003) *Failing our Kids: How we are Ruining our Public Schools*. Toronto, McClelland & Stewart.

Part C
Reflections and Analysis

14 Oppositions and Possibilities

Walter Parker

Citizenship education and multicultural education (with various names and meanings) have been rather distinct curricular programmes in more than a few school systems around the world, as we have seen in the revealing chapters of this volume. They are embedded, of course, in unique national contexts; both initiatives are of the nation. Conceptually and empirically, they are its products. Cosmopolitanism is also making brief appearances in educational discourse—minor in relation to the two stronger, national discourses, but provocative as a harbinger of a different kind of political community: world citizenship.

These three projects are intersecting more frequently now in education circles, clashing and sometimes merging and then diverging again, like awkward dance partners. Contradictions and ironies are plentiful, as we see in these rich and insightful case studies. Ours is an era, not unlike prior eras, of curricular foment and possibility. It is loaded with opportunities and constraints, and it moves in fits and starts. No single discourse is hegemonic, not even neo-liberalism. There are flows and counter-flows, programmatic initiatives and push-back. This makes a fertile site for knowledge construction and contestation. And there is, as Erickson (2004, p. 197) puts it, 'wiggle room' for creative agency.

I want to reflect on the national case studies collected in this volume by focusing on oppositions (dichotomies, binaries) that, in my judgment, are central in this work and could benefit from further exploration. Of several that could be called 'central', I am struck by two:

> *multiculturalism versus nationalism*
> *nationalism versus cosmopolitanism*

Numerous expressions of these oppositions appear in the chapters of this volume. In this brief analysis, I focus on only two. The first, multiculturalism versus nationalism, I take from Bryan's chapter on Ireland. She quotes a text-book used in Civic, Social and Political Education, an examination subject recently added to Ireland's lower secondary curriculum:

Over the last decade Ireland has become a *multicultural* society. This means there are people living and working in Ireland from many other cultures and countries. (emphasis in original)

As Bryan explains, diversity is othered and abnormalised in these sentences. It is treated as new and aberrant. The connotation, quoting Bryan, is that 'it is something which is at once unusual and alien to the Irish nation'. The pre-diversified Irish person was ethnically Irish; the post-diversified Irish person is the same, except that others are present; thus 'Ireland has become a multicultural society' while a homogeneous Irish nation is reinscribed.

Turning to the second opposition, I take an example from Baildon and Sim's chapter on Singapore. The authors quote a government minister:

[Singaporeans] must balance this contradiction between being cosmopolitan and being nationalistic. We cannot be a trading nation, if we are not cosmopolitan. We cannot be a nation, if we are not nationalistic. We must be both at the same time.

These are 'new times', Baildon and Sim observe, when the two terms in the opposition are to be nurtured 'at the same time'. National Education is launched in the curriculum to instill patriotism and harmony while another government initiative, Thinking Schools Learning Nation, encourages hyperflexibility in the productive capacity of the people themselves. A new subjectivity is encouraged on the model of a citizen who is loyal to the nation yet at the same time cosmopolitan, and who is, meanwhile, a nonstop, adaptive learner.

Having identified examples, we can see that each opposition has a conceptual network that extends beyond the given binaries. Let us take each in turn.

The opposition *Multiculturalism/Nationalism* has not just two but at least four possibilities: Multiculturalism, Nationalism, Not Multiculturalism (the negation or opposite of Multiculturalism) and Not Nationalism (the negation or opposite of Nationalism). Not Multiculturalism includes more than just Nationalism (Nationalism is only one possibility in the category Not Multiculturalism; racism, for example, is another); and Not Nationalism includes more than just Multiculturalism (Multiculturalism is only one possibility in the category Not Nationalism; cosmopolitanism, for example, is another). And there are at least two more possibilities: Multiculturalism and Nationalism, and neither Multiculturalism nor Nationalism.

The opposition *Nationalism/Cosmopolitanism* also has not just two but at least four possibilities: Nationalism, Cosmopolitanism, Not Nationalism and Not Cosmopolitanism. Not Nationalism might include, in addition to cosmopolitanism, ethnocentrism and sectarianism—each another kind of affinity. Not Cosmopolitanism might include, in addition to nationalism, provincialism and familism (kinship). And the additional two: Nationalism and Cosmopolitanism, and neither Nationalism nor Cosmopolitanism.

If this sort of analysis strikes the reader as semantic, it is. But it is not 'merely semantic' because it also is pragmatic: language gets things done (discourses simultaneously shape the phenomena they purport to describe). The purpose of peering more deeply into these two oppositions and their orbiting systems of meaning is to make visible the array of meanings that stem from the simple binary, destablilising it and opening it up in the process. The aim is to not get stuck, one could say, in the initial, given opposition, accepting the dichotomy and closing down the possibilities at two, as if there was a choice to be made between two alternatives.

This elementary structure of meaning was conceived by Greimas (1987) as a 'semiotic square'. Let's look at our two oppositions and extend the analysis as before to four, and then six meanings, and this time to eight. We will see that the last two hybrids (7 and 8) reinforce and intensify one term in the binary as a consequence of negating its contrary (Hébert 2006).

Consider a semiotic square on the opposition *multiculturalism versus nationalism* (see Figure 14.1). First, note that the terms in the given binary make the contraries found inside the square on the upper horizontal. Their contradictions or negatives ('nots') are diagonally located on the lower horizontal. Second, note the hybrids. These are represented outside the square on the four sides by combining the four possibilities inside the square. This takes us to eight possible meanings.

5. At the top of the multiculturalism/nationalism square, we have the hybrid Multiculturalism and Nationalism composed by adding the terms on the upper horizontal. If one can imagine or has found empirically this combination on the ground, in schools or education policy statements, then this demonstrates that a contrary or tension is not to be confused with a contradiction.

6. At the bottom we have the hybrid Neither Multiculturalism nor Nationalism, created by combining the terms on the lower horizontal. This is a broad field of possibility that excludes only these two categories.

7. To the left, we add the verticals on that side of the square and arrive at Multiculturalism and Not Nationalism—a sort of strong multiculturalism with no hint of nationalism. I have not seen this, and I suspect it is because multiculturalism is normally practised, where it is found, rather thoroughly within the national framework (see Beck 2006 on methodological nationalism).

8. To the right, we add the verticals on that side of the square and arrive at Nationalism and Not Multiculturalism—a sort of strong nationalism with no hint of multiculturalism: somewhat rare today as gestures toward multiculturalism routinely make their way into education policy and school practice.

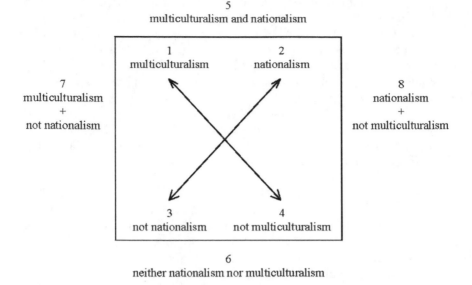

Figure 14.1 Multiculturalism/Nationalism.

What is the Irish text-book doing? This is open to debate. Perhaps it is persuading its audience toward the primary hybrid based on the upper horizontal: Multiculturalism and Nationalism. Or is it gesturing toward the hybrid on the right: a continuation of ethnic nationalism as usual? This seems unlikely. Perhaps it is invoking the negative hybrid based on the lower horizontal, Neither Multiculturalism nor Nationalism.

Now consider a semiotic square for the opposition *nationalism versus cosmopolitanism* (see Figure 14.2). Again, the terms in the given opposition compose the upper horizontal: a contrary or tension. Their contradictions are diagonally located. Second, note the hybrids. Again, these are represented outside the square by combining the four possibilities inside the square. This takes us to eight possible meanings, the last two being, again, strong as a consequence of negating the contrary.

5. At the top of the Nationalism/Cosmopolitanism square shown in Square 2, we have the hybrid Nationalism and Cosmopolitanism composed by adding the contraries on the upper horizontal. Again, if one can imagine or has found empirically this combination on the ground, in schools or education policy statements, then this demonstrates that a contrary is not to be confused with a contradiction.

6. At the bottom we have the hybrid Neither Nationalism nor Cosmopolitanism, created by combining the contradictories on the lower horizontal. This is a broad field of possibility that excludes only these two concepts.

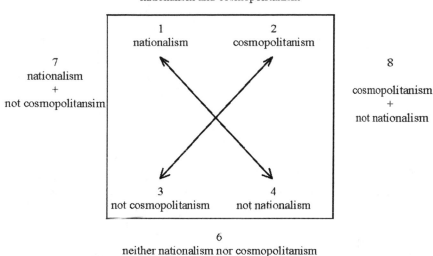

Figure 14.2 Nationalism/Cosmopolitanism.

7. To the left, we add the verticals on that side of the square and arrive at Nationalism and Not Cosmopolitanism—strong nationalism with no hint of cosmopolitanism: ethnocentrism or chauvinism, perhaps.
8. To the right, we add the verticals on that side and arrive at Cosmopolitanism and Not Nationalism—strong cosmopolitanism with no hint of nationalism: world citizenship or the *Earth Charter*, perhaps.

What is Singapore's government minister doing? This, too, is open to debate. He appears to be imploring his audience in the direction of the primary hybrid: Nationalism and Cosmopolitanism. But there is the possibility that such a hybrid is a rhetorical convenience, a lexical flourish, and that in fact the result is neither one nor the other, but something else altogether—perhaps the lower hybrid.

CONCLUSION

From this perspective, an opposition and its accompanying either/or logic is only a starting point, a first step in a broader analysis. Any text or social practice, such as curriculum decision making, can be understood from this point of view as a set of constraints and possibilities, not a determinate, finished thing. My opening remark—that the foment of the present social moment makes a fertile field for curriculum and other education policy work—refers to the jumble of meanings at play on the discursive field of Citizenship Education, Multicultural Education and Cosmopolitan Education today *and* to the openings that lie among them. There is 'wiggle room'.

I share the chapter authors' keen interest in these phenomena. In studies of what is now called 'international education' in the public schools of the United States (Parker 2008, in press; Parker & Camicia 2009), I have found nationalism to be the dominant discourse: the goals of national economic competitiveness and national military readiness are driving the 'international education' movement from the power-and-funding heights. Yet it is nationalism in tension with cosmopolitanism and, more so, with a global variant of multiculturalism called 'global perspective'. In a related study (Mitchell & Parker 2008), a group of U.S. adolescents expressed multiple allegiances and flexible citizenship that together undermined any simple oppositions such as multiculturalism/nationalism or nationalism/ cosmopolitanism. 'I don't have a national identity', a tenth-grade student said (p. 792).

As Foucault (1980, p. 114) demonstrated, relations of power, not relations of meaning, furnish the history of the present moment. Power asymmetries matter at sites of knowledge construction because these are political sites: some meanings are ushered into official knowledge while others are cast out to the margins. The practice of ethnocentrism by dominant groups and the global weight of the neo-liberal juggernaut of recent decades, to name two forces, bear down on the possibilities for creative agency, limiting the wiggle room. Whether in Ireland or Singapore, or Mexico, Australia, Hong Kong or elsewhere, at least one useful undertaking is to understand the discursive field well enough to engage the possibilities and mobilise the creative agency that would move citizenship education, multicultural education and global education toward greater empathy, equity and fairness. The chapters in this volume have done a great deal in this regard.

REFERENCES

Beck, Ulrich (2006) *Cosmopolitan Vision*. Cambridge, U.K., Polity.

Erickson, Fred (2004) *Talk and Social Theory*. Cambridge, U.K., Polity.

Foucault, Michel (1980) *Power/Knowledge: Selected Interviews and Other Writing, 1972–1977* (C. Gordon, trans.). New York, Pantheon.

Greimas, Algirdas J. (1987) *On Meaning: Selected Writings in Semiotic Theory* (P.J. Perron & F.H. Collins, trans.). Minneapolis, University of Minnesota Press.

Hébert, Louis (2006) The semiotic square, *Signo*, http://www.signosemio.com\ (accessed 8 May 2009).

Mitchell, Katharyne & Walter C. Parker (2008) 'I pledge allegiance to' . . . Flexible citizenship and shifting scales of belonging, *Teachers College Record*, 110(4), pp. 775–804.

Parker, Walter C. (2008) 'International education': What's in a name? *Phi Delta Kappan*, 90(2), pp. 196–202.

Parker, Walter C. (in press) 'International education' in U.S. public schools. *Globalisation, Societies and Education.*

Parker, Walter C. & Steven P. Camicia (2009) Cognitive praxis in today's 'international education' movement: A case study of intents and affinities, *Theory and Research in Social Education*, 37(1), pp. 42–74.

15 Citizenship and the Nation-State
Affinity, Identity and Belonging

Audrey Osler

INTRODUCTION

At the beginning of the twenty-first century and in our global age, citizenship education programmes typically remain focused on the nation and citizens' supposed natural affinity to the nation-state. This is confirmed, to varying degrees, in the contributions to this volume, one of the aims of which is to explore and theorise the relationship between civic or citizenship education and the nation-state, in the context of globalisation.

In this response, I reflect on national citizenship as a status, a feeling and a practice. I examine some of the different ways in which education for citizenship is constructed to support a primary affinity to the nation, considering some of the pitfalls and tensions which arise when such policies are pursued.

The impact of globalisation on the demographics of different nation-states has led to a renewed focus on civic education which promotes national belonging and loyalty, often targeting, either explicitly or implicitly, students from minority or migration backgrounds. I consider scales of belonging, other than that of the nation, focusing on the local, regional and global. I consider how official policies for democratic citizenship address diversity, reflecting on the relationship between democracy and diversity. Finally, I examine the potential of education for cosmopolitan citizenship (Osler & Vincent 2002; Osler & Starkey 2003, 2005).

CITIZENSHIP AS STATUS, FEELING AND PRACTICE

Citizenship can be conceptualised as a status, a feeling and a practice (Osler & Starkey 2005). It is most commonly conceived by governmental bodies as a status. Citizenship as status is, in many ways, exclusive: although individuals can hold dual citizenship, so that, for example, an individual can be a Pakistani citizen and a British citizen (holding two passports), either a person is a citizen of a nation-state, or s/he is not. This conception of citizenship contrasts with the status of all individuals as holders of human rights. The status of human rights holder, unlike that of citizenship, is inclusive. All human beings, including those who are stateless, are holders of human rights.

Citizenship can also be conceived as a feeling or sense of belonging. The degree to which a person feels they belong is not necessarily related to formal status, although legal entitlements obtained through citizenship status may be among those goods which enable a person to feel they belong. Prerequisites for belonging are likely to include: access to services and resources; legal rights of residence; social and psychological security; an absence of discrimination and/or legal redress if discrimination occurs; and acceptance by others within the community.

Citizenship can also be conceptualised as practice. Citizenship as practice is the everyday citizenship engagement in which each individual can participate, in working alongside others to make a difference. Citizenship in this sense is the everyday political, social, economic and cultural activities in which people engage to shape the community, most commonly in the immediate locality or at the level of a town or city, but also at other scales, including national and global.

Citizenship as status, feeling and practice are interlinked: citizenship status may give an individual a sense of security and enable them to feel they belong and so enhance their engagement in the affairs of the community. Nevertheless, the three elements are also discrete; so, for example, it is not necessary to have citizenship status in order to be an active, contributing member of society, engaged in the practice of citizenship.

EDUCATION FOR DEMOCRATIC CITIZENSHIP AND NATIONAL BELONGING

Education for national citizenship focuses on one or more elements of citizenship, but tends to emphasise citizenship as status. So citizenship education programmes typically address knowledge about the constitution and the legal entitlements and duties of citizenship, such as voting, knowing and obeying the law and paying taxes (even though these responsibilities are not necessarily restricted to those who hold the formal status of citizen).

This emphasis on knowledge-based learning is sometimes seen by policy makers and educators to stand in tension with that of education for citizenship as practice, which is often locally or community focused, and is likely to include community engagement or service learning. Education for citizenship as practice is sometimes targeted at students who are perceived to be less academic in their interests, or who are judged to be lower achievers. For example, Scott and Cogan (this volume) report that a course entitled 'Community Civics' was proposed in the United States during the second decade of the twentieth century. It aimed to prepare school-leavers to fulfill their roles in participatory citizenship. The proposal was in tension with what remains today a standard U.S. knowledge-based civics education almost a century later. The same tension between traditional civics and community-focused learning also continues in England at the beginning of the twenty-first century, where some teachers argue that lower-attaining students are better suited to locally based community learning than to knowledge-based citizenship courses focusing on the nation and beyond (Osler & Savvides 2009).

Nevertheless, education for national citizenship also stresses, in many contexts, citizenship as feeling as well as citizenship as status. Taking the case of Singapore, Baildon and Sim (this volume) discuss the challenge faced by government of 'managing identities'. They report that, in Singapore, official discourse stresses a sense of belonging as something critical to the national curriculum, and to 'national survival'. According to this perspective, without such education, there is a real danger that young Singaporeans will pack their bags and take flight if they see better opportunities elsewhere. Therefore, they need to be encouraged to develop a stronger sense of national pride and learn 'the Singapore story', which recalls the struggles of political leaders and past generations. The aim is to encourage young citizens to recognise a duty and vital obligation in protecting their country, and overcoming its apparent vulnerability.

Senior politicians in Britain have also stressed the importance of a strong sense of national identity, through the study of British history and the British story of democracy, with such calls gaining momentum after the suicide bombings in London in 2005. In this development within citizenship education, a new emphasis is attached to the nation's ethnic diversity. This is welcomed by Davies (this volume), but this development needs critical analysis, stemming as it does from a concern about terrorism (Osler & Starkey 2006), yet largely avoiding discussion of continuing barriers to democracy such as inequalities and racism (Osler 2008).

DEMOCRACY, DIVERSITY AND HIDDEN HISTORIES

At the beginning of the twenty-first century, references to diversity within citizenship education policies usually imply ethnic and cultural diversity. Some policy documents celebrate the diverse populations of the nation-state, but fail to take into consideration the differential access that different groups encounter in accessing citizenship rights. They neglect to examine power relations or barriers to citizenship, historical or contemporary. As Audrey Bryan (2008 and this volume) reminds us, citizenship education policies and other related policies addressing, for example, intercultural or multicultural education need to be contextualised within a broader legislative framework relating to citizenship, immigration and social cohesion.

As we have seen, history is sometimes harnessed to tell a national story of citizenship, as in the Singapore story, and this telling of the national story can be found not only in school texts and promoted through formal education, but also in museums, where it is often presented in a compelling way, as in the National Museum of Singapore, where it is retold for children and adults alike, and for citizens, residents and, indeed, visitors and tourists to the country.

Of course, in Singapore as elsewhere, there are many different histories to be told, and it is these different perspectives, when explored, that can engage young people as critical learners. In examining diversity, it is important to identify the silences around certain forms of diversity, particularly silences around gender and women's citizenship. In national stories it would appear that the citizen is rarely gendered; that ethnic and cultural diversity is often portrayed either as new or as something which must be carefully managed; and political dissent is rarely seen as progressive, unless part of a struggle against a colonial power, or in a story where the nation has (re)-established democracy, after a period of dictatorship.

Interestingly, the British story of democracy is set largely within the territorial confines of the United Kingdom, and Prime Minister Brown calls for a new sense of patriotic pride, which aims to be inclusive and to avoid any basis in ethnic exclusivity and which will be realised through the teaching of British history. Unfortunately, the rhetoric ignores the multiple histories and perspectives of a diverse nation (Osler 2009). It also ignores the legacy of empire. It is interesting to note that the authors of the chapters on a number of territories and nation-states represented in this volume that were tied to Britain during the imperial age (notably Australia, Canada, Hong Kong, Ireland and Singapore) make at least passing reference to colonialism and/or independence in their analysis of the historical context of citizenship education, whereas the legacy of empire is not examined in the chapter addressing citizenship education in England, even when the discussion touches on gender, diversity and twenty-first-century appeals to refocus on Britishness.

The modern international institution of the Commonwealth remains an important institution and a key forum for international dialogue for many member states, significantly within Africa, with key meetings reported in the media and regular celebrations and holidays. Yet this institution is largely overlooked among the British public and receives, at best, passing mention in British schools.

National political and educational programmes in progress at the beginning of the twenty-first century continue to draw a line between rightful, deserving citizens and an alien Other; within this outsider grouping are some who hold citizenship status, but who are nevertheless portrayed as an alien threat. In such an atmosphere of fear, refugees and asylum seekers are no longer vulnerable people in need of assistance and with an entitlement to have their claims considered, but are portrayed as unscrupulous individuals exploiting both international law and those who rightfully belong. Reid and Gill (this volume) show how the Australian government, under

Prime Minister Howard, promoted such a message of fear, in the wake of the 2001 attacks on the United States, preventing migrants seeking refugee status from landing in Australia and making their claims.

In the revised national curriculum for citizenship in England (Qualifications and Curriculum Authority 2007) the British story of democracy is presented as a completed project, as it was in the curriculum's important founding document, the Crick Report (Qualifications and Curriculum Authority 1998), rather than a process which needs continual renewal. Particular groups are identified as 'vulnerable', less likely to identify with the nation and therefore in need of specific targeted compensatory education. British government funds are thus being set aside for programmes aimed at preventing 'violent extremism' and the radicalisation of young Muslims (Home Office 2008). Effectively, whole groups of citizens are classed as having a deficit in terms of their loyalty to the polity.

Sears (this volume) considers education for citizenship within the context of diversity, observing that the reconciliation of different positions has always been part of the Canadian framework. Following Kymlicka (2003), he notes how Canada is distinctive in having to address three types of diversity (national minorities, immigrants and indigenous peoples). What is curious is that diversity in so many national contexts continues to be seen as a problem, or at best, a challenge, rather than an asset to democracy (Osler 2008; Parker 2002). The vision that democracy needs diversity (political, cultural and social) in order to flourish and regenerate is lost.

EDUCATION FOR COSMOPOLITAN CITIZENSHIP AND HUMAN RIGHTS

In our global age, not all young people at school are citizens of the nation-state in which they are studying. Citizenship education cannot be premised on the notion that all students are citizens or aspirant citizens. From 2002 to 2003, James Banks at the University of Washington in Seattle convened an international panel of scholars, who produced a report designed to inform teachers and policy makers and to act as a starting point for discussion in developing or reviewing citizenship education programmes appropriate for multicultural democracies in a global age. While all students may not necessarily be citizens, all are holders of human rights. It is partly for this reason that I would stress the principle of the Banks panel, that: 'The teaching of human rights should underpin citizenship education courses and programs in multicultural nation-states' (Banks et al. 2005). This principle, I would argue, should apply in all schools, regardless of the ethnic or cultural composition of the student population or the nation in question.

Recognition that all human beings are holders of human rights is also an underpinning principle of education for cosmopolitan citizenship. The human rights project is a cosmopolitan project, which assumes the equal entitlement to rights of all human beings. I understand education for cosmopolitan citizenship as a theoretical construct in which citizenship at all scales, from the local to the global, is reconceptualised, to enable young people to recognise our common humanity and express solidarity with others at all levels from the local to the global, accepting and valuing diversity at all these levels (Osler & Vincent 2002; Osler & Starkey 2003, 2005).

Education for cosmopolitan citizenship is thus conceptualised, not as an alternative to national citizenship education, nor, as has sometimes been interpreted, as a synonym for global citizenship education. It requires that we reimagine the nation as cosmopolitan, and that we reconceptualise education for national citizenship so that it meets more adequately the needs of contemporary nation-states and the global community. It demands we acknowledge there are many ways of being Australian, Brazilian, British, Canadian, Japanese, Mexican, Singaporean and so on.

Citizenship does not necessarily require a deep love of country; it requires minimally a commitment to the polity. It is policy and legislative frameworks designed to promote greater social justice and remove barriers to full participative citizenship which will allow individuals to develop affective ties to the nation. Efforts by nation-states to promote national identity and affinity through education, in response to perceived threats, risk unintended outcomes, provoke concerns about propaganda and threaten, rather than secure, social cohesion and democratic participation.

Interestingly, within EU member states, an assumed binary between education for national and global citizenship (Marshall 2009) is troubled by the issue of European citizenship and belonging (Osler & Savvides 2009; Osler, forthcoming). Evidence is also emerging that many young people do not identify primarily or exclusively with the nation-state but have flexible and shifting identities (Mitchell & Parker 2008; Osler & Starkey 2003). At all levels, national, regional, global and especially at the local level, education for cosmopolitan citizenship responds to the realities of learning to live together and to develop a dialogue with those whose perspectives are different from our own. Education for cosmopolitan citizenship recognises these realities and offers an alternative way of reconceptualising education for citizenship in our globalised world and globalised communities.

REFERENCES

Banks, James A., Cherry A. McGee Banks, Carlos Cortes, Carole L. Hahn, Merry M. Merryfield, Kogila A. Moodley, Stephen Murphy-Shigematsu, Audrey Osler, Caryl Park & Walter C. Parker (2005) *Democracy and Diversity: Principles and Concepts for Educating Citizens in a Global Age*. Seattle, University of Washington, Center for Multicultural Education.

Bryan, Audrey (2008) The co-articulation of national identity and interculturalism in the Irish curriculum: Educating for democratic citizenship? *London Review of Education*, 6(1), pp. 47–58.

Home Office (2008) *£12.5m Allocated to Prevent Violent Extremism*, London, Office for Security and Counter-terrorism, http://security.homeoffice.gov.uk/news-publications/news-speeches/millions-fight-extremism (accessed 19 June 2009).

Kymlicka, Will (2003) Being Canadian, *Government and Opposition*, 38(3), pp. 357–385.

Marshall, Harriet (2009) Educating the European citizen in the global age: Engaging with the post-national and identifying a research agenda, *Journal of Curriculum Studies*, 41(2), pp. 247–267.

Mitchell, Katharyne & Walter Parker (2008) 'I pledge allegiance to . . . ' Flexible citizenship and shifting scales of belonging, *Teachers College Record*, 110(4), pp. 775–804.

Osler, Audrey (2008) Citizenship education and the Ajegbo report: Re-imagining a cosmopolitan nation, *London Review of Education*, 6(1), pp. 11–25.

———. (2009) Patriotism, multiculturalism and belonging: Political discourse and the teaching of history, *Educational Review*, 61(1), pp. 85–100.

———. (Forthcoming) Teacher perceptions of learner-citizens in a global age: Cosmopolitan commitments, local identities and political realities, *Journal of Curriculum Studies*.

Osler, Audrey & Nicola Savvides (2009) Teachers' perceptions of student needs and identities, in G. Weisseno & V. Eck (eds.) *Educating European Citizens*. Munich, Waxmann, pp. 97–114.

Osler, Audrey & Hugh Starkey (2003) Learning for cosmopolitan citizenship: Theoretical debates and young people's experiences, *Educational Review*, 55(3), pp. 243–254.

———. (2005) *Changing Citizenship: Democracy and Inclusion in Education*. Maidenhead, Open University Press.

———. (2006) Education for democratic citizenship: A review of research, policy and practice 1995–2005, *Research Papers in Education*, 21(4), pp. 433–466.

Osler, Audrey & Kerry Vincent (2002) *Citizenship and the Challenge of Global Education*. Stoke-on Trent, Trentham.

Parker, Walter C. (2002) *Teaching Democracy: Unity and Diversity in Public Life*. New York, Teachers College Press.

Qualifications and Curriculum Authority (1998) *Education for Citizenship and the Teaching of Democracy in Schools (Crick Report)*. London, QCA.

———. (2007) *The National Curriculum. Citizenship: Programme of Study for Key Stage Three and Attainment Target*. London, QCA, http//curriculum.qca.org.uk/uploads/QCA-07-3329-pCitizenship3_tem8–396.pdf?return=/key-stages-3-and-4/subjects/citizenship/keystage3/index.aspx%3Freturn%3D/key-stage-3-and-4/subjects/zitizenship/index.aspx% (accessed 9 May 2009).

16 Neo-Statism and Post-Globalisation as Contexts for New Times

Kerry Kennedy

CITIZENSHIP EDUCATION: COMPLEXITIES AND ISSUES

If there is any doubt about the complexities of citizenship then the chapters contained here put that doubt to rest. From Ireland to Brazil and from Canada to Singapore we read about the different ways in which societies struggle with the challenges of preparing young people for citizenship. There are some common themes I want to explore in this chapter and these relate both to what has been included in these chapters and to what has not. These themes are centred on the nation-state and its centrality in the lives of citizens, including new and emerging issues. Despite the attention that globalisation and consequently global citizenship has attracted, there is increasing evidence that nation-states continue to be significant sites when it comes to citizenship issues.

Thus the focus on the nation-state is quite deliberate. There is a growing literature that suggests globalisation itself is mediated through local values, conditions or processes. Interestingly, some of this literature comes out of psychologically oriented research (Silbereisen, Best & Haase 2007; Schoon & Silbereisen 2008; Nafstad–et al. 2009) as well as sociologically oriented studies (Steiner-Khamsi & Stolpe 2006; Grossman, Lee & Kennedy 2008). This trend of resistance to globalisation will be extended in this chapter to suggest that we now live in an era of neo-statism that can be seen as a post-globalisation era. This is not to herald the 'end of globalisation', although a discourse is emerging on this issue (Altman 2009). Rather I want to view globalisation through a different lens—the lens of strong nation-states that become stronger on a daily basis.

THE NATION-STATE, POLITICS AND CITIZENS

Keating (2009, p. 36) has commented that 'the nation-state model continues . . . to have a grip on the intellectual imagination and its normative elements survive in much writing about politics'. The statement also appears to be true when it comes to citizenship education since the chapters in this book focus exclusively on the nation-state. This may simply reflect the way in which the book has been organised, with chapters solicited from writers representing different countries. But it may also reflect another reality: like it or not, citizenship is embedded in nation-states and no amount of theorising can get away from this reality. Advocates of global citizenship or even global education may be disappointed at this focus. Yet theorists need to come to grips with this important reality: citizenship is a legal status and it is only conferred by nation-states. Even advanced suprastates such as the European Union do not confer citizenship status; the legal instruments for doing so, such as a constitution, have more often than not been rejected by national citizens of the European Union. Nation-states, therefore, are not just a reality in the social and political landscape but they have the capacity to reinforce their role and status through citizen action.

It is important, then, to understand nation-states and the citizenship issues they engender. This is not to dismiss a process such as globalisation but it is to place it in perspective. Nation-states have not withered under the onslaught of globalisation. Indeed, it can probably be argued that the opposite is the case. This is certainly true in the Asian region where 'strong' states such as Singapore, Korea and Taiwan have deliberately forged a local citizenship education to counter globalised influences. Nation-states, therefore, can pose resistance to globalisation in order to preserve local cultures and values. There is nothing inevitable about globalisation because nation-states can always be mobilised against it.

A number of authors in these chapters highlight the significance of nation-states by pointing to the strength of politicians and their potential for shaping citizenship values. Obama is given Messiah status by Scott and Cogan, John Howard is demonised by Gill and Reid and there is suspicion of his successor, Kevin Rudd. This is the politics of personality and charisma (or lack of it!) and it is a characteristic of many nation-states. Tony Blair came to characterise British politics for more than a decade and George Bush was unassailable in the United States for eight years. Focusing on politicians is understandable because they mediate an everyday politics that impact on the lives of citizens. At the same time, however, an emphasis on politicians and the process of government obscures the political lives of ordinary people. When the focus is on 'high' politics the assumption is that such politics construct citizens' lives. It is the same when the focus is on history and politics.

We can observe in these chapters the powerful forces of history and how these histories shape the lives of citizens. It may be the growth of the 'Celtic Tiger', the complex ethnic history of Canada, the transition from totalitarianism in Russia or the 'Landless Movement' in Brazil. Citizens cannot help but be affected by these broad historical processes. Often, however, these historical processes are portrayed as though they are inevitable—almost an historical determinism as though citizens have no options. Yet we have seen recently—as well as in the past—that citizens themselves are capable of exerting considerable influence within nation-states, with or without the consent of politicians and despite the so-called forces of history.

Iran provides the most recent example where citizens and citizens' technology sent a real and powerful message to the ruling elite—although the exact import of this Iranian resistance is still under debate. We have seen 'people power' in the Philippines, the 'Orange Revolution' in the Ukraine, the 'Rose Revolution' in Georgia, the 'Saffron Revolution' in Myanmar. Not all of these have been successful and tyranny has often triumphed, but the point is that citizens can exercise political influence of their own often against great odds. Politicians may be powerful and historical directions may appear set, but when citizens come together they too can be powerful. Witness the five hundred thousand Hong Kong people who protested 1 July 2003 against national security legislation that has not been enacted to this day. As many people protested worldwide against the Iraq war, but with no effect. Citizen power does not always work. But it is always there and we should hear more about it, otherwise it is too easy to believe that only 'high' politics and history matter in the construction of citizenship issues.

'STRONG' STATES, NON-STATE ACTORS AND CULTURE

Not only is it necessary to accept that nation-states are the inevitable brokers of citizenship in the twenty-first century, but there is now evidence they are growing even stronger. It could well be argued that we are now witnessing a neo-statism, even in liberal democracies, where only the state can respond to the problems of our times. First, 'strong states' characterise governance in many parts of the world. Some, like China and Myanmar, are totalitarian states where citizenship rights and responsibilities are both prescribed and rigidly monitored by the state. Others, like Singapore and Malaysia, have the apparatus of democracy but citizens are closely monitored, traditional freedoms are not always respected and one-party rule, despite elections, has predominated. While the four examples provided here might seem more like exceptions, a worrying trend even in traditional liberal democracies has been a shoring up of state power at the expense of democratic liberties. Post-9/11 security legislation now in place in the United States, Australia and the United Kingdom, for example, has been much more republican than liberal in its orientation. In order to protect the public against terrorism, many democratic states can now hold citizens without warrants for longer periods of time, monitor citizens extensively through closed-circuit television systems and deny citizens access to legal representation when it is thought that the state is under threat. Thus the distinctions between 'totalitarian' and 'democratic' states are not as rigid as they used to be—states have flexed their muscles in order to protect against what are seen as security threats.

Linked to these security issues in the twenty-first century have been issues of wars between nation-states. The almost unilateral declaration of war by the United States against Iraq and Afghanistan immediately after 9/11 both reinforced and questioned the Westphalian doctrine of national sovereignty. International criticism did not deflect the Bush administration, although the necessity to couple together a 'coalition of the willing' was perhaps recognition that national sovereignty could be more effective with some modicum of international support. At the same time, the national sovereignty of the two countries that were invaded was completely disregarded. The 'power of the sword' in the service of noble objectives was seen both to rationalise and rectify any wrong that was being done. Just as each side in the early crusades thought it had 'God on its side', so too did the United States in these invading actions. 'Might and right' make powerful nation-states even more powerful and less accountable.

A quite different manifestation of the 'strong state' in the twenty-first century has been the reactions forced on governments by the financial crisis that characterised the latter part of 2008. As stock markets crashed, banks foundered and investment companies declared bankruptcy, it was governments that had to act to stave off even more dire financial consequences. Stimulus spending, company buyouts and other acts of deleveraging had to be put in place in Washington, London, Berlin and Canberra. It was only the limitless power of governments to call on what often appeared like a limitless supply of money that could rescue national economies from ruin. Neo-liberal free market economics, the handmaiden of globalisation, had brought nation-states to the brink of disaster; it was a Keynesian injection of public funds that seems to have held then back from the precipice. Nation-states, therefore, were not mere referees in market-dominated economies. They were not just idle bystanders watching the invisible hand do its work. They intervened to protect citizens from the failure of deregulation, sheer greed, blatant dishonesty and economic distortions of the worst kind.

The point of alluding to the 'strong state' status of nation-states is that citizenship education must be much more mindful of the implications of this status for democratic citizenship. It is one thing to opine for a greater emphasis on global citizenship in this age of globalisation. But we shall miss the forest for the trees if we believe this means we no longer need to examine national citizenships carefully. It is something akin to many Christian groups who wish to focus on a 'citizenship that is in heaven'. This may well be, but before Christians can appropriate their 'heavenly citizenship', they need first to negotiate their everyday citizenship that is right here on earth. So it is with global citizenship: it may represent a noble ideal but it should not deflect us from focusing on national citizenships in the first instance since it is these that have the potential to influence the ordinary lives of people.

If there remains any doubt about the importance of nation-states, we should perhaps take a lesson from those non-state actors that constantly make nation-states their target. It was such actors who perpetrated 9/11 against the United States, the Bali bombings against Indonesia and Australia, the underground train bombings against Great Britain, train bombings against Spain and India, political assassination in Pakistan and so on. Ironically, it is these non-state actors that attest to the strength of nation-states to the point where there seems an almost nihilistic urge to obliterate them. Again, this needs to be a focus for citizenship education since understanding such individuals and groups, knowing how to respond to them and knowing how to respond to state actions against them should be part and parcel of any citizenship education programme. Citizens must be equipped to handle complex ideas and ideologies if they are to contribute to their societies in a constructive way—traditional approaches to citizenship education may not always achieve this end. Traditional ideologies such as progressivism may not be robust enough to handle these new developments and we may need to think in new and different ways about them.

Finally, there are two issues that stand out from the cases presented in this book that deserve some comment. The issues are not unrelated to the main themes discussed previously. One is concerned with voices and who speaks for citizenship and citizenship education and the other is concerned with methodology and how we interrogate citizenship education.

Academics are privileged in many ways and this is particularly so for those who work in citizenship studies. They get to portray the values and understandings of citizenship and citizenship education within their particular jurisdictions. The cases in this volume demonstrate the power of academics in constructing citizenship issues in particular ways. Yet we need to be aware that there are many other voices that might construct the same issues in very different ways. For example, if these chapters were written by students or youth workers, or women or ethnic groups or marginalised people, we might get very different perspectives. We should not discount these alternative voices and we should find a way to include them in academic debates and discussions. On the issue of students, for example, the Youth Citizenship Commission (2009) in the United Kingdom has just released a report canvassing the issue of lowering the voting age to sixteen. Should governments proceed to act on this issue, then the views of sixteen-year-olds will take on a new significance. At one level, academic constructions of citizenship have a role to play but we also need to ensure that academic texts contain other voices as well so we can see the full range of community interests and concerns around citizenship issues.

Methodologically, what is reported in these chapters is largely analytical/conceptual/philosophical in nature. This kind of work is important but it tends to privilege a particular way of knowing, a way that suits academic discourse very well. Broadening methodological approaches to investigating citizenship can provide a more inclusive view of citizenship issues. Empirical approaches, for example, can focus on those individuals and groups mentioned in the previous paragraphs. These approaches might be qualitative or quantitative—the techniques do not really matter so much. What does matter is that we get to hear more views from those people who themselves have experiences of citizenship that are often masked because they do not get the opportunity to express them. A broader methodological approach to citizenship and citizenship education can help to resolve this problem.

CONCLUSION

It is always instructive to learn about citizenship issues in different geographic, social and political spaces. The sheer breadth of the cases presented in this volume is not disappointing in this regard. As governments increase their control over different aspects of citizens' lives, it is important that we constantly monitor the status of citizens' rights and responsibilities in these new times. As globalisation exerted its pressures in the 1990s and early part of this century it seemed that the key issues were global and that the local was under threat. Security issues challenged this scenario towards the end of 2001 and financial issues challenged it even more severely in mid-2008. We are now confronted with strong states—what I referred to earlier as neo-statism. This is the new reality for citizenship educators.

As Altman (2009) has pointed out, it is strong states such as China and India that have fared best in the post–financial crisis environment. It is not clear what lesson there is to draw from this politically since one of these states is totalitarian and the other is democratic. Yet the problem with all strong states is that they can become very introspective and governments can become very complacent—especially about competing demands that need to be addressed in a politically acceptable way. Democracies have historically known how to do this—totalitarian regimes have not. In this current environment, therefore, we need to watch closely that democratic impulses continue to fuel strong states—especially where these states are liberal democracies. These are new times for citizenship educators and once we recognise this we can rethink how best to gear citizenship education for the future.

REFERENCES

Altman, Roger (2009) Globalization in retreat: Further geopolitical consequences of the financial crisis, *Foreign Affairs*, 88(4), pp. 2–7.
Grossman, David, Wing-On Lee & Kerry Kennedy (2008) *Citizenship Curriculum in Asia and the Pacific*. Hong Kong and Dordrecht, CERC and Springer.
Keating, Michael (2009) Rescaling Europe, *Perspectives on European Politics and Society*, 10(1), pp. 34–50.
Nafstad, Hilde, Rolv Blakar, Albert Blotchway & Kim Rand-Hendrickson (2009) Globalization, ideologies and well-being: A study of a West African and a North European Society, *Journal of Positive Psychology*, 4(4), pp. 305–315.

Schoon, Ingrid & Rainer Silbereisen (2008) *Transition from School to Work. Globalisation, Individualisation, and Patterns of Diversity.* Cambridge, Cambridge University Press.

Silbereisen, Rainer, Heinrich Best & Claudia Haase (2007) Agency and human development in times of social change, *International Journal of Psychology*, 42(2), pp. 74–76.

Steiner-Khamsi, Gita & Ins Stolpe (2006) *Educational Import: Local Encounters with Global Forces in Mongolia.* London, Palgrave MacMillan.

Youth Citizenship Commission (2009) Old enough to make a mark? Should the voting age be lowered to 16? http://www.ycc.uk.net/publications/YCC_18–16_summary.pdf (accessed 15 July 2009).

17 Politics, Citizenship Education Policy in Twelve Countries and Cosmopolitanism
A Commentary

Yvonne Hébert

INTRODUCTION

A close consideration of the case studies in this volume brings to the fore several strong points cutting across most of the countries. As I write this commentary upon my return from a two-week trip to China, my third such trip in recent years, preceded the month before with travel in France, one of many visits, I am particularly struck, in analysing these chapters, by the many different ways a society can be conceptualised and operationalised. In both countries visited and in many of the countries covered in this book, state governments loom large. These are oft ripe with tensions linked to long-term or even short-term diversity in hostile environments usually marked by repressive measures. Moreover, in many countries under consideration, the globalising context is perceived as problematic by policy makers and practitioners alike, who do not know how to prepare young people for this reality. Given this preamble and my wanderings, three strong points are of particular interest to me: (a) the influence of the state government on civics or citizenship education; (b) the centrality of diversity; and (c) a call for expansion of citizenship education to include globalisation, intercultural education, peace studies, gender education and so on, which I understand in terms of cosmopolitanism. These three topics will be discussed each in turn. In so doing, common directions, issues, future directions, need for further conceptual clarification and the possible shape(s) of civics and citizenship education for the future will be interwoven in the fabric of my commentary. Look for the threads . . .

THE IMPACT OF STATE POLITICS ON CITIZENSHIP EDUCATION

The first topic is the impact of state politics, not only on schooling in general, but especially on civics or citizenship education as this subject serves the state by creating the kinds of citizens preferred by the reigning political party. This means that schooling is organised, structured and practised by the state to serve particular versions of what it means to be a citizen in a particular democracy at specific historical moments in accordance with the prevailing government's ideology and in light of the country's political legacy and its conception(s) of the learner over time. With fundamental changes in government, be it a change of regime, of ideology or of governing political party, education is not only affected by the change but is expected to foster the new political order by means of citizenship education. Indeed, citizenship education appeared with the rise of the nation-state to pursue the fiction of a homogeneous nation co-terminous with the state.

In other words, not only is citizenship a profoundly historical and embedded concept inseparable from the definition of the polity, but it is also inseparable from the determination of the educational services regardless of the type of ruling polity. Schools are expected to successfully foster integration into the political and national community, as well as sub-national groups, especially official minorities. Delivering civics and citizenship education is, however, no simple or easy task, for delivery or implementation involves at least three educational modalities: the structure of schooling; the culture and processes of school; and the representation of formal knowledge of civics and citizenship education. The latter may include structures of power and governance, citizen's rights and responsibilities and the skills and dispositions for participation in the polity and civil society. Thus, citizenship education is reflective of the balance, or struggle for balance, between sub-national, provincial, territorial, national and supranational levels of government, as can be seen in the various chapters.

State influences, however, are variable. By stressing the collective character of society and its common cultural roots, a nation-state can provide a common identity binding mutually distinct social groups for centuries to follow, even if its character and roots are constructed for this purpose and even if the notion of nation-state is largely fictitious, there being very few such entities without the presence of others within their boundaries. Moreover, historical experiences of oppression, be these internal or external, and in the case of colonialisation either as colonisers or as the colonised, including military rule, have left in their wake strong tendencies to justify and laud oneself, to control the historical narrative and thus, history and civics text-books.

Among the commonalities though, it can be noted that the control of the state has been strengthening over the educational process generally and specifically citizenship education/social studies. For example, this can be seen in the conception of the student as a self-motivating independent individual, i.e. as a 'responsible' learner. The evaluation and overview of teaching materials is similarly subject to greater state control in most countries. States are also systematically reducing the autonomy of teachers, deprofessionalising educators and instigating greater accountability of teachers for school results.

The uneven ideologies of ruling parties and their influence on the educational system have had a considerable effect on teachers and students alike. These ideologies, as changeable as they are, tell a tale of state and governmental development over time. In some countries, the fluctuations between dictatorships have had devastating effects especially on citizenship education, for example, in Brazil and Pakistan. Yet, even within supposedly stable countries, there has been a tremendous influence of ruling ideologies on market economy agendas on school systems, be it, for example, in Australia and Alberta, a Canadian province which followed the ideas of the former. Both jurisdictions implemented in the social studies curriculum notions of individual choice, accountability, standardised testing, publication in the media of school comparisons and funding of private schools, all key elements of a neo-liberal political and conservative economic agenda. Yet in Alberta, the Social Studies Program of Studies includes a sophisticated multiple perspectives approach to curriculum and critical inquiry pedagogy, while incorporating Anglophone, Francophone and Aboriginal perspectives, and later adding voices of polyethnic groups in the province within the curriculum. This Program of Studies was developed over an eight-year cyclical process of literature reviews, consultations, proposals and partial trials, thus resulting in a complex balancing of multiple voices and perspectives in the province. Moreover, it was developed within the Western Protocol Agreement between the three Western provinces and Northern Territories, thus instigating a balancing process of views and voices from the very onset. As a result of inviting input from multiple voices and taking up the responses seriously, the curriculum avoids the excesses of the current market economy approach to education.

Why the differences from jurisdiction to jurisdiction? One such difference is clearly the developmental process in which the roles of the Internet, the media, civil society as well as the voices of professional and teachers' organisations, community leaders and other voices serve to counterbalance dominant state views. Other possible influences on citizenship education and civics stem from the discourses of international organisations and declarations, foreign agencies working within a country on citizenship education; for example, in Russia and South Africa. Elsewhere, the complex political, social, cultural and religious history of a country, such as in Pakistan, leads to conservative religious discourses relegating women to secondary roles in society and reducing minorities to second-class citizens without rights, thus denying both women and minorities equal citizenship. Different countries also hold and embed different values in their curricula, for example, dictatorial, authoritarian governments tend to emphasise the links between morality and/or ethics, democracy and citizenship education, as exemplified in Brazil. There is consequently no emerging general agreement, as this part of democratic education is particularly sensitive to government pressures and policies, especially in this age of neo-liberalism.

Overwhelming political pressures, concomitant with financial pressures and negative public media coverage of supposedly low-quality schools, impact negatively upon the cultures and processes of schooling in Alberta, Australia and the United States, to name but a few. In the United Kingdom, the competitive systems for distributing school choice are counter-productive, creating closed and negative environments, impacting on school offerings, especially on personal and social education programming. In South Africa and Mexico, the lack of implementation plans with realisable goals, strategies and knowledgeable supporting teachers as well as civics teachers is discouraging, in spite of dramatic policy announcements and sophisticated policy documents, compounded with the opposing strong effects of the conduct and communication of daily politics, thus effectively broadcasting to students and the populace, a counter-productive 'hidden' curriculum.

Nonetheless, transformation is possible. Local municipal and community initiatives in conjunction with schools have their own ability to change, as three initiatives demonstrate. The now well-known processes of collective policy making involving an investigation of the main issues affecting schooling, such as the Citizen School of Porte Allegro, as well as the Plural School initiative which emerged as a grass roots teachers' movement, were so successful that they are now extended throughout schools in all Brazil. Moreover, in Latin America, the development of citizenship/democratic education movements, such as the Landless Rural Workers or 'Landless Movement' (MST[1]), operated schools with public funding and is now widely recognised as the largest and most influential social movement in Latin America, organised around agrarian reform, responding to severe inequalities of landownership, worker exploitation and gender inequities. Central to these initiatives is citizenship and political participation, understood broadly along Freirean lines in conjunction with the explicit realisation that education is a political practice with democracy as a pedagogical principle. Thus, with an emphasis on dialogue, collective work is a key element to develop competencies as well as collective values, so as to effectuate change in society.

THE CENTRALITY OF DIVERSITY

The second topic to be addressed here is the centrality of diversity across all chapters, although various terms may be used to refer to the presence of peoples, citizens and workers and remind them of their non-sanguine relationship to the 'founding ethnos' of the country in question, even if the existence of 'ethnos' is a socially constructed reality or perhaps fiction. The focus on diversity is accompanied by more inclusive understandings of pluralism, often termed multiculturalism, although only one country has an explicit policy of multiculturalism and formal law, Canada. Sometimes the political discourse is articulated as 'managing identities' as, for example, in Singapore, or as 'diversity management' in Ireland, Canada and many other countries, or as 'managing national minorities' in China, a country that is not represented in this book. In some if not most countries, this notion of managing 'others' lies in tension with conceptions of unity and of social cohesion, as articulated by bureaucrats and politicians alike, and sometimes scholars eager for research and contract funding. Moreover, in some countries, the perceived need to maintain social cohesion is usually accompanied by a sense of crisis and by measures that suppress recognition and rights to self-determination.

The centrality of diversity, in its various guises, includes the common stance of most authors who note that citizenship education dwells within local and national perspectives and yet ought to take up global perspectives so as to effectively include the experiences of learners who are likely to have multiple identifications and attachments. Moreover, the scholars propose active forms of democracy, blending deliberative and participatory practices for most countries surveyed in this collection. Doing so effectively broadens the content and contexts of civics and citizenship education beyond the historical, so as to include contemporary economic, political and environmental forces.

There are, nevertheless, aspects of education for diversity which are yet to be developed. For example, there is a lack of consent on values education, often linked to moral education and/or ethics, and its relevance to democratic or citizenship education. Given the lack of consent, the ruling party may step in and impose its own values. There is similarly a lack of theoretisation and modeling for dialogical and conceptual purposes. Moreover, there are historically inconsistent and contradictory discourses within the domain of citizenship, for example, within Russia, Australia, South Africa and the United Kingdom, as well as France and Switzerland. Finally, there are unresolved relationships between the public and the private domains, between the individual and community, as noted for the United Kingdom.

Making it difficult to deal effectively with diversity and other pressing issues, the term *citizenship* has a multiplicity of meanings, all closely dependent upon political ideologies, class identities, the historical experience of cultural groups, gender differences and racialised identities. It is important then to establish acceptable definitions of what it means to be a 'citizen' in a milieu of fluid and conflicting politics, and at the same time trying to cope with quickly shifting identity politics. The same urgency holds for the competing, uneven, conflicting definitions of democracy and hence of citizenship education. Conceptual clarity is needed.

Most scholars in this collection bemoan the lack of attention to diversity, to international or global education, to peace education, to gender equity and to gender education. Moreover, youth voter participation is down in most countries, except for the recent U.S. election. Obama's campaign galvanised young voters through extensive use of the Internet. This has considerable importance for bringing in the disenfranchised, the disenchanted and the marginalised, including the youth. Given the extensive use of the Internet and its rapid communication, no election campaign will ever be the same.

The acceptance of others is key to learning to live together. This cannot happen without quality work, not only on definitions of terms such as integration, but also on the origins and forms of multiculturalism. According to Kymlicka, states that have successfully dealt with diversity have put into policy and practice three general ideas:

- repudiating the idea of the state as belonging to the dominant group
- replacing assimilationist and exclusionary nation-building policies with policies of recognition and accommodation
- acknowledging historic injustice and offering amends for it—all are common to virtually all real-world struggles for multiculturalism (2009, p. 66)

Restructuring schools as sites for the inclusive education of all young people as democratic citizens will require that schools themselves be structured democratically and use democratic processes at all levels. This will also require that those directly involved in schools, head teachers, teachers, students and parents, be involved in making policy decisions and in governance guided by democratic values. Thus, the school itself will be inclusive, belonging to all groups attending it; students will be recognised and accommodated, and amends will be made for historic injustices, all as part of the processes of becoming and being multicultural.

COSMOPOLITANISM AS FUTURE DIRECTIONS

Civics, citizenship education and social studies all are circumscribed by national boundaries and national notions of citizenship, and thus concomitantly neglect globalisation and its impact on states, schooling and young people. Yet there are many young people in schools today who have extensive knowledge of the world, be it virtual or experiential, especially the children and adolescents of immigrant backgrounds. In a recent study in three Canadian cities, second-generation participants demonstrated their capacity to engage in three forms of mobility: mobility of mind, body and boundary, all forms of mobility responding to globalisation (Hébert, Wilkinson & Ali 2008). While the data and analysis may be innovative, there are many studies which document young people's eager participation in a world well beyond narrow national borders (Hoerder, Hébert & Schmitt 2005).

The many forms of cosmopolitanism provide much leavening for thought and consideration for curriculum as a possible theory and orientation to the world. *Cosmopolitanism* is a complex term with many definitions, the most common one is a vague notion of being a 'citizen of the world', loosely holding attachments to particular issues, perhaps environmental ones, and to real and imaginary places. This sense of being part of something bigger than one's country is pervasive among many young people today who insist that they are part of a greater world, moving well beyond the confines of local ethnos, local community, local schools and religious institutions. Cosmopolitanism involves multiple belongings as noted earlier, dual or multiple citizenships, an awareness of global issues, events and trends and their relevance to everyday lives. It may also involve ethical stances in intercultural situations (Appiah 2006). Cosmopolitan studies may also consider excessive consumerism as an effect of globalisation, as well as other aspects of the market economy (Klein 2001). Knowledge of, and interaction with, international civil society could also be of interest, particularly in recognition of the power of NGOs, trade unions and social movements to interact with, advise and/or counsel governments.

Cosmopolitanism could also involve an awareness of self as well as the development of an intercultural or transcultural competence linked to language learning, situated, for example, within the European Common Frame of Reference (Zarate et al. 2004; Lázár et al. 2007). Ideally it would entail knowledge of the significance and relevance of the corpus of international human rights legislation, such as the UN Declaration of Human Rights and the Convention on the Rights of the Child, and their links to state-specific laws; the mandate and operationalisation of international courts; an awareness of issues of security and of peace efforts; and comparative study of cultural rights around the world, for possible incorporation into educational curriculum.

To serve as a basis for curriculum development, this notion must be theorised and yet remain practical. Appiah sees cosmopolitanism as ethics in a world of strangers, thus taking up the great human project of trying to live together. His is a moral manifesto for a planet we share with billions of strangers, redefining our moral and civic obligations to others based on a very humane and realistic outline and love of art. For Appiah, cosmopolitanism 'begins with the simple idea that, in the human community, as in national communities, we need to develop habits of coexistence: conversation in its older meaning, of living together, association' (2006, p. xix). Along the way, he tells stories and makes the point that to be a citizen of the world is to accept and understand difference without feeling the need to change it for something more familiar.

Thus, Appiah articulates the need for kindness to strangers as a moral commitment to others who are our global neighbours, by assuring first of all, that all states respect the rights and meet the needs of their citizens. If they fail to do so, providing resources can be part of our collective obligation and an equally fundamental cosmopolitan commitment. Secondly, it is not our obligation to carry the whole burden alone but to do our fair share. Thirdly, our basic obligations must be consistent with our being. Whatever our obligations to the poor far away, these do not trump our basic obligations to our family, our friends and our country. However, a genuinely cosmopolitan response to need is to ask why it is occurring, who has the power to make changes and to join with others to set priorities, to make a difference, to bring about positive change. Thus, a cosmopolitan curriculum would present learners with specific cases and call upon them to think critically about who benefits from the situation and why, about who has the power to change and about the issues and plausible solutions set in a worldwide context. Involving students in projects of their own initiative could be a particularly powerful form of learning. This form of criticality is central to the cosmopolitan position as it questions power structures and the ideological constructions of truth and belief beyond critical thinking as technical problem-solving skills.

Another part of cosmopolitan studies may involve consideration of how international human rights cross over into domestic law. Attempting to do so, Benhabib (2006) proposes a dynamic process through which universal principles of human rights are progressively incorporated over time into the positive law of democratic states, for example, assuring the human rights of legal and illegal aliens. Will Kymlicka suggests that connecting these to liberal nationhood is a step towards the integration of aliens into the status of full national citizenship. Benhabib distances herself from this solution as she makes the point that modern nation-states in the European Union are typically based on a common ethnos, 'a community bound together by the power of a shared fate, memories, solidarity and belonging' (2006, p. 65). Thus, she invites us to consider a future in which 'civil, social, and some political rights' are maximally unbundled 'from national belonging' (p. 171). While her conception of the future is not fully worked out, it at least involves separating the demos from the ethnos and renegotiating the boundaries in more universalistic terms. Nonetheless, universal cosmopolitan law faces two problems. One is the necessary boundedness of democratic authority; the second is the historically specific forms of national solidarity represented by the ethnos. Nonetheless, some countries have moved beyond ethnic solidarity as the basis for demos, for example, those countries which value and recognise diversity.

CONCLUSION

The ideas and experiences described in this collection are very rich. Further work is needed to develop common understandings of democratic concepts, such as multiculturalism, participation, integration, civil society and bringing together educators, researchers/scholars, politicians and interested citizens, in national and international forums, whether online or face-to-face or both. Moreover, critical comparative conceptual studies are needed to support such dialogue, as well as the development of ideas for possible programmes or partial programmes, focusing on international education, peace education, international human rights and citizenship education as sites of contestation and resistance.

Given the weight of neo-liberal and conservative economic philosophies on civics and citizenship education, several types of critical comparative studies are greatly needed:

- the development and negotiation of an epistemology of citizenship education; studies of learning for citizenship activity and identity
- studies of teaching practices as well as the practices of other agents, organisations and initiatives involved in curriculum implementation
- studies of democratic identity formation and of the values actually espoused by citizens with respect to those espoused by the respective governments
- studies of the development and implementation of models of cosmopolitan, global, peace and/or international citizenship education

Some basic research is also needed, for example, to study understandings of diversity beyond a sanitised perspective, to include schools as sites of contestation and of mobilisation with respect for others, with respect to rights of minorities around the world, and for the development of political activism among young people, be it at the local level of a political party, an environmental agency, a community group, workers' party or group. Finally, as new economic models are foreseen (Casey 2009), studies must be launched of social citizenship in the workplace, in the face of increased control of workers, including teachers. There is so much to do.

NOTE

1. Movimento dos Trabalhadores Rurais Sem Terra.

REFERENCES

Appiah, Kwame Anthony (2006) *Cosmopolitanism: Ethics in a World of Strangers*. New York and London, W.W. Norton & Company.
Benhabib, Seyla (2006) Another cosmopolitanism, with commentaries by Jeremy Waldron, Bonnie Honig and Will Kymlicka, in Robert Post (ed.) *The Berkeley Tanner Lectures*. Oxford and New York, Oxford University Press, pp. 13–80.
Casey, Catherine (2009) Organizations, workers, and learning: New prospects for citizenship at work? *Citizenship Studies*, 13(2), pp. 171–185.
Hébert, Yvonne, Lori Wilkinson & Mehrunnisa Ali (2008) Second generation youth in Canada, their mobilities and identifications, *Brock Education*, 17(1), pp. 50–70.
Hoerder, Dirk, Yvonne Hébert & Irina Schmitt (eds.) (2005) *Negotiating Transcultural Lives: Belongings and Social Capital among Youth in Comparative Perspective*. Göttingen, V & R Unipress.
Klein, Naomi (2001) *No Logo*. Toronto, Vintage Canada.

Kymlicka, Will (2009) *Multicultural Odysseys: Navigating the New International Politics of Diversity.* Toronto, University of Oxford Press.

Lázár, Ildikó, Martina Huber-Kriegler, Denise Lussier, Gabriela S. Matei & Christiane Peck (eds.) (2007) *Developing and Assessing Intercultural Communicative Competence.* Strasbourg, European Centre for Modern Languages.

Zarate, Geneviève, Aline Gohard-Radenkovic, Denise Lussier & Hermine Penz (2004) *Cultural Mediation in Language Learning and Teaching.* Strasbourg, European Centre for Modern Languages.

Contributors

Mark Baildon is Assistant Professor in the Centre for Research in Pedagogy and Practice and the Humanities and Social Studies Education Academic Group at the National Institute of Education in Singapore. His teaching and research interests include inquiry-based social studies education and the uses of technology to support inquiry and new literacies.

Audrey Bryan currently teaches sociology in St. Patrick's College, Drumcondra, Dublin. Previously, she was a Lecturer in the School of Education, University College Dublin. She holds a PhD in Comparative and International Education (with a specialisation in sociology) from Columbia University. Her research interests include: international educational development, global citizenship education, globalisation and social stratification. To date, her research has examined how schooling and the state interact to shape the life experiences of members of marginalised minority groups. She has examined these dynamics in the context of how social policies and school practices affect the educational and life experiences of racialised minorities and individuals who identify as Lesbian, Gay, Bisexual and/ or Transgender (LGBT).

John J. Cogan is Professor Emeritus of Comparative and International Development Education and Social Studies Education at the University of Minnesota. His research specialisations are educating for citizenship and educational reform. He is an internationally recognised authority on educating for citizenship. He is the author of four books, seventeen book chapters and more than one hundred published journal articles.

Ian Davies is Professor of Education at the University of York, U.K. He is the director of the MA in International and Global Citizenship Education at York. Recent publications include the edited (with James Arthur and Carole Hahn) *SAGE Handbook of Education for Citizenship and Democracy*. He has extensive international experience which includes working as an expert consultant for the Council of Europe and as a Fellow of the Japan Society for the Promotion of Science.

Bernadette Dean is Professor of Education and Principal of Kinnaird College, Lahore, Pakistan. Her research interests span teaching and learning and citizenship and human rights education, and she has published numerous articles, books and book chapters in these areas. She has served as consultant to the Ministry of Education, Pakistan, and to the text-book boards of the provinces of Pakistan, facilitating the development of the national curriculum and writing of text-books in keeping with the curriculum.

Judith Gill is Associate Professor in Education at the University of South Australia. She has carried out research on the ways in which young people understand the political dimensions of their life-worlds and the degree to which they identify as citizens. Her latest work relates to the ways in which teacher education students see their role in relation to the current directives around citizenship education. Her most recent book, written with Sue Howard, is *Knowing Our Place: Young People Talking about Power, Identity and Citizenship*, published by ACER Press (2009).

Yvonne Hébert is a Professor of Education, University of Calgary, with research interests in youth, identity, democracy, minority studies, policy and educational reform. Her current research projects focus on the impact of French language immigration on an urban francophone community; francophone youth's mobility and identity construction in postsecondary education in minority contexts; and youth's negotiation of difference and democracy, a comparative study in three Canadian cities. Her books include: *Negotiating Trans-Cultural Lives: Belongings and Social Capital among Youth in Comparative Perspectives* (with Dirk Hoerder and Irina Schmitt) and *Citizenship in Transformation in Canada*.

Kerry Kennedy is Chair Professor of Curriculum Studies at the Hong Kong Institute of Education. His main research interests are in curriculum policy and theory and citizenship education. He is Series Editor of the *Routledge Series on Schools and Schooling in Asia*. He is the co-author of *Changing Schools in Asia: Schools for the Knowledge Society* (Routledge, 2008) and author of *Changing Schools for Changing Times: New Directions for the School Curriculum in Hong Kong* (Chinese University Press, 2005).

Bradley A.U. Levinson is Associate Professor in the Department of Educational Leadership and Policy Studies at Indiana University, where he also directs the Center for Latin American and Caribbean Studies. He is the co-editor of two recent volumes, *Reimagining Civic Education* (Rowman & Littlefield) and *Advancing Democracy through Education?*

(Information Age Publishing). He edits the *Inter-American Journal of Education for Democracy*.

Tristan McCowan is Lecturer in Education and International Development at the Institute of Education, University of London. His current research focuses on the right to education, citizenship and the curriculum in an international context. He is the author of *Rethinking Citizenship Education: a Curriculum for Participatory Democracy* (Continuum, 2009) and has recently published articles in *Theory and Research in Education*, *Journal of Curriculum Studies* and *Journal of Philosophy of Education*.

Kogila Moodley is Professor Emerita at the University of British Columbia, Vancouver, Canada, where she was the first holder of the David Lam Chair in Multicultural Studies. She has served as President of the International Sociological Association's Research Committee on Ethnic, Minority and Racial Relations (RC05), and is currently on the editorial board of several journals including *Ethnic and Racial Studies* (London). She is annually affiliated with the University of Cape Town's Centre for African Studies and conducts research on xenophobia, political education and comparative multiculturalism. Her most recent co-authored book, with Heribert Adam, is *Seeking Mandela: Peacemaking between Israelis and Palestinians* (Temple University Press).

Audrey Osler is Professor of Education and Founding Director of the Centre for Citizenship and Human Rights Education at the University of Leeds. In 2007 she was Visiting Scholar at the Center for Multicultural Education at the University of Washington, Seattle. Her research addresses citizenship, children's human rights and racial justice. She is author of *Changing Citizenship: Democracy and Inclusion in Education* (2005, with Hugh Starkey) and is currently completing a book entitled *Students' Perspectives on Schooling*.

Walter Parker is Professor of Education and Adjunct Professor of Political Science at the University of Washington, Seattle. He studies civic education and international education in schools. His books include *Educating the Democratic Mind* (1996), *Teaching Democracy: Unity and Diversity in Public Life* (2003) and *Social Studies Today: Research and Practice* (2009).

Nelli Piattoeva's research interests focus on citizenship and nation-building in the realm of compulsory education. In her ongoing doctoral research Piattoeva explores how citizenship education in Finland and Russia has changed in the face of socio-political changes triggered by the collapse of the iron curtain and intensifying globalisation. Piattoeva has previously published in *European Education, Comparative Education* and *Journal of Curriculum Studies.*

Cleonice Puggian is Senior Lecturer in Education at the University of Grande Rio, Brazil. She holds a PhD in Education from the University of Cambridge and a Master's in Brazilian Education from the Catholic University of Rio de Janeiro. She is also a member of the Nucleus of Ethnography in Education at the State University of Rio de Janeiro. Her studies focus on young people's identity in a context of urban conflict, exploring the role of formal and non-formal education in the constitution of citizenship ideals and youth participation in civil society.

Alan Reid is Professor Emeritus of Education in the School of Education at the University of South Australia. His research interests include education policy, civics and citizenship education, curriculum politics and change and the history and politics of public education. He has led a number of national and state curriculum initiatives.

Thomas J. Scott, PhD, teaches American Government and Citizenship and College in the Schools American Democracy at Rosemount High School, Rosemount Minnesota. He is also Adjunct Associate Professor of Education at Saint Mary's University in Minneapolis and an Adjunct Professor of Social Science at Metropolitan State University in St. Paul, Minnesota.

Alan Sears is a Professor in the Faculty of Education at the University of New Brunswick in Canada. His research interests include citizenship education; children and young people's understanding of key democratic ideas; and educational policy.

Jasmine B-Y Sim is Assistant Professor in the Curriculum, Teaching and Learning Academic Group at the National Institute of Education, Singapore. Her research interests include civics and citizenship education, social studies education and critical thinking. She is also the Principal Investigator of a fairly large-scale project researching Singaporean students' civic engagement involving twenty-one schools and twenty-five hundred students.

Thomas Kwan-choi Tse is currently an Associate Professor of the Department of Educational Administration and Policy, The Chinese University of Hong Kong, Hong Kong. He teaches and publishes in the fields of citizenship education, moral education, educational policy and sociology of education.

Index